Jonah
An Expository Commentary

To Mike –
May God continue to bless
your service to Him.

Russ Reaves

Russ Reaves
Jonah 2:9

Third Printing: November, 2012

Unless otherwise indicated, all Scripture taken from the
NEW AMERICAN STANDARD BIBLE®,
© Copyright 1960, 1962, 1963, 1968, 1971, 1972, 1973, 1975, 1977, 1995 by
The Lockman Foundation
Used by permission.
(www.lockman.org)

ISBN: 1466450797
ISBN-13: 978-1466450790
Suggested Dewey Decimal Classification: 224.92

For Donia, Solomon, and Salem

A fruitful vine in my house,
And olive plants around my table.
Thus I have been blessed by the LORD

Psalm 128:3-4

CONTENTS

ACKNOWLEDGMENTS

Beginning in the Spring of 2011, I delivered these messages to the congregation of Immanuel Baptist Church of Greensboro, North Carolina. I am grateful to this church and to the Lord for granting me the privilege of serving as pastor there since 2005.

I am also thankful for the men whom God has used to shape my life and ministry. Each sermon I preach bears the fingerprints of the influence of these men. My pastor, the late Dr. Mark Corts, influenced me as a pastor and preacher in countless ways. I am particularly indebted to Kenneth Ridings (who introduced me to expository preaching), Ron Owen, Robert Spender, and Walter Kaiser (who instilled a love for the Old Testament in me), Allen Moseley and John Sailhamer (both of whom instructed me in the Hebrew language at Seminary).

The numerous citations throughout the book will indicate the scholars whose works on Jonah have influenced my study of the book. I am thankful for their respective works.

I am thankful to numerous fellow pastors who have encouraged me in the course of my ministry in general, and in the task of preparing this volume in particular. I mention a few here whose friendship through the present season of life has been a great blessing: Billy Belk, Dennis Conner, Jim Upchurch, and Bryan Rhoden. Several friends have made suggestions for improving this work. Most notably I am grateful for Joan Whitcomb and Andrea Barnes for their painstaking editorial review of the work.

Most of all, I am grateful to my family, to whom this volume is dedicated. Their constant love and encouragement is a special blessing of the Lord in my life.

Foreword

Throughout my years of service in pastoral ministry, people have often said that my style of preaching is more like teaching (and I have yet to discover if that is meant as a compliment or a critique). I believe that there is one fundamental difference between teaching and preaching. In teaching, the goal is the transfer of information. In preaching, the goal is the transformation of a person's life. I believe that all good preaching teaches, though not all good teaching is preaching. It is my aim in each message I deliver to do both—to teach and to preach. I believe that good sermons are those which are biblical, theological, historical, edifying, evangelistic, Christ-centered, personal, and practical.

We read in 2 Timothy 3:16-17, "all Scripture is inspired by God and profitable for teaching, for reproof, for correction, and for training in righteousness; so that the man of God may be adequate, equipped for every good work" (2 Timothy 3:16-17). These Scriptures are "able to give you wisdom that leads to salvation through faith which is in Christ Jesus" (3:15). Jesus expounded the Old Testament to His disciples, saying that "all the things which are written about Me in the Law of Moses and the Prophets and the Psalms must be fulfilled" (Luke 24:44). Two of the Gospels record the Lord Jesus pointing specifically to the book of Jonah to proclaim truth about Himself (Matthew 12:38-41; 16:1-4; Luke 11:29-32). He identified Himself as One who is "greater than Jonah" (Matthew 12:41; Luke 11:32). These foundational truths have informed my study of the book of Jonah.

The first section of this volume is a lengthy and semi-technical background study that deals with issues such as the authorship, date, genre, and historical circumstances of the book. Readers who are inclined to find such information tedious and laborious (or who grow weary of reading it) may choose to move immediately to the first exposition that follows the background study. For those with interest in who wrote this book, what kind of literature it was intended to be, and questions regarding historicity, I would commend the background study and the works that are cited therein.

Each subsequent chapter contains a message that can stand alone or build upon the information that comes before it. Because they were originally sermons, I had to keep in mind that my audience may vary from week to week. Someone may be present to hear the exposition of a text from Jonah

3 who was not there to hear a text expounded from Jonah 1. Therefore, from time to time, summary details of the preceding information are repeated. Also, because each message can stand alone, each one concludes with a practical application. Most of these are aimed in two directions at the same time. To those who do not believe on the Lord Jesus Christ, there is the repeated call to repentance and faith. To those who believe, there are points of specific application for the Christian life.

It is my prayer that as these words are read God will use them to feed hungry souls with the bread of life, to quench spiritual thirst with living water, and to scatter broadly the good seed of the Word that it may find good soil in which to grow. There may be areas in which the reader disagrees with me, and some of those may be of greater or lesser importance. There is always the potential for typographical errors or mistaken citations, and the reader's grace is appreciated where those are found. Feel free to share any that you find and we will gladly take them into consideration for future printings. Where the reader suspects that a biblical or theological error is found, I would welcome feedback, not to mention earnest prayer on my behalf.

I submit the project to you, the reader, in humility. If God should honor these words by using them to touch your life in some way, then He alone should receive the glory. Preparing and proclaiming expository messages from God's word is a delightful duty. I do it for His glory, and I give Him the glory for any good that should come from it.

Russ Reaves
Immanuel Baptist Church
Greensboro, NC

The Background of Jonah

The book of Jonah is so named because of the primary human character in the story. His name in Hebrew means "dove." The prophet featured in the book is the same one mentioned in 2 Kings 14:25, as indicated by the repetition of the name of his father Amittai. The sudden introduction of Jonah in the book that bears his name indicates that the original audience was likely familiar with him. As Estelle writes, "We do not know how long our protagonist lived, yet his life, or at least his influence, seems to have overlapped with Jeroboam II's reign."[1] According to 2 Kings 14:25, some of Jonah's prophecies were fulfilled during Jeroboam II's reign, which can be dated to approximately 786-746 BC.[2] Jonah may have been a contemporary of Jeroboam II, or may have preceded him by some time. He was possibly (not to say, likely) an immediate successor of Elijah and Elisha.

A number of rabbinic traditions surround the life of Jonah, but none of them have any historical evidence to validate them. One of these suggests that Jonah may have been a disciple of Elisha.[3] Others have speculated that Jonah was the son of the widow at Zarephath who was restored to life by Elijah (1 Kings 17:17-24). There are also unreliable traditions stating that he was buried in Meshad of Galilee or in Nineveh.[4] Many other creative theories have been put forth in the rabbinic literature, however Scripture is silent on all of these details therefore it is best to ignore them for the purpose of historical reconstruction.

The only accurate biographical information we have about the prophet comes from the book that bears his name and the brief mention of him in 2

---

[1] Bryan D. Estelle, *Salvation Through Judgment and Mercy* (The Gospel According to the Old Testament; Phillipsburg, NJ: P & R Publishing, 2005), 19.

[2] Scholars vary on the specific dates. Some have his dates a bit earlier.

[3] Richard D. Phillips, *Jonah & Micah* (Reformed Expository Commentary; Phillipsburg, NJ: P & R Publishing, 2010), 4. Phillips offers this as a legitimate possibility but offers no argumentation or supporting evidence. This seems to have been an oral tradition that found its way into Rabbinic literature at some point in Israel's history.

[4] Frank Page and Billy K. Smith, *Amos, Obadiah, Jonah* (New American Commentary 19B; Nashville: Broadman & Holman, 1995), 204. Hereafter, cited as Page.

Kings 14:25. This amounts to his name, that of his father (Amittai), that he was a prophet, and that he was from Gath Hepher. From Joshua 19:10-13, we learn that Gath Hepher was located in the territory of Zebulun, in what became the Northern Kingdom following the division of the monarchy. Aside from these basic facts, the rest of Jonah's story must unfold from the details we find within the book of Jonah itself. As Stuart has noted, "The book ... is self-contained. It is not necessary to know much of anything about Jonah's life otherwise to appreciate the story."[5]

Author

The book of Jonah has traditionally been attributed to the prophet whose name it bears. Within the book itself, there is no explicit reference to an author. Therefore, when the title was assigned to it, it may have intended that the book was written by Jonah or that the book is about Jonah. If it is assumed that Jonah intends to be a historical account, then certainly much of its content must come from Jonah, either directly (as the author) or indirectly (as a source consulted by the anonymous author). Those who hold that it is not a historical account do not put forth any effort to connect it to Jonah as an author or source. Yet there is much agreement that the book is not a piecemeal collection of multiple sources but the work of a single writer.[6] As Stuart has pointed out, "The book ... is short and sufficiently united in theme and style ... so as to be rather clearly the work of a single author."[7]

Might this single writer have been the prophet Jonah himself? Even among those who argue for the historicity of the book, there is not a consensus on this question. Stuart, for instance, suggests that it is unlikely that Jonah wrote the book given that it is "so consistently critical" of him. He points to the writer's portrayal of Jonah's "hypocrisy and inconsistency," culminating in "his almost childish stubbornness." While recognizing that much later in his life, "a contrite Jonah ... might have chosen magnanimously to characterize himself this vividly and embarrassingly,"

---

[5] Douglas Stuart, *Hosea-Jonah* (Word Biblical Commentary 31; Waco, TX: Word, 1987), 431

[6] The only portion of the book where literary unity comes into question is the poetic prayer of Chapter 2, which will be discussed below.

[7] Stuart, 431.

Stuart asks, "Where else in the Scriptures (or any ancient literature, for that matter) does an author of a narrative so thoroughly deprecate himself or herself?"[8] One counter example comes to mind immediately from the New Testament. It is nearly unanimously agreed among evangelical scholars that Peter was the source behind the Gospel According to Mark, and this Gospel paints a truer picture of Peter ("warts and all," we might say) than perhaps any other. Likewise, Moses is widely defended by conservatives as the substantial author of the Pentateuch, yet therein we see glimpses of him in which his faith and conduct are deficient. So an autobiographical self-deprecation may be surprising in the book of Jonah, but it is not entirely without parallel in Scripture. It certainly does not eliminate Jonah as a candidate for the author or primary source behind the book that bears his name.

Much of the debate concerning "source material" behind Jonah ignores or else disregards the phenomenon of divine revelation. Among those who confess to a belief in an inspired Bible, it is entirely plausible for the Holy Spirit to reveal information that would have been otherwise unknown to a human author. Yet, as Stuart observes, "virtually all the data from which the story is constructed could have been supplied by two sources: Jonah and the sailors."[9] While the sailors could have informed a narrator of incidents on board the ship that occurred while Jonah was asleep and after he was thrown overboard, Jonah himself could have supplied every other detail.

An evangelical conviction on the truthfulness of Scripture leads one to affirm the historicity of the events described in this book (a discussion that will be developed below). Since the book does not specify that Jonah wrote it, it is no issue of inerrancy or biblical integrity to question whether or not he wrote it. It does seem to entail that the book, if not written by Jonah, was written *at least* by someone who knew him or was sufficiently close to the events to know vivid details, many of which would have only been known to Jonah. Otherwise, it could have also been written by someone who received this information as a direct result of divine inspiration. The issue of Jonah's authorship seems to bear most directly on the psalm of

---

[8] Ibid., 432.
[9] Ibid., 442.

Chapter 2. If this psalm does not come directly from Jonah, then it seems that much literary license has been taken by a writer to put words into his mouth. Such license in this case may exceed the bounds of biblical integrity. Therefore, we would conclude that at a minimum, the psalm of Chapter 2 and other direct quotations from Jonah were composed by the prophet himself. Having concluded this, it is not a far reach to suggest that he could have written the entire document or provided information to another author. On the other hand, it is no sin to leave the identity of the substantial author, editor, or narrator a mystery.

Date

As indicated above, the issues of authorship and date are closely intertwined. If Jonah is the author, then, on the basis of his mention in 2 Kings 14:25, the date of writing could be no later than the first half of the eighth century BC (799-750). Similarly, if it can be demonstrated that the writing took place after this timeframe, then Jonah is eliminated from consideration as a possible author. As Walton points out, even a late date of composition would not lead to the conclusion that the information is historically inaccurate.[10] Seldom, however, does the proposal of a late date accompany a historical interpretation. Frank Page may be excessively generalizing when he says, "A parabolic or allegorical interpretation invariably accompanies the view that the book was a late anonymous composition," yet evidence to the contrary is not easily found.[11]

The book could not have come into existence later than 200 B. C. Around that time, the apocryphal book *Sirach* (also called *Ecclesiasticus*) was written, in which there is reference to "the twelve prophets." This number would include Jonah among the prophets.[12] This presents a broad set of boundaries for dating the book of Jonah between the eighth and third centuries BC. Many scholars attempt to close the window significantly to a range between the sixth and fourth centuries BC, thus placing the book during or immediately following the Babylonian exile. There are four primary reasons set forth by these scholars to validate this time period:

---

[10] Cited in Bill T. Arnold and Bryan E. Beyer, *Encountering the Old Testament* (Grand Rapids: Baker, 1999), 486.
[11] Page, 206.
[12] Ibid.

linguistic data; divergent views on Jewish nationalism and exclusivism; alleged historical inaccuracies; verbal and thematic parallels with later biblical writings.

Concerning linguistic data, it is suggested that several words and phrases found in Jonah are of late origin, being found only during and following the period of exile. Some of these include "Aramaisms," words that were absorbed into the Hebrew vernacular from Aramaic. If this is so, then a late date (post-586 BC) is said to be preferable on the basis that pre-exilic Jews would not likely make use of Aramaic expressions. Of the seven so-called Aramaisms in Jonah, none decisively fit the criteria "necessary to constitute a 'genuine' Aramaism according to O. Loretz."[13] It remains a possibility that the expressions in question do not come from Aramaic but from the influence of Canaanite and Phoenician languages which influenced both Hebrew and Aramaic. This Canaanite and Phoenician influence would have been particularly strong in the northern territories of Israel from whence Jonah hailed. G. M. Landes examined the alleged Aramaisms of Jonah in detail and discovered that many of them are actually found in preexilic texts.[14] Other research has demonstrated that Aramaic was in use during the reign of Sennacherib (705-682 BC) as a language of correspondence.[15] Texts discovered at Ras Shamra dating to 1400 BC or earlier also contain some Aramaic similarity.[16] Landes further notes that there is other linguistic data within Jonah to suggest an early date, which the evidence of these so-called Aramaisms is not persuasive enough to overrule. Landes' conclusion, therefore, is that the linguistic data is not sufficient to date Jonah any later than the sixth century BC (500s).[17] Furthermore, T. D. Alexander concluded that, given a northern Israelite origin, it is "not inconceivable that the book of Jonah could have been written prior to the sixth century, possibly even in the eighth century BC."[18] Therefore, while linguistic data may not be able to conclusively

---

[13] Stuart, 433.
[14] Page, 207.
[15] C. Hassell Bullock, *An Introduction to the Old Testament Prophetic Books* (Chicago: Moody, 1986), 52.
[16] Edward J. Young, *An Introduction to the Old Testament* (Grand Rapids: Eerdmans, 1960), 279.
[17] Cited in Page, 207.
[18] Ibid.

establish the book within the timeframe of Jonah's lifespan, neither does it demand a significantly later time. As Bryan Estelle says, "dating books on linguistic criteria alone is a risky endeavor and the results of such studies are often debated for a number of other reasons."[19]

A second argument for a late date involves what is perceived to be a shift on the matter of Jewish exclusiveness and nationalism. It is argued that even as late as Ezra and Nehemiah (following the exile), there was a narrow view of Israel alone being the privileged recipients of God's favor, while other nations were noticeably outside of both His covenant and His concern. One frequently cited text is Nehemiah 13 in which the Ammonites and Moabites are forbidden from entering the assembly, and mixed marriages are prohibited and forcibly annulled. It is questionable whether or not this is an "apples to apples" comparison. The situation with the Ammonites and Moabites in Nehemiah is restricted and qualified by an explicit cause and a unique set of circumstances. A ban on two nations does not equal a ban on all Gentiles. Further, the issue with the mixed marriages seems to center upon the Jews being led astray into idolatry (like Solomon was) by their unequal yokes with pagan peoples. The issue was idolatry, not ethnicity. To the contrary, throughout the Old Testament we find emphasis on God reaching out to bless all peoples (nations) and to bring them into His covenant. This was stipulated in God's covenant with Abraham (Genesis 12:1-3). Young writes, "As to the universalistic ideas of the book [Jonah], they are in perfect keeping with the universalistic emphasis which appears throughout the Old Testament. ... There is no objective warrant for regarding such teaching as characteristic of post-exilic times alone."[20] Therefore, this reason for accepting a late date of Jonah seems misguided. Rather than suggesting that the book must be late because early books did not look on the nations in this way, Jonah may well be one of several early books that do, in fact, look upon the nations in

---

[19] Estelle, 11-12.

[20] Young, 279. It should be clarified that Young's use of the word "universalistic" is in no way related to the doctrine of "universalism" that teaches that all people will be saved ultimately regardless of their response to the gospel. In the context of Young's statement, "universalistic" clearly means that the purposes of God have the whole world and all the nations in view.

this way. Because of the many flaws with this line of reasoning, Page writes, "This argument ... is generally rejected today."[21]

Though the arguments involving linguistic data and Jewish exclusivism may be inconclusive and easily set aside, the allegation of historical inaccuracy is vital. If there are historical inaccuracies within the book of Jonah, then there are bigger issues at stake than just who wrote it and when. Verifiable historical flaws would be a smoking gun in the case against biblical inerrancy and authority.

Critics say that Jonah must be a late writing (which actually becomes a very small concern in light of the bigger issues at stake) because it contains errors of history and geography. Several of the alleged historical inaccuracies involve the city of Nineveh. It is suggested by critics that Nineveh appears in the narrative as the capital of Assyria, which it was not officially until the reign of Sennacherib (705-682 BC). It should be noted that even if this is assumed to be the case, the book could still originate far closer to the lifetime of Jonah than the exilic or post-exilic periods. It is, however, far from certain that such an assumption is warranted. Upon looking carefully at the text one discovers that Nineveh is never referred to as "the capital." The expression that gives rise to this notion is the phrase "king of Nineveh" in 3:6.[22] Whether or not Nineveh was an official capital of Assyria at the time of Jonah's ministry, it is known that several of Assyria's kings maintained a royal residence there both before and after the lifetime of Jonah. These include Tiglath-Pileser I (1114-1076), Ashurnasirpal II (883-859), and Sargon II (722-705).[23] The phrase "king of Nineveh" may also refer to a period of time in which there were numerous internal revolts in Assyria (763-746 BC). Hallo writes of this period that, "even the central provinces maintained only a tenuous loyalty to Assyria,

---

[21] Page, 207.
[22] It is noted by some that this exact phrase never occurs in the Assyrian annals, indicating that it is a mistaken title. The unusual phrase may well be a case of synecdoche, in which a part of something is used to refer to the whole thing. This occurs twice (1 Kings 21:1; 2 Kings 1:3) in reference to Ahab as "king of Samaria," where the implication is clearly "king of Israel." Though the title "king of Nineveh" is unattested in Assyria's historical records, it is not necessarily inaccurate, nor is it inappropriate for a Hebrew prophet (or his chronicler) to speak of the Assyrian king or a more local regent as such.
[23] Page, 209.

for the various governors ruled in virtual independence."[24] Thus, the "king of Nineveh" may have been a provincial ruler rather than the king over the entire Assyrian empire, or Nineveh may have been the extent of the true king's unquestioned authority. In light of these various possible explanations, the narrator can speak factually of a "king of Nineveh" though it may not have been the actual capital at that time.

Another concern regarding Nineveh relates to its size. In 3:3, we read that "Jonah arose and went to Nineveh ... a three days' walk," or "a journey of three days." It is suggested that this expression refers to the size of Nineveh—that is, that it would take a person three days to traverse or circumnavigate it on foot. If this is the intended meaning, then Nineveh would have been some forty to sixty miles in either diameter or circumference. As Page admits, "All agree, however, that cities in ancient Mesopotamia were not this large" during the time in which Jonah lived.[25] The walls of the ancient city of Nineveh encompassed two mounds, separated by the Khoser River which flows into the Tigris. Archaeological digs have revealed that Nineveh's somewhat rectangular ancient walls measured only about eight miles in length and enclosed approximately 1,800 acres.[26] It is likely that these walls represent an enlargement made later by Sennacherib, so in Jonah's day the city would have been even smaller. It should also be noted that great cities of that region were also not forty to sixty miles in diameter or circumference even by the third century BC. So, on either view of dating the book, if "three days' walk" is a reference to the time it would take one to walk through or around the city, it would be either an intentional or accidental exaggeration. If accidental, this would mean that errors had crept into the Bible. Worse, if intentional, it would mean that the biblical writer is being deceptive, unless the exaggeration is chalked up to hyperbole. Edward J. Young seems to hint at this without affirming that it is hyperbole when he says of the phrase, "possibly it is nothing more than a rough expression to indicate that the city was a large one."[27] If this is hyperbole, then the figurative use of language should be evident to all who encounter it as an indication of the

---

[24] cited in Page, 205.

[25] Page, 208.

[26] LaMoine F. DeVries, *Cities of the Biblical World* (Peabody, Mass.: Hendrickson, 1997), 31.

[27] Young, 279.

city's "inestimable" size. However, this figurative sense is not so plain on the surface and therefore hyperbole seems unlikely. Therefore, either the description is an error or it has been commonly misunderstood.

Perhaps the notion of "a three days' walk" being a reference to the enormous size of the city is not the best understanding of the phrase. Some have suggested that "three days walk" refers not to the size of the city, but rather to the duration of the mission. On this view, "three days' walk" may indicate Jonah's itinerary: a day of arrival (3:4), followed by a day of preaching, then a day of departure. The phrase could also be understood to mean that Jonah's mission in Nineveh would require three days in order to get the message to the entire population. Presumably, he would have needed to speak to a sizeable portion of the city's inhabitants and perhaps make an official visit to the royal residence in order to have the effect that is described in the book. This task would have likely required several days to complete. So, when 3:4 says that Jonah "began to go through the city one day's walk," Young writes, "This does not mean that he walked as far as it is possible to walk in one day. It merely means that he entered the city and went about, doubtless here and there, preaching his message."[28] As Bullock writes, "It is conceivable that he could have delivered the bad news to all of Nineveh's citizens in a period of three days, stopping at the main gates (Nineveh had over a dozen), the temple courts, and perhaps the king's palace."[29] Walton points out that when a distance requiring three days to travel is intended in other passages, a different Hebrew phrase is used than that which is found here.[30] Furthermore, the "three days' walk" could refer to what we might call "Greater Nineveh" as opposed to "Nineveh Proper", comprising the area including Nineveh, Asshur, Calah, and Dur-Sharrukin. Bullock notes, "All three of those were occupied

---

[28] Ibid., 279.
[29] Bullock, 47.
[30] Cited in Bullock, 47. The Hebrew word rendered "walk" in Jonah 3:3 and 3:4 is *mahalak*, also found in Nehemiah 2:6 (where it may well allude to the duration of the task rather than the distance of the journey), Ezekiel 42:4 (where it describes a "walk", as in a "walkway" or "corridor"), and Zechariah 3:7 (where the plural *mahlkim* is used in a sense that is difficult to pinpoint with precision). In Genesis 30:36, Exodus 3:18, 5:3, and Numbers 10:33, where the sense is plainly a distance requiring three days to travel, the Hebrew word *derek* (a word commonly denoting "road" or "way") is used.

within the period between 850 and 614 BC, and all were within one to three days' walk of each other."[31]

A related concern has to do with the population of Nineveh, which 4:11 specifies to include "more than 120,000 persons who do not know the difference between their right and left hand." There are varying interpretations on the exact meaning of this phrase: does it refer to children only?; does it signify moral and spiritual ignorance?; etc, which affect estimates of *total* population. These estimates are called into question by some who suggest that the city was too small to accommodate 120,000 or more people in that day. Yet, a text discovered at Calah (the neighboring city which may have been part of "Greater Nineveh") states that King Ashur-nasir-apli entertained 69,574 guests, undoubtedly from several surrounding cities, at a major dedication event in 865 BC.[32] It is no stretch to assume that *everyone* did not attend the event, and even among those who did, there may be children, elderly relatives, and others in their families or homes who did not attend. This being so, it is not unreasonable to suggest that the Greater Nineveh area, if not Nineveh Proper, could have had well over 120,000 residents.

Though Nineveh is repeatedly called a "great" city in Jonah, its greatness is not necessarily one of size or population (though it may have been great in both of these as well). In the Hebrew text, the phrasing of Jonah 3:3 reads literally that it was "a great city to God." While there are numerous interpretations of this statement (evidenced by the variety of creative attempts to translate it into English), Stuart says, "The point is that Nineveh was a city God was concerned for, one that was by no means insignificant to him. Nineveh's physical size may have figured prominently into its importance, as may have its population, but there is no ground for assuming that size per se is the issue" when Nineveh is referred to as "great."[33]

Some have suggested that the book must have originated at a date later than 612 BC, for it was at that time that Nineveh fell from its position of prominence in the region. This is based on the description of Nineveh in

---

[31] Bullock, 47.
[32] Ibid.
[33] Stuart, 487.

3:3: "Now Nineveh *was* an exceedingly great city." The use of the past tense here is said to indicate that, while Nineveh had been an important city in the past, it was no longer at the time Jonah was written. Young rightly observes that the past tense "does not describe Nineveh as a city that had existed long ago in the past but simply indicates the condition or size as Jonah found it."[34] Pointing to Luke 24:13, where it is said of Emmaus that it "*was* about seven miles from Jerusalem," Young says that the words "simply describe the location and do not imply that Emmaus was a city which had existed in the distant past but was no longer in existence."[35] Neither does the past tense in that text suggest that Emmaus was *no longer* seven miles from Jerusalem. Reading the phrase as it occurs in Luke, we understand that it *was* that distance from Jerusalem, and *still is*, at least at the time of writing.[36]

Caution must be exercised when interpreting a "time sense" of Hebrew verbs, because it has been well argued that Hebrew tenses do not carry the same idea of past, present, and future that is found in the verbs of English and many other languages. The form of the verb translated here in Jonah 3:3 as a past tense ("was") is Qal perfect (or *qatal*). This form is by far the most common of all verbs in the Hebrew Bible. Sailhamer notes, "In narration, the *qatal* [perfect] denotes an action lying behind the main sequence of verbal events. It is a part of the background of the narration. … The *qatal* expresses events previous to the moment of narration … and concurrent with … the moment of narration."[37] According to Ross, the perfect tense may be translated several ways depending "on the kind of sentence and the meaning of the word itself. The perfect tense is in the indicative mood (which presents the action as an objective fact) and essentially reflects completed action (i.e., 'perfect' action in a linguistic sense)."[38] This is why the Qal perfect is so commonly rendered in English in the "past" tense. However, Ross notes that a Qal perfect verb may be

---

[34] Young, 279.

[35] Ibid.

[36] This is not a "special hermeneutic"; it is normal use of language. I recently visited a rural village in Nepal and I have told many people that the hotel where I stayed there *was* a terribly uncomfortable place. It is still there (though from the shape it was in I do not care to speculate how much longer it will be there), and undoubtedly it is still uncomfortable.

[37] John Sailhamer, *A Grammar of Biblical (Tanak) Hebrew* (unpublished course material from Southeastern Baptist Theological Seminary), 76.

[38] Allen P. Ross, *Introducing Biblical Hebrew* (Grand Rapids: Baker, 2001), 89.

translated as a simple past, a perfect (stressing continuing effects of a past action), a present, or a present in the sense of setting forth a general truth. Use of the present to render a Qal perfect is especially appropriate with verbs "that are stative (i.e., describe a state) or that signify thinking, knowing, or perceiving (rather than an action directly performed on an object)."[39] Therefore, though the past tense makes good literary sense in the reading of 3:3, we must not think that it exclusively means that Nineveh had been great at one time was not great at the time of writing. It may well mean that it was a great city, and still was when Jonah visited and when the book of Jonah was written. Stuart writes, "the Hebrew narrative style calls for the past tense regardless of proximity to events. Thus the importance of the verb in 3:3 is easily overrated."[40]

In addition to concerns regarding literary data, Jewish nationalism, and historical accuracy, some have stated that the book of Jonah must have been written much later than the lifetime of Jonah because it shows marks of dependency upon other, later biblical literature. Frequently cited are parallels in both wording and subject matter found in Kings, Jeremiah, and Joel. For example, the argument of parallels between Jonah and Joel focuses on the near identical words found in Jonah 3:9, 4:2 and Joel 2:13-14.

Before even examining the wording of the text, one obvious factor here is that those who would argue that this similarity proves a dependency of Jonah upon Joel and therefore a late date are making some bold assumptions. First, there is the assumption that this similarity proves dependence, and further that it proves Jonah is the book which is doing the borrowing. Second, and related, there is an assumption or reasoned conclusion that Joel definitely originates from a late, post-exilic date. The various arguments for the dating of Joel are beyond the scope of this study. Scholars of all theological persuasions differ with one another in their conclusions, and many are uncommitted to a position because of the difficulty of nailing down a specific date for Joel. A survey of popular, conservative, evangelical study Bibles demonstrates the slipperiness of this issue. The NIV Study Bible says, "a good case can be made for its being

---

[39] Ibid., 90.
[40] Stuart, 432.

written in the ninth century BC,"[41] while the ESV Study Bible provides a five-point argument for dating Joel after the Babylonian exile in 586 BC.[42] This alone should warn us against being dogmatic about date claims for Joel. After all, if Joel dates to the ninth century BC as some suggest, then it could both precede and inform Jonah without requiring Jonah to be postexilic. Additionally, since there is some measure of elasticity in the dating of both of these books, and the author of Jonah remains anonymous, Stuart has gone so far as to suggest, "It could even be the case, after all, that the prophet Joel was the anonymous narrator of the book of Jonah."[43]

Beyond this, the similar wording in these passages includes a description of God as "gracious and compassionate, slow to anger, abounding in lovingkindness and relenting of evil." This description of God is one of the most frequently recurring statements about His nature in all Scripture. God revealed Himself to Moses in Exodus 34:6 with these very words. Therefore, it is entirely possible, if not plausible, that both Jonah and Joel are repeating frequently stated words about the nature of God without one of them borrowing from the other.

As Page well states, "Arguments based on literary dependency ... are seldom convincing because of the difficulty of proving the direction of dependency."[44] What this means is that when two writings bear similarities, it is very difficult to determine which one borrowed from the other. This is particularly true when it comes to inspired Scripture, whose ultimate author is God the Holy Spirit. Therefore, it must not be a shocking discovery to find similar statements and content from book to book; it should be expected! If Scripture is inspired in the way that it claims to be, then the greater surprise would be to find significant variance between the ideas expressed in biblical literature. It is this very line of reasoning that Stuart applies to the allegations of the dependency of Jonah upon Jeremiah (the evidence of which he calls "both minimal and ambiguous"), saying, "sharing of concepts is not the same as a dependency of concepts. ... The similarity of Jonah and Jeremiah is far more cogently attributable to the

---

[41] *The NIV Study Bible* (Grand Rapids: Zondervan, 1995), 1330.
[42] *ESV Study Bible* (Wheaton, Ill.: Crossway, 2008), 1643.
[43] Stuart, 433.
[44] Page, 209.

univocal nature of divine revelation throughout the Scripture than to a borrowing from Jeremiah on the part of the book of Jonah."[45]

As Page has written, "Perhaps the most convincing argument for the probability of a preexilic date is to recognize that Jonah's ministry was clearly in the vein of preclassical prophecy. His writings and prophecy preserved the tensions present in the prophetic community of the eighth century BC."[46] The events of the book are narrated as if they occurred in that time, and contain details that would only be known to the prophet himself or someone very close to him. Since, as Richard Phillips has written, "there is no compelling reason to doubt that this book of Scripture dates from the time frame it describes, the eighth century B.C.,"[47] it may be best to leave the date of origin at that early period unless further evidence and information comes to light to persuade us otherwise. However, academic integrity and Christian humility should prevent us from making the dating of this book a litmus test for orthodoxy, unless one's conclusion required one to depart from a commitment to biblical inerrancy and authority or to compromise core Christian doctrines.

Historical Circumstances

As mentioned above, the ministry of the prophet Jonah can be dated roughly to the reign of Jeroboam II of Israel (786-746 BC). The reference to Jonah in 2 Kings 14:25 indicates that his prophecy came to pass under Jeroboam II's reign, so the prophet may have lived and ministered at some time prior to Jeroboam II's reign. King Solomon had been dead for upwards of 150 years by this time, and it was immediately following the death of Solomon that the Kingdom of Israel experienced upheaval. The northern tribes began to chase after false gods (1 Kings 12-14) and the Kingdom was divided in two. The northern ten tribes came to be called Israel, and the two tribes of the south were called Judah. Because of God's fatherly love for His people, He disciplined them whenever they became unfaithful, often using foreign powers as His agents of judgment.

---

[45] Stuart, 433.
[46] Page, 209.
[47] Phillips, 4.

Assyrian threats toward Israel were in full swing by the time of the reigns of Shalmaneser in Assyria and Jehu in Israel (842-815 BC) when the Assyrian king demanded payment of a tribute from Israel. The Black Obelisk of Shalmaneser bears an inscription that reads in Akkadian, "I [Shalmaneser] received the tribute of the inhabitants of Tyre, Sidon, and of Jehu, son of Omri."[48]

Jonah had prophesied good news for Israel which came to fruition under Jeroboam II. In 2 Kings 14, we read:

> He [Jeroboam II] restored the border of Israel from the entrance of Hamath as far as the Sea of the Arabah, *according to the word of the LORD, the God of Israel, which He spoke through His servant Jonah the son of Amittai, the prophet, who was of Gath-hepher.* For the LORD saw the affliction of Israel, which was very bitter; for there was neither bond nor free, nor was there any helper for Israel. The LORD did not say that He would blot out the name of Israel from under heaven, but He saved them by the hand of Jeroboam the son of Joash. (2 Kings 14:25-27).

That this reprieve of Assyrian dominance and restoration of Israel's territory was all a gift of divine mercy and grace is evident in the preceding context of those verses. Second Kings 14:24 makes clear that Jeroboam II "did evil in the sight of the LORD; he did not depart from all the sins of Jeroboam the son of Nebat, which he made Israel sin."

When Israel was advancing to reclaim the territories of their ancient boundaries, Assyria seemed to be preoccupied with other, more pressing concerns. New skirmishes with the Arameans and Urartians, a severe famine (from 765-759 BC, or perhaps multiple famines within that timeframe), and various internal revolts (763-760 BC, and 746 BC) contributed to a state of affairs in which, "for 36 years (781-745 BC) Assyria was practically paralyzed."[49] At roughly the half-way point of this period, the *Eponym Chronicle* records that a total solar eclipse occurred (763 BC). A major earthquake also occurred in the region during this time.

---

[48] Estelle, 14.
[49] Page, 204-205.

These events would have undoubtedly have been considered ominous, and may have increased the spiritual receptivity of the people of Nineveh.

Perhaps it was during the period of Assyria's diminished power that Jonah was called to go and prophesy there. For its entire history, Israel had not only been called to be the privileged recipients of divine favor, but also the specially commissioned messengers of God's truth and grace to the nations. Though God had, at least temporarily, spared Israel from destruction at the hands of the Assyrians, there was still a proclamation of repentance and redemption to be announced to the unbelieving peoples of Nineveh and its surrounding regions. Old Testament scholar Samuel Schultz writes, "From the human standpoint, Assyria was the last place any Israeli would choose for a missionary venture."[50] Just as Elisha, Jonah's predecessor, knew that anointing Hazael as king in Aram would mean destruction for Israel (2 Kings 8:7-13), so Jonah must have known that announcing judgment to Nineveh may provoke them to repentance, thus sparing them from disaster and preserving them to bring destruction upon Israel.

Though the threat of Assyrian domination over Israel had temporarily diminished, it did not disappear. Assyria would remain a potential force to be used as agents of divine judgment if God should choose in His appointed time. Jonah's prophetic successors, Hosea and Amos, foretold of this very judgment coming upon Israel at the hands of the Assyrians. Beginning with Tiglath-Pileser III (744 BC), who reasserted Assyrian power and once again subjugated Israel and Judah (2 Kings 15-16), and continuing through the reigns of Shalmaneser V (726 BC) and Sargon II (721 BC), Assyria would reassert itself and ultimately conquer the Northern Kingdom of Israel in 722 BC.[51] But this took place under the sovereign hand of God, who had raised Assyria up to bring judgment on the idolatry and unfaithfulness of Israel. Israel had spurned repeated prophetic warnings. Assyria heeded the only prophetic warning it ever received when Jonah came to Nineveh, and though they did not necessarily turn to orthodox monotheistic faith on a widespread or long-term scale,

---

[50] Samuel Schultz, *The Old Testament Speaks* (New York: HarperCollins, 1990), 380.
[51] Estelle, 14.

that temporary revival spared them from certain judgment and preserved them for the use of God to bring judgment upon Israel.

Style and Genre

The issue of Jonah's literary style and genre is wrapped up in the question of its author and dating. If the book was written as a narrative of historical events, then a stronger case can be made for Jonah or one of his close contemporaries as the author, and the date being close to the eighth century BC. However, if the genre is parable, allegory, or some other non-historical form, then the date and authorship of the book become much more elastic.

The book of Jonah is short, with only four chapters and forty-eight verses. Yet, nearly every scholar who examines the book remarks univocally about the sophisticated style and superb skill of the writer. Estelle writes, "The prophecy of Jonah is an extremely subtle and complex piece of work," and remarks that its writer is a "very thoughtful and skilled author."[52] Bullock says, "His Hebrew is smooth and simple, and his literary ability to tell a story is unsurpassed by any other author in the Old Testament."[53] Page comments on the "high degree of literary excellence" by citing Allen, who calls Jonah a "model of literary artistry, marked by symmetry and balance." Further, Page quotes Brichto as saying that it is "a masterpiece of rhetoric. ... As an aesthetic achievement the marvel of its creation is surpassed, if anything, by the marvel of its pristine preservation and transmission over a period of 25 centuries and more."[54] Stuart says, "Jonah is *sensational* literature; that is, the book is clearly composed with a high concentration of elements designed to arouse the imagination and emotion of the audience (the storm at sea, the fish story, the plant story, etc.)."[55]

Many scholars assume that the literary sophistication of the book stands as evidence against a simple historical interpretation of it. According to Page, this assumption involves "a false dichotomy between history and literature or history and prophecy, as if a work cannot relate historical events in a rhetorically sophisticated fashion for didactic purposes." Yet, as Page

---

[52] Ibid., 2.
[53] Bullock, 52.
[54] Page, 219.
[55] Stuart, 435.

counters, "the Bible is full of literature that does this very thing."[56] Stuart notes that, in spite of the stylistic richness of Jonah, a "relatively simple vocabulary prevails throughout the book, something to be expected if the inspired narrator did not wish the didactic impact of the story to be missed at any point by reason of the intrusion of an overly complex style."[57] In other words, the simple, historical interpretation yields itself easily to the reader through a straightforward vocabulary. Yet many scholars remain convinced, for various reasons, that the historical position must be jettisoned in our day. Once the historical genre is assumed to be without merit, there seem to be few limits placed on the possible kind of literature before us in Jonah.

To assign Jonah to the category of a parable or allegory is to immediately alleviate many questions and concerns about the book. Brevard Childs has said, "By determining that the book of Jonah functions in its canonical context as a parable-like story, the older impasse regarding the historicity of the story is by-passed as a theological issue." Childs does not dismiss the presence of some "historical features" in the story, but he concludes that it is "theologically irrelevant" whether the events occurred.[58] From his comments one can easily see the pragmatic expediency of relegating Jonah to the status of parable or allegory, but the merits of the position must rest on more than a pragmatic footing if it is to be adopted.

An allegory is, as Stuart defines it, "a kind of extended analogy, sometimes including extended metaphors, in which the meaning of the story is not to be found in the concepts and actions presented, but in concepts and actions outside the story, to which the story points analogically."[59] There are several examples of allegory within the Old Testament, including Ecclesiastes 12:3-5, Jeremiah 25:15-29, Ezekiel 17:3-10, 19:2-9, 24:3-5, and Zechariah 11:4-17. It is evident that Jonah is considerably lengthier than these other biblical allegories. Allegories do not *have to* be short, but in the Bible they are typically much shorter than Jonah.

---

[56] Page, 210.
[57] Stuart, 437.
[58] cited in Page, 210.
[59] Stuart, 436.

In order to qualify as an allegory, the various elements of the story within Jonah must represent certain aspects in the life of Israel. Those who hold to an allegorical interpretation often point to Jonah's name, which means "dove," as one of the story's symbolic elements. Based on references to Israel as a dove in Psalm 74:19, Hosea 7:11, and Hosea 11:11, Jonah is thought by many to be a symbol of Israel. The fish is sometimes likened to Babylon, who swallowed up Judah in the captivity of 586 B.C. This exile took place in part because of their failure to take the good news of God to the nations. This failure is represented in the story by Jonah's decision to flee to Tarshish rather than accept God's call to Nineveh. The regurgitation of the prophet onto dry land is seen to be indicative of the restoration of the Israelites from Babylon. At first glance, this proposal seems to "work"; it successfully incorporates authentic biblical teaching from the latter Old Testament era without denying the historicity of any of them (albeit, while denying the historicity of Jonah). However, the theory is not without its difficulties.

Because figurative literature requires a "suspension of the rules" of normal interpretation, the presence of an allegory must be clearly recognizable, to the extent that any ordinary reader would detect that literal, historical meaning is not intended. A writer of allegory has failed to communicate well if a sizeable portion of his readership leaves the story under the impression that historical events have been factually described therein. Yet this is precisely what has happened over the centuries with the book of Jonah. Time and time again, the readers of this book have come away from it believing that it intends to relate a historical, factual account. If this was not the writer's intention, then he (or she) is a tremendous failure at the task of writing, which is, interestingly, precisely the opposite point that defenders of non-literal interpretations want to make. They insist that the literary greatness of the book demands a non-literal interpretation, but to quote Stuart, "style is largely irrelevant to factuality."[60] As Bullock states, "no Old Testament allegory is written so straightforwardly as historical narrative as is Jonah." He cites Perowne who comments that Jonah's

[60] Ibid., 440.

19

setting "is too exact, too detailed, too closely in accordance with facts, to be in keeping with the allegory itself."[61]

Further, in an allegory, nearly every element of the story has a symbolic reference to something other than itself. Defenders of the allegorical position go to great lengths to demonstrate how Jonah refers to Israel and the fish refers to Babylon (though not all are agreed), etc., but the system breaks down in two crucial areas. The part of the pagan nation is played in this allegory by a pagan nation. Nineveh cannot stand, allegorically, for the pagan world because Nineveh is part of that pagan world. It might be argued that Nineveh is later depicted in the story by the plant, but this only further complicates the interpretation. On this reading, the plant symbolizes Nineveh, which in turn symbolizes itself and the larger collection of nations of which it is a part. That is stretching the bounds of allegorical interpretation on nearly every definition of it. Similarly, in the story, the element that is said to symbolize God is none other than God Himself. As Page says, "The point of a biblical allegory or parable is to clarify a spiritual or heavenly truth on the basis of analogy with common earthly experience. Having God as a main character in such a story would be counterproductive."[62]

Related, if the allegorical genre is so plainly present in this book, then we might expect for the symbols to reveal themselves in an easily recognizable way. Yet, when one surveys the allegorical treatments of Jonah, there is seldom agreement on the symbols and referents contained therein. For example, though many argue that Jonah, the "dove," is a picture of Israel, Page notes, "One work associates the 'dove' with Nineveh, the chief sanctuary of the goddess 'Ishtar,' whose sacred bird was the dove."[63] Page also notes that there are erroneous biblical references in some allegorical handlings of Jonah. One of these involves Jonah's flight to Tarshish, which is supposed to represent the sin of Israel that precipitated the Babylonian captivity, namely their failure to spread the truth of God to the nations. However, in Scripture, the reason revealed for the Babylonian captivity is Israel's unfaithfulness to God's covenant in their rampant idolatry and

---

[61] Bullock, 44-45.
[62] Page, 212.
[63] Ibid.

immorality. Additionally, the Babylonian captivity was primarily a judgment against the Southern Kingdom, Judah. However, Judah does not figure into the story at all. The prophet hails from the Northern Kingdom of Israel. This tension could be alleviated by arguing that the fish represents the Assyrian domination of Israel in 722 BC, but then one would be hard-pressed to identify symbolically the regurgitation of the prophet, for Israel never "bounced back" from the Assyrian conquest. Similarly, the fish cannot represent God's judgment of His people, whether at the hands of Babylon or Assyria, for in the story the fish is clearly seen as a means of deliverance rather than punishment. Beyond this, Jonah actually asked to be thrown into the sea for the sake of the other sailors, and nothing in any biblical narrative concerning the destruction of Israel or Judah can be shown to reflect this scenario.[64]

In the end, Burrows is correct when he says that the "greatest weakness of this kind of [allegorical] exposition is that it is only to a small degree controlled by the text."[65] It is a good general rule that interpretation of a text must be rooted within the text, and where this is not the case, any proposed interpretation can be considered invalid. For these reasons, it seems that an attempt to identify Jonah as an allegory fails.

Others have claimed that Jonah is not an allegory, but rather a parable. Parables and allegories are similar, both having a figurative interpretation that signifies a truth beyond the events, characters, and actions of the story itself. However, there are significant differences between the two genres as well. Parables are typically shorter than allegories, and normally consist of a single scene.[66] In an allegory, nearly every detail can carry symbolic meaning, while in a parable there may be few symbolic elements. It is the story as a whole that carries the symbolic meaning. An allegory may have many "points" or "lessons" to teach, but a parable typically only seeks to reinforce one primary truth. In a parable, there is typically some unexpected twist, what Stuart calls a "shock" or "punch line," which has the effect of drawing "the hearer up short as it teaches a lesson, the reader

---

[64] Ibid., 212-213.
[65] Cited in Page, 213.
[66] Stuart, 436. Stuart notes that in some cases a parable may have two or three scenes, such as the story of the prodigal son in Luke 15. These would be rare exceptions, as evidenced by a survey of Jesus' parables.

seeing himself or herself in the story."[67] Additionally, characters in a parable tend to be anonymous, and are certainly not well-known figures from history. The fact that Jesus names a character in Luke 16 (Lazarus) has caused some to ponder if that pericope can be rightly called a parable. If so, it is one of the only known parables in which one of the primary characters is not anonymous. In Jonah, not only is the main character named, he is identified as a well known prophet from Israel's history. This would be a highly unusual feature in a parable. Stuart also notes that a significant feature of a parable is that it is "obviously fictional."[68] Thus, regardless of whether one believes that Jonah is factual or fictional, the very fact that there is a debate on the question at all suggests that it is not "obviously fictional." Page has concluded that "its multiple elements and the complexity of its themes are not characteristic of the parabolic form."[69]

Perhaps in light of the difficulty posed by the appearance of a notable historical figure in the story, other scholars have abandoned the parabolic or allegorical interpretation in favor of a more nuanced view. It is the opinion of some that Jonah represents an example of midrashic literature. As Trible explains, "a midrash is a commentary on a portion of ancient Scripture whose purpose was to adapt it to an immediate situation." In a midrash, a story takes the form of a legend, "a narrative with a historical core embellished by imagination."[70] Trible claims that Jonah is a midrash on Exodus 34:6, by which the merciful character of God which was declared in Exodus is illustrated through this non-historical, embellished account concerning the prophet. On her view, the historical core includes Jonah and "the geographical locations referred to," but this core has been "embellished considerably by mythological and folk-tale motifs."

In Trible's argument for this position, she states that the text which is being expounded by the midrash should be "evident in the midrash itself."[71] However, among those who claim that Jonah is a midrash, there is little agreement on which text is being expounded. Though Trible points to Exodus 34:6, others have argued that Jonah is a midrash of 2 Kings 14:25,

---

[67] Ibid.
[68] Ibid.
[69] Page, 214.
[70] Cited in Page, 211.
[71] Page, 211.

Jeremiah 18:8, Joel 2:13-14, or Amos 7:9-11, to name a few. This lack of agreement should cause us to question whether Jonah could rightly be identified as a midrash. Stuart notes that, in order for Jonah to be "convincingly identified as a midrash, it would need to be demonstrated that the story was composed to serve as an illustrative explanation of something taught elsewhere in the Old Testament." He asserts that Jonah "appears far more likely to be not the midrash but the primary material, so that any midrash would be secondary, i.e., a discussion of the truth contained in Jonah."[72] Additionally, even if one dates Jonah to a post-exilic period, it would be one of the earliest examples of midrash known to exist, for the form did not develop until significantly later.[73] Though the word *midrash* occurs in the Hebrew Old Testament in 2 Chronicles 13:22 and 24:27, its meaning there is hard to determine and does not seem to have much similarity to the later known form of midrash. For these reasons, it seems improbable to identify Jonah as a midrash.

While others have proposed various other kinds of non-historical literature as the genre for Jonah, a common element in nearly every non-historical approach is a suspicion of the supernatural features of Jonah. Brewer can be cited as an example of this kind of approach, as he admits that this is the primary reason to treat Jonah as unhistorical. The miracles of Jonah, including his three day and three night sojourn in the belly of the great fish, are more than can be considered within "the limits of credibility," according to Brewer.[74] However, this approach may be due to an anti-supernatural bias rather than an objective examination of the text. After all, the miraculous elements of Jonah are not without parallel in numerous other texts of the Old and New Testaments. As Stuart notes, "one can reject these on the basis of a systematic anti-supernatural bias, but one cannot single out Jonah in this regard. The argument that 'miracles can't happen, therefore they don't' is a subjective, not an objective, basis for discounting the factuality of the miracle narratives in Jonah."[75]

Walton's eloquent observation is worthy of full quotation:

---

[72] Stuart, 436.
[73] Page, 211, notes that even Trible admits this in her defense of the position.
[74] Cited in Page, 214.
[75] Stuart, 440.

If these be miracles, it is useless to discuss the gullet sizes and geographical habitats of dozens of species of whales, or the chemical content of mammalian digestive juices and their projected effect on human epidermis over prolonged periods. If we wanted to discuss this sort of thing, we would have to begin with first things first, and ask whether or not God could talk to man, as he did in Jonah 1:1.[76]

Elsewhere, Walton and Hill write similarly,

Affirming the factual nature of the book does not require one to attempt to identify what species of fish was involved (not necessarily a whale) on the basis of gullet size and having the Mediterranean as a natural habitat, etc., as many conservative interpreters have felt obliged to do. The fish's action was ordained by God, and if the possibility of the miraculous is accepted philosophically, further identification is irrelevant and may be impossible.[77]

If the miraculous elements of Scripture are considered from a biblically and theologically informed vantage point, one will likely observe that there are periods of redemptive history in which miracles occurred with greater frequency and intensity. These periods seem to involve new revelation from God, transitions from one source of revelation to another, and periods in which the revealed truth of God is made known in new places and to new peoples. So, we find the epochs of creation, the giving of the Law, the institution of the ministry of the prophets, the ministry of Jesus Christ and His apostles, and the spread of the Gospel into pioneer territories as eras in which the miraculous occurred with somewhat extraordinary frequency and intensity. If Jonah is among the earliest of the prophets, perhaps being an immediate successor to Elijah and Elisha, and if the truth about God is being revealed for the first time to the pagans of Assyria through Jonah's ministry, then it would not be unusual, unprecedented, or entirely unexpected, for miracles to dominate this story. Keil has noted that "the book of Jonah is similar in content and form to the history of Elijah and

---

[76] Cited in Page, 215.

[77] Andrew E. Hill and John H. Walton, *A Survey of the Old Testament* (Second Edition; Grand Rapids: Zondervan, 200), 496.

Elisha (1 Kings 17-19; 2 Kings 2:4-6)," and surely this inclusion of the miraculous is one evident way in which it is.[78]

Dillard and Longman are careful to point out that we must not categorize "all people who argue for a parabolic interpretation as deniers of the miraculous. Clearly some are driven to a non-historical reading of the book because they do not believe the fish incident is possible. But others, such as Allen, are convinced that the inspired author intended his book to be read as a parable, not as a historical report."[79] Further, they add that there are other characteristics within Jonah "that may further signal that the author did not intend his readers to understand his account to be historical." They cite as an example, "a level of vagueness in the world of the story," noting that "Jonah is the only character with a name."[80] Yet, it seems that this argument could also be advanced as evidence of the opposite point. After all, someone composing a fantastical narrative would have no objection to manufacturing names and other details to eliminate some of the vagueness. If there is a vagueness about the story, it could just as easily demonstrate historical accuracy as unhistorical authorial intent. All of this notwithstanding, it does seem that a lion's share of those who reject a literal, historical reading do so on the basis of an anti-supernatural bias. Though a small number of witnesses may be called forth who reject a historical interpretation on a strictly literary basis, their cases for a figurative genre are not without problems, as indicated above.

If, as Trible says, the book of Jonah is so "clearly non-historical," then Page is right to note that "it only became so in the nineteenth century," for "prior to that virtually every biblical scholar and reader of the book assumed that it at least claimed to recount actual events."[81] T. D. Alexander appropriately asks, "Were these earlier generations completely blind to features which we are asked to believe are immediately apparent?"[82] The book of Jonah deals with known historical figures and

[78] Cited in Bullock, 45.
[79] Raymond B. Dillard and Tremper Longman III, *An Introduction to the Old Testament* (Grand Rapids: Zondervan, 1994), 392. "Allen" refers to L. C. Allen, *The Books of Joel, Obadiah, Jonah and Micah* (New International Commentary on the Old Testament; Grand Rapids: Eerdmans, 1976).
[80] Dillard and Longman, 392.
[81] Page, 217.
[82] Cited in Page, 218.

geographical locations. It bears no internal indicators of a non-historical intent. Therefore, internal evidence suggests that the book's writer intended for it to be understood as a historical narrative. The question of its historicity, then, becomes a theological one rather than a literary one.

Jesus pointed to the story of Jonah as a picture of His resurrection in Matthew 12:38-42 and Luke 11:29-32. Some have suggested that the story does not have to be historically accurate in order to be used by Jesus in this way, however the context indicates that Jesus *was* speaking of the story in a historical way. He identifies the men of Nineveh (from the story of Jonah) along side of the Queen of the South (or Queen of Sheba, whose historical identity is nowhere under serious question) as those who will rise up and testify against the unbelieving generation of Jesus' own day. Bullock writes, "If the reference to the Ninevites is taken to be merely illustrative and not historical, then we have a confusing mixture of non-historical and historical material in the same analogy. Further, the condemnation of Jesus' generation is far less effective if the repentance of the Ninevites is non-historical."[83] On the basis of Christ's reference to Jonah, the church fathers understood Jonah to be historical. Cyril of Jerusalem, writing around 370 A.D., exemplifies this as he writes, "If that [the story of Jonah and the fish] is credible, this [the resurrection of Jesus] is credible also; if this [the resurrection] is incredible, that [Jonah and the fish] also is incredible. For to me both are alike worthy of credence. I believe that Jonas was preserved, for all things are possible with God; I believe that Christ also was raised from the dead."[84] Writing around the turn of the twentieth century, J. W. McGarvey stated, "It is really a question as to whether Jesus is to be received as a competent witness respecting historical and literary matters of the ages which preceded His own."[85]

In the final analysis, it seems advisable to conclude that the book does not neatly fit into any unhistorical genre of literature and appears to be intended as a historical narrative. Objections against this line of

---

[83] Bullock, 46.

[84] Cyril of Jerusalem, *Catechetical Lecture XIV, On the Words, And Rose Again from the Dead on the Third Day, and Ascended into the Heavens, and Sat on the Right Hand of the Father.* http://www.ccel.org/ccel/schaff/npnf207.ii.xviii.html. Accessed April 5, 2011.

[85] Cited in Page, 218.

interpretation have reasonable answers. As Stuart writes, "There is ample evidence to support the historicity of the book, and surprisingly little to undermine it."[86] It seems to be something of a cop-out to suggest that the historicity of the events have no bearing on the didactic importance of the book. Dillard and Longman lean toward this when they say with regret that "the debate that surrounds the historicity of this story has obscured its literary beauty and theological significance."[87] They further say "that the question is irrelevant to the interpretation of the book. This is not to say that the issue is unimportant. If the book intends to be historical, but makes a historical error, that is theologically significant. But the question of the intention of historicity is totally without effect on the interpretation of the book's theological message or even the exegesis of individual passages."[88] However, Stuart rightly asserts,

> ... the issue of historicity has implications beyond the formal didactic function of the narrative. If the events described in the book actually happened, the audience's existential identification with the characters and circumstances is invariably heightened. People act more surely upon what they believe to be true in fact, than merely what they consider likely in theory. If it really happened, it is really serious. ... it is not simply a narrator's desire, it is God's enforceable revelation.[89]

---

[86] Stuart, 440.

[87] Dillard and Longman, 391.

[88] Ibid., 393. Their statement here is nearly nonsensical. They seem to want to have their cake and eat it too. While admitting that a historical error in a historical work is theologically significant, they seek to push that question from the table by asserting that it is insignificant for the theological understanding of the book to determine if it is historical or not. This line of reasoning is akin to the phenomenon of "theological doublespeak" that once plagued evangelical seminaries. During a previous era, some professors understood that the views which they felt they must hold to be "academically credible" would not be considered "biblically faithful" by the rank and file Christians in the local church. Therefore, they spoke one way in the classroom and another way in the pulpit. Dillard and Longman seem to suggest by this statement that they are caught between the Scylla of "academic credibility" and the Charibdis of "biblical faithfulness." Many times, the narrow strait between the two can be navigated safely, but often the ship must run aground on one bank or another. One might wish that more scholars were willing to run aground on the shores of biblical faithfulness rather than steering toward the acceptability of an academic culture which has no regard for biblical faithfulness.

[89] Stuart, 440.

Some scholars have advanced nuanced positions on the style and genre that maintain its historical accuracy while further seeking to delineate a specific literary form. Suggestions have included simple prose, poetry (and some who advance the poetic argument reject historicity), tragedy, comedy, didactic prophetic narrative, and satire. Each of these has strengths and weaknesses and involves issues that are more complex than is necessary to engage herein. It is sufficient to say based on the arguments above, a commitment to biblical inerrancy, and the reality of miracles, that the book intends to be historical, and that the events actually did happen just as the narrator records. Further specificity of genre or subcategory beyond this can be attempted so long as these matters are not compromised, and room for disagreement can be allowed within the camp among those who agree on historical accuracy.

While Dillard and Longman's insistence that this is "an area where room for disagreement must be allowed to exist"[90] can be affirmed, it is essential that all positions be articulated carefully and thoroughly defended. As Feinberg has warned, one must not "mistake a case of bad hermeneutics (e.g., genre misidentification or ignoring altogether the genre of a passage) for a theological defection (rejection of biblical inerrancy). That is, we must be careful not to call an unusual interpretation of a passage a rejection of the passage's inerrancy."[91] And this is certainly true. However, many "unusual interpretations" are based on a faulty foundation that calls into question the inerrancy of Scripture and the power of God to work in human affairs in miraculous ways. Where those assumptions underlie an interpretation, it may be more than just bad hermeneutics at play. It may well be a theological defection of the highest order.

The Psalm (Jonah 2): A Genre Within A Genre

D. L. Christensen has said, "At the very point in the narrative where Jonah makes his final descent to the depths of hell itself, the language soars to lyrical heights."[92] He is, of course, referring to the brilliant psalm of praise found in chapter two of Jonah. Yet, some consider the psalm of Jonah 2 to

---

[90] Dillard and Longman, 393.
[91] John Feinberg, "Literary Forms and Inspiration", in D. Brent Sandy and Ronald L. Giese, Jr., *Cracking Old Testament Codes* (Nashville: Broadman & Holman, 1995), 64.
[92] Cited in Page, 222.

be a strong piece of evidence against the unity and integrity of the book. Dillard and Longman claim, "The only serious issue surrounding the literary unity of the book of Jonah arises with the psalm in the second chapter."[93] Critics of the book of Jonah have asserted that the psalm does not fit with the rest of the book and is therefore likely an insertion of an independent piece of literature into the midst of Jonah's narrative. They argue that the section could be removed from the story without harming the flow of the narrative. They also suggest that a psalm of praise and thanksgiving is inappropriate at this juncture when a lament or plea for deliverance would be more naturally expected. Additionally, it is claimed that the psalm does not connect smoothly with the remainder of the book, bearing unusual style, vocabulary, and theology. Upon closer examination of the book as a whole, however, these objections can be easily overruled.

Regarding the "excisability" of the psalm, the ability to remove it without disrupting the story, several responses have been offered by those who maintain the unity and integrity of Jonah. In most literary works, there are certain portions that could be removed without affecting the flow of the story. Therefore, as Stuart insists, "excisability is never a legitimate indication of lack of integrity in a literary work."[94] On further consideration, the psalm may in fact not be so easily removed. Stuart suggests that this is only possible "when the story is actually misunderstood to some degree," and therefore it may be "genuinely integral ... within the overall message of the book."[95] Rather than disrupting the story, the psalm actually serves to reinforce the central theme of divine deliverance in the book. Not only will God spare Nineveh from certain destruction, He will also deliver His prophet from the judgment that he deserves for his defection from the divine call. The Psalm acknowledges this is happening and expresses Jonah's gratitude to God for His merciful salvation. Jonah's heartfelt song of worship for God's saving mercy then helps us to see how hypocritical his resentment toward God for sparing Nineveh is. Without this psalm, that ironic contrast would disappear from the text.

---

[93] Dillard and Longman, 393.
[94] Stuart, 439.
[95] Ibid., 439.

The second criticism of the inclusion of the Psalm is well-expressed by B. W. Anderson, who writes, "In the belly of a fish a cry for help (that is, a lament) would be appropriate, but not a thanksgiving for deliverance already experienced!"[96] This would be true if in fact the fish had been sent as an agent of judgment against Jonah. However, this blatantly misses the point of the entire fish episode. The storm was sent as a judgment, and Jonah being tossed into the sea appears to be the final outpouring of wrath against the belligerent prophet. His death by drowning is all but certain as soon as he breaks the surface of the water. The fish enters the scene not "to add insult to injury," but rather as an agent of divine mercy. The fish is the vehicle God has appointed to save and deliver His prophet from certain destruction. If Jonah prayed a prayer of lament (and he may well have), it would have been offered as he splashed around in the sea. Once inside the belly of the fish, he is able to recognize that God is saving him in a miraculous and merciful way. "Jonah was not complaining about his predicament inside the fish; rather, he was thanking God for delivering him from death," as Hill and Walton note.[97] Therefore, it seems perfectly fitting for him to offer a prayer just like this one at the time and in the circumstances he finds himself.

Related to this are the arguments that reject the historicity of the book on the basis of expressions within the psalm. Wellhausen, for one, claimed that Jonah erred when he described "weeds" in 2:5, saying, "weeds do not grow in a whale's belly." Young responds, "Of course weeds do not grow in whale's bellies. But this is *not* a psalm of thanksgiving for deliverance from a whale's belly. It is rather a psalm of thanksgiving for deliverance from drowning." [98] The "weeds" Jonah describes are those that entangled him in the depths of the sea before he was ingested by the fish. This is yet another example of how "the school of negative criticism has unjustly imputed to this psalm a meaning which it never was intended to bear."[99]

As for the objection that the psalm diverges from the rest of the book in its style, vocabulary and theology, fairly simple responses can be offered. It has already been demonstrated that there is significant theological harmony

---

[96] Ibid.
[97] Hill and Walton, 500.
[98] Young, 281.
[99] Ibid.

between the psalm and the larger context of the book. The book concerns divine deliverance, and that is precisely the theme of the psalm. There seems to be nothing in the psalm which differs from the theological ideas set forth in the rest of the book. There is a difference in style and vocabulary, and this is not a cause for concern. The fact that we have here a Hebrew poem necessitates a shift in style and language. Differences in language and style are the most evident distinctions between Hebrew prose and Hebrew poetry. Stuart writes, "The language is generalized, so as to maximize applicability; the style is formalized so as to fit the meter, tune, and function" of the poetic genre.[100] Many books of Scripture incorporate poetry into the midst of narrative passages, and Jonah is no different from any of them.

It should not surprise the reader to encounter a highly stylized poem in the midst of a story about a prophet. Many of the prophetic books make heavy use of poetry, and some are entirely poetic. Stuart suggests that the prophets were trained poets, and as such, Jonah may have been drawing from a repertoire of memorized psalms as he expressed his praise to God.[101] There are parallels between a number of Psalms, including 5:7, 18:6, 31:22, 42:7, 120:1, 142:3, and 143:4.[102] Being a student of the Scriptures, including the Psalms, texts such as these may have informed Jonah's psalm directly, in the form of explicit borrowing, or indirectly, in the form of filling his vocabulary with expressions of praise.

While critics suggest that the psalm has been crammed into the book like a large foot in an ill-fitting shoe, it can be demonstrated to serve a significant purpose in the book. This has already been hinted at above in the discussion of it's theological consistency and the question of its excisability. But its appropriateness can be demonstrated stylistically as well. Young has said, "If 2:2-9 be removed, the symmetry of the book is

---

[100] Stuart, 439.
[101] Ibid.
[102] Bullock, 50. Hill and Walton, 51, also mention similarity with Psalm 69. Moeller (cited in Young, 282) provides a helpful comparison between Jonah and the Psalms which show similarity between 2:3b and Psalm 18:7 and 120:1; between 2:4b and Psalm 18:6 and 30:4; between 2:5 and Psalm 42:8; between 2:6 and Psalm 31:23 and 5:8; between 2:7 and Psalm 18:8 and 69:2; between 2:8 and Psalm 18:17, 30:4; and 104:4; between 2:9 and Psalm 142:4, 143:3, 18:7, and 5:8; between 2:10 and Psalm 88:3; as well as additional parallels with Psalm 31:7, 26:7, 50:14, 50:23, 42:5, and 116:17.

destroyed."[103] As it stands, the psalm not only rounds out the opening half of the book, but also provides a needful balance with the second half. It is quite evident in the Hebrew text that 1:1-3a and 3:1-3a are nearly identical in wording and form. Nearly every scholar observes and expounds on this similarity as a key element of the book's structure. However, what is often overlooked is the similarity between 2:2 and 4:2. Both of these verses mention Jonah praying. In 2:2, Jonah begins to pray a prayer of thanksgiving, while in 4:2 he begins to lodge a complaint against God. Therefore, it is not likely to be a later interpolation, but rather was intentionally incorporated by the original author for reasons of theological and literary significance.

Did Jonah pray this exact prayer inside the fish, or was it composed later to reflect his sentiments while inside the fish? This question only matters in relation to the issues of authorship and date. If Jonah did not pray, compose, or compile the psalm himself, then this may be the work of a later editor putting words into the prophet's mouth. This suggestion was dealt with above where it was concluded that the book likely comes from Jonah or one of his contemporaries. Therefore, these may be the exact words that the prophet prayed, or words that he composed or compiled himself upon later reflection of his experience. These may have been written by him or related to another who recorded them in the form we now have. Speculations concerning the psalm's allegorical reference to the Babylonian captivity would be dismissed in similar ways as those presented above when the allegorical treatment of the entire book was under consideration.

Message

In John's Gospel, the writer tells us why he wrote the book (John 20:31). Several other books also include clear statements of purpose. Jonah, however, contains no such statement. Therefore, views on purpose have varied greatly among those who have treated this small book academically. Brevard Childs has said that it is the purpose of the book, rather than the issues of authorship, date, or genre, which is "the most crucial and

---

[103] Young, 281.

perplexing problem of the book."[104] It is often mistakenly assumed that the message of the book of Jonah has to do primarily with an incident involving a whale. Forgetting for a moment that the book never identifies the sea creature as a whale at all (rather, it is called a "great fish"), this is actually a very minor detail in the story. The great fish only appears in three verses (1:17; 2:1; 2:10), and is one of several objects or phenomenon in the story which are described as being "appointed" by the Lord to accomplish His divine purposes. Therefore, there is a complexity to the story of Jonah that transcends the Sunday School lessons from childhood memories. As Phillips says, Jonah is "not so much about a great fish, but a gracious God."[105]

Unlike other prophetic books, Jonah does not focus on the message that the prophet proclaimed, but on a series of events in the prophet's life. The message Jonah proclaimed to Nineveh is contained within a single verse, and it does not even mention the name of God. It simply says, "Yet forty days and Nineveh will be overthrown" (3:4). Yet upon reading the book, it is evident that God is the primary figure in the story. It seems that Estelle is correct when he writes, "This little book of Jonah is not intended to communicate merely a message, but messages."[106] And each of these messages serves to clarify truth about who God is and what He is doing in the world. As Page writes, "Its purpose is to instruct God's people more fully in the character of their God, particularly his mercy as it operates in relation to repentance. ... This does not deny that there are many other lessons to be found in the Book of Jonah ... concerning such subjects as monotheism, obedience, and motivation."[107]

The attributes of God most clearly evident in the book of Jonah are His holiness, His mercy and His sovereignty. The holiness of God is demonstrated in His pronouncement of judgment against Nineveh because of it sins (1:2) and His dealings with His prophet who refuses to reflect His true nature. His mercy is evident as He does not abandon Jonah, though Jonah would have gladly abandoned God. His mercy is also seen in withdrawing the promised judgment from Nineveh in response to their

---

[104] Cited in Bullock, 50.
[105] Phillips, 4.
[106] Estelle, 29.
[107] Page, 219.

repentance. His mercy and holiness are seen to be in balance, as indicated by Hill and Walton: "His justice is not negated by the offering of extensions by grace. ... Yet God is not obligated to offer extensions endlessly. His just punishment will eventually be carried out (cf. Jeremiah 13:14; Ezekiel 7:1-9)."[108] The key to this balance between a holiness that must issue just judgment and a mercy that wills to forgive sin is found in God's sovereignty. As Hill and Walton say, "God must be granted the freedom to exercise either. ... God must be free to act as He sees fit."[109] And this "freedom" of God is assured by His complete sovereignty.

God's sovereignty is on display throughout the book. Bullock refers to God's sovereignty in terms of His "irresistible will in His world," and suggests that this in fact is the central purpose of the book.[110] God sovereignly chooses Jonah and commissions Him to go to Nineveh, which God has sovereignly determined to judge. His sovereignty extends over all nature as He appoints a storm, a fish, a plant, a worm, and a scorching east wind to perform His will. Of all that God appointed to serve Him only Jonah is disobedient; but God's sovereign plan to use Jonah prevails in spite of his rebellion. The withdrawal of judgment from Nineveh also demonstrates God's sovereignty, illustrating that great truth, "I will have mercy on whom I have mercy, and will have compassion on whom I have compassion" (Romans 9:15). Though these divine attributes are found throughout Scripture, the story that unfolds in the pages of Jonah provides rich demonstrations and illustrations of these and other characteristics of God. Each of these divine attributes is reflected by the questions that God asks of His prophet. In Jonah in 4:4 and 4:9, "Do you have good reason to be angry?" If Jonah could comprehend the holiness of God, then he should understand that his own sin is as vile as that of the Ninevites. If he understood the mercy of God, he would see that he cannot be angry about divine mercy when he owes his very life to it. If he had a healthy concept of the sovereignty of God, then he would realize that God does not need Jonah's approval to do as He wills. But God asks again in 4:11, "Should I not have compassion on Nineveh?" This question also gets at the issue of who God is, and expects an answer that affirms His holiness, His mercy,

---

[108] Hill and Walton, 501.
[109] Ibid., 501.
[110] Bullock, 51.

and His sovereignty. So, Stuart says of this question, "Anyone who replies, 'Why is that such an important question?' has not understood the message. Anyone who replies, 'No!' has not believed it."[111]

An additional divine attribute that is evident, though less so than those discussed above, throughout Jonah is the omniscience of God. One's view of omniscience will affect one's interpretation of this entire book, for here God declares through His prophet that something is going to happen (without condition or exception). A few paragraphs later, God declares that He will not bring that promised state of affairs to pass. If one has a view of God's omniscience which has no room for any measure of human freedom at all, then one must appeal to mystery (perhaps as a copout) for how God can relent when Nineveh repents. On the opposite extreme, we find the Open Theists whose extreme adherence to libertarian freedom chips away at God's omniscience. They say that God could not have known when He announced the coming judgment that Nineveh would repent, therefore they took Him by surprise and forced His hand to change His plans. The absurdity of this position can be illustrated by observing Jonah 4:2, in which Jonah says that *even he knew* what would happen. How then can anyone suggest that God did not know what Jonah knew? But if one's view of God's omniscience allows for Him to have perfect knowledge, not only of what *is* but also of what *may be*, then one can interpret the events of Jonah in a different way. If God has what has been called "middle knowledge," then He knows what choices free creatures will make in any circumstance. Therefore, He could know that Nineveh will only repent (which is His ultimate desire for them) if they are presented with such a devastating warning about the coming judgment. This proclamation will cause them to recognize their sins and their desperation for God's mercy, and it will cause them to turn to Him. Thus, if God has this kind of knowledge, sparing Nineveh is not "Plan B," but "Plan A," which He knew would only come to pass if the message that He commissioned Jonah to preach was delivered to the Ninevites.

Jonah is a book that teaches well the truth that God desires and works toward bringing salvation to all nations. Israel had been appointed by God, in the words of E. J. Young, "to bring the knowledge of the Lord to the

---

[111] Stuart, 435.

world."[112] This is seen from the beginning of Israel's existence with the calling of Abraham (Genesis 12:1-3). It may even be argued that this desire of God was expressed in His mandate to Adam and Eve to "be fruitful and multiply, and fill the earth, and subdue it" (Genesis 1:28). In many of the great acts of God in the Old Testament, we see that the motivation and result often included making the nations aware of God and bringing them to faith in Him. Therefore, the Great Commission in the New Testament (Matthew 28:18-20; Acts 1:8; et al.) was not a new idea, but was a renewing of God's commission for His covenant people. The church which stands on this side of the Cross can therefore find in the book of Jonah an illustration of the truth that God finds "no pleasure in the death of the wicked; but rather that the wicked turn from his way and live" (Ezekiel 33:11).

Another lesson easily seen in Jonah, related to the previous one, is that no single nation, not even Israel, can claim to have an exclusive relationship to God. Young states, "the mission of Jonah served to impress upon the Israelites the fact that the Lord's salvation was not to be confined to one nation."[113] Jonah demonstrates that when Israel loses sight of this truth and takes for granted the blessings they have received through God's sovereign choice of them among all the nations, God will act in ways that take them by surprise and provoke them to jealousy. This is not a "new thing" that God is doing by extending His grace toward a pagan nation. As already indicated, God has always had a desire to extend His truth and grace beyond Israel to the rest of the world. But God has also declared from the beginning of His covenant with Israel that if they turn away from Him He will harden them and provoke them to jealousy by showering other nations with grace. Deuteronomy 32:21 promised this, saying, "They have made Me jealous with what is not God; They have provoked Me to anger with their idols. So I will make them jealous with those who are not a people; I will provoke them to anger with a foolish nation." So, Stuart points out that "in ancient Judaism the book served as a bulwark against the narrow

---

[112] Young, 280.
[113] Ibid., 289.

particularism that allowed Jews to think they alone were worthy of God's blessing while other peoples were not."[114]

This book, like all Scripture, also points clearly to Jesus Christ. Estelle is correct when he says, "We must read Jonah through Christocentric glasses."[115] R. T. France put it this way, "Jesus understood the Old Testament Christologically: in its essential principles, and even in its details, it foreshadows the Messiah whom it promises. The whole theological system of the Old Testament points forward to His work, and in His coming the whole Old Testament economy finds its perfection and fulfillment."[116] Jesus made this clear throughout His earthly ministry, but nowhere more clearly than in Luke 24:25-27, when He said, "O foolish men and slow of heart to believe in all that the prophets have spoken! Was it not necessary for the Christ to suffer these things and to enter into His glory?" Then, Luke says, "beginning with Moses and with all the prophets, He explained to them the things concerning Himself in *all the Scriptures*." Luke goes on to record in 24:44-47 how Jesus spoke to His disciples saying, "These are My words which I spoke to you while I was still with you, that all things which are written about Me in the Law of Moses and the Prophets and the Psalms must be fulfilled."[117] Then Luke says that "He opened their minds to understand the Scriptures, and He said to them, 'Thus it is written, that the Christ would suffer and rise again from the dead the third day, and that repentance for forgiveness of sins would be proclaimed in His name to all the nations, beginning from Jerusalem.'" The book of Jonah was one of those places where the Lord Jesus saw His death, burial, and resurrection typified in the Old Testament (Matthew 12:39; 16:4; Luke 11:29-30). It is clear that the book of Jonah teaches that repentance for forgiveness of sins must be proclaimed to all nations. With that understanding, it is easy to see how Young can conclude, "The fundamental purpose of the book of Jonah is not found in its missionary or universalistic teaching. It is rather to show that Jonah being cast into the

---

[114] Stuart, 434.

[115] Estelle, 3.

[116] R. T. France, *Jesus and the Old Testament*. Cited in Estelle, 3.

[117] In using this tripartite division (the Law, the Prophets, and the Psalms), Jesus is referring to the entire Old Testament, the Tanakh. The term Tanakh (which describes the entire Old Testament) is actually an acrostic, referring to the Torah (Law), the Nebiim (Prophets), and the Writings (Kethubim, of which the Psalms are the largest part).

depths of Sheol and yet brought up alive is an illustration of the death of the Messiah for sins not His own and of the Messiah's resurrection."[118] Estelle says similarly, "Jonah, first and foremost, plain and simple, has this most important message for the Christian church today: *Christ, the risen One who is greater than Jonah, brings salvation through judgment and mercy to his people, those inside and outside of Israel who call on his name.* What is foreshadowed and illustrated in Jonah becomes a reality in Christ."[119] If Jonah's reluctant obedience to God brings mercy to the nations, then the One who is greater than Jonah (Matthew 12:41; Luke 11:32), who perfectly obeys the will of His Father, brings this all the more. "While Jonah reluctantly preached to save a city against his will, Jesus freely gave up his life to save many."[120]

There are perhaps many other lessons in Jonah, lessons which are theological, spiritual, moral, and missional. Only those which can be shown to be rooted in the text can be considered legitimate, but the lessons have by no means been exhausted here.

Textual Tradition

The book of Jonah comes to us with rather strong manuscript support. Brichto comments on its "pristine preservation and transmission over a period of twenty-five centuries and more."[121] Variations among the surviving manuscripts are few and minor. At least two things can be gleaned from this. First, the book of Jonah was obviously precious to Israel, and was seen as complete and self-sufficient. Therefore, it was preserved with integrity and did not undergo expansion, elaboration, editing, or excise through its long history of transmission (a history that is long on any theory of dating). Second, it also assures readers that this text can be approached with confidence that the Word of God has been purely preserved in the book as we now have it.

---

[118] Young, 263.
[119] Estelle, 3. Emphasis original.
[120] Dillard and Longman, 395.
[121] Cited in Page, 219.

Significant Dates

810-743 BC – Reign of Adad-nirari III in Assyria

c.790-745 BC – Reign of Jeroboam II in Israel[122]

781-745 BC – Assyria experiences significant internal turmoil, including famine (765-759), plague (765), eclipse (763), and internal revolt (763-760, 746).

771-754 BC – Reign of Ashur-dan III in Assyria[123]

c.745 - 727 BC – Reign of Tiglath-Pileser III in Assyria

726-722 BC – Reign of Shalmaneser V in Assyria

722 BC – Fall of Israel to Assyria (end of the Northern Kingdom).

---

[122] Dates vary among scholars, with some proposing a span from 786-746, others 793-753, and others 783-743. The differences are relatively insignificant in the bigger picture because of the close proximity of these suggestions.
[123] Others suggest 773-756.

Outline

There are many outlines available in the literature on Jonah, but there is little variation among them. The book's dividing lines are evident. Therefore, what follows is the outline suggested by Frank Page in his volume in the New American Commentary Series[124]:

I. God's first call and Jonah's response (1:1-16)

    1. God's instruction and the prophet's flight (1:1-3)

    2. The storm at sea (1:4-6)

    3. Unveiling of responsibility and identity (1:7-10)

    4. Stilling of the storm (1:11-16)

II. God's rescue of the rebellious prophet (1:17-2:10)

    1. God's protection and Jonah's prayer (1:17-2:9)

    2. The prophet's deliverance (2:10)

III. God's second commission and Jonah's obedience (3:1-10)

    1. God's renewal of His commission (3:1-2)

    2. The prophet's preaching and Nineveh's response (3:3-9)

    3. God's response (3:10)

IV. Jonah's displeasure and God's response (4:1-11)

    1. The prophet's displeasure (4:1-3)

    2. God's response (4:4-11)

---

[124] Page, 222

I

The LORD of the Word Which
Was Revealed to Jonah
Jonah 1:1-2

The word of the LORD came to Jonah, the son of Amittai saying,
"Arise, go to Nineveh the great city and cry against it,
for their wickedness has come up before Me."

While visiting Nepal in early 2011, some friends and I visited a breeding ground for elephants. We had an opportunity to feed them, to touch them, and to just behold these magnificent creatures. As I stroked the long trunk of an elephant, it didn't feel at all like I thought it would. It was very rough and dry, and the tiny hairs along the trunk felt like the bristles of a coarse brush. As I reflect on that wonderful experience, I think about an old Asian folktale about six blind men and their encounter with an elephant. One of them felt the massive torso of the elephant and concluded that he was feeling a wall. Another felt the trunk and determined that he must have a tree branch in his hands. The third wrapped his arms around the leg of the elephant and figured that he must be at the base of a large pillar. One gripped the tail and said that it must be a rope. Another felt the ear, and proclaimed that he was holding a fan. The last man ran his hands along the tusk and determined that it was a pipe. In one version of the story, there was a king present with the men, and he said to them, "All of you are right."

This story has become popular here in the postmodern West. It illustrates the principle of religious pluralism and universalism by saying that everyone has different ideas about God, but that we are all right because we are doing the best we can with the information we have. It is said that each of us only perceives a limited spectrum of reality, and the best we can do is offer a conjecture about what seems true to us. Of course, the problem with this story is that they were not all *right*. They were, in fact, all *wrong*. What these men perceived to be a rope, a tree, a pillar, a pipe, a fan, and a wall, was actually none of those things. It was an elephant. And what we often do not take into account in this story is the elephant itself. What if the blind men in the story began to treat the elephant as if it really was what each one perceived it to be? What if one began to tie knots in the elephant's tail? What if another tried to cool himself by flapping the ears of the elephant back and forth? Suppose the one who thought it was a wall tried to nail something to that wall? Needless to say, the elephant would be none too pleased with that. If he could talk, he might say, "I am not what you think I am! I am an elephant." Well, we all know that elephants can't talk. There was that one elephant, Babar, who could talk, but he could also walk on his hind legs, wear a business suit and a crown. Aside from him though, no other elephants can talk. Unlike elephants, God can and does speak.

The Bible tells us that God has made Himself known to every person in the world through the things that He has made. But sin has so warped our perception of Him in creation, that if this was all we had, we would certainly be like blind men groping an elephant. This is why every culture of humanity is inherently religious (they all know that a divine being is there), but also why every culture's religion is inherently idolatrous (they all get it wrong about who God is). The Apostle Paul says this very thing in Romans 1:20-23—

> *For since the creation of the world His invisible attributes, His eternal power and divine nature, have been clearly seen, being understood through what has been made, so that they are without excuse. For even though they knew God, they did not honor Him as God or give thanks, but they became futile in their speculations, and their foolish heart was darkened. Professing to be wise, they became fools, and exchanged the glory of the incorruptible God for an image in the form of corruptible man and of birds and four-footed animals and crawling creatures.*

And Paul goes on to say that because our sinful nature corrupts our perception of what can be known about God through creation, this information alone is insufficient to save anyone. It is enough to condemn humanity, for we are without excuse when we do not realize that there is a

God who will hold us accountable for our sin. But in order for humanity to be saved, we need the specific revelation of God: a direct word from Him about who He is and what He requires of us. Without some word *from* God *about* God, we will be throwing out guesses like blind men conjecturing over the anatomy of an elephant. And like them, we will be wrong. The only information we can know for certain about God is that which comes from God Himself. And He is not silent. He has spoken to us in His Word.

The book of Jonah is classified with the twelve Minor Prophets in the Old Testament. They are not called "minor" because they are of lesser importance, but because they are shorter than the much longer books called the Major Prophets. If we were asked, "What is the book of Jonah about?" I imagine many of us would say, "It is about a man who was swallowed by a whale." I knew that much about the book of Jonah before I ever read it. But as you will see through the study of this book of Scripture, Jonah is not a story about a whale. In fact, the Bible doesn't even call the creature a whale, but instead *a great fish*. And that great fish is only mentioned in three verses. It is also not primarily a story about Jonah. As Sinclair Ferguson writes, "It is really a book about God, and how one man came, through painful experience, to discover the true character of the God whom he had already served in the earlier years of his life. He was to find the doctrine about God (with which he had long been familiar) come alive in his experience."[125]

The book begins with the statement, "The word of the LORD came to Jonah." In fact, in eight of the twelve books of the Minor Prophets, the very first verse makes reference to "the word of the LORD." More important than the identity of the prophet, the mission for which he has been chosen, or anything else, is that *God is speaking!* A more significant miracle than Jonah being alive in the fish or anything else in this story is that God has chosen to speak to humanity. And the words which God speaks always reveal something about who this God is. And so it is here. The word of the Lord which comes to Jonah tells us much about this Lord of the word which comes to Jonah.

---

[125] Sinclair Ferguson, *Man Overboard!* (Carlisle, PA: Banner of Truth, 2008), xi.

I. The Lord is sovereign.

Not long ago someone came to me following a worship service and said, "I hear you use the word 'sovereign' a lot in your sermons, and I was wondering what it meant." I absolutely love it when I get questions like that! What does this word "sovereign" mean? It is a word we hear sometimes in the news, for instance when the UN or some country takes action against "a sovereign nation." When I preached on this passage in our church, it was the weekend of the royal wedding of Prince William and Kate Middleton. In all the media coverage about the royal wedding, we heard much about England's historical monarchy, which at one time was sovereign, meaning that the king or the queen held total power. So, we get the idea that "sovereign" has something to do with authority or control. And it does, but it also means more than this. When we speak of God's sovereignty, we are speaking of "His kingly, supreme rule and legal authority over the entire universe."[126] It is to say that God's will is supreme, and is not subject to the dictates of another. No one compels God to do something that He does not will to do. He doesn't answer to anyone. A. W. Pink said that the doctrine of God's sovereignty is "the foundation of Christian theology."[127]

We see God's sovereignty at work in many ways throughout Scripture, but often it is seen in how He takes initiative. We see that in the opening words of the very first verse of Jonah: *the word of the Lord came to Jonah.* God is not required by any condition or circumstance to make Himself known to anyone at anytime. If He reveals something about Himself or His purpose and plan in the world, it is because He chooses to do so according to His own will. Jonah was not knocking on the door of heaven begging to hear some word from God. For all we know, he was going about his daily routine when suddenly, somehow (we are not told how) he was confronted with the Word of God. Why did this happen? It happened because God chose for it to happen and took the initiative. Amos 3:7 says that the Lord does nothing unless He reveals His secret counsel to His prophets. But this is not because the prophets demand it or require it of the Lord. It is because

[126] Stanley J. Grenz, David Guretzki & Cherith Fee Nordling, *Pocket Dictionary of Theological Terms* (Downers Grove, Ill.: Intervarsity, 1999), 109.
[127] Arthur W. Pink, *The Sovereignty of God* (Grand Rapids: Baker, 1969), 263.

in His sovereignty He chooses to communicate to them and through them the secrets of His divine nature and will.

We see God taking sovereign initiative in choosing Jonah as a prophet for Himself. Once you've read the whole story, you will know that Jonah does not appear to be a likely candidate for the ministry. But then again, who is? If God didn't use imperfect people, there would be no people at all for God to use. But surely there was someone out there whom God could have used who would not be so stubborn and rebellious as Jonah proves to be, and there probably was. Why didn't God choose them? He is sovereign, and He took the initiative to call Jonah as His prophet. This happened long before the book of Jonah begins. We are told that Jonah was the son of Amittai, which is a detail that serves absolutely no purpose here in the book except to connect this prophet Jonah to the same prophet who was mentioned earlier in Second Kings 14:25. There we read that Jonah, the son of Amittai, was a prophet, a servant of the Lord, prophesying during the reign of Jeroboam II in the Northern Kingdom of Israel. We don't know when God initially called Jonah to be His prophet. Perhaps he was like Jeremiah, who was set apart for the Lord's service before birth (Jeremiah 1:5). It doesn't matter much, because the point is that Jonah had not volunteered for this job or chosen it from a range of possible career options. God, in His sovereignty, had taken the initiative to call Jonah into this service.

We find God's sovereignty at play in our own lives as well. It is God who makes Himself known to us as we hear the Gospel and read the Scriptures. He is revealing Himself to us on His own initiative. It is God who takes the first step in calling us into a saving relationship with Him through faith in Jesus Christ. It is God who initiates our service for Him, calling us and preparing us for the specific ways in which He chooses to use us. It is God who opens and closes doors of opportunity for us to serve Him in various ways. The only reasonable response to the sovereign will of God is to trust and obey. To do otherwise is to rebel against His ultimate authority like a traitor who opposes the rightful rule of a king. God is sovereign, always taking the initiative, and we are always in the position of reacting or responding to what He says and does. And it is precisely here that human beings have always choked on this doctrine of God's sovereignty. When we come up against it, we are forced to recognize that we are not in control of our own little universes, and we do not like that idea. We are small and finite, with delusions of grandeur blinding us to the reality of an all-powerful sovereign God who has complete authority over every aspect of the universe. We are born believing the lie of our own sovereignty, but God will not let us believe it forever. In life, or ultimately at death, we will come to realize that He is sovereign, that He takes all the initiative, and we are reactors and responders to His first moves.

II. The Lord is unlimited.

I often say jokingly that I skipped my Pastoral Ministry class on the day when the professor taught how to be in two places at one time. Sometimes I need to be in two places at one time, but I just can't. It is one of many ways in which I am limited by my humanity. There's a lot I don't know and a lot I can't do. The same is true of each of you. But none of this is true of God. We are limited, finite creatures. He is infinite and unlimited.

We see in these verses that God is not limited by time. He is eternal. He has always existed, and always will. He has always been at work in the world, ever since He created it, and will be until the end. Where do we see this in the text? Well, if we are reading an English Bible, we probably don't. If we were reading it in Hebrew, we would see that the first verse begins with a conjunction. A conjunction connects a word, a phrase, or a sentence with something that came before it. I did a little research on this subject as I was preparing this study by pulling up the old "Schoolhouse Rock" video on YouTube. Did you see that when you were younger? The little ditty said, "Conjunction-junction, what's your function? Hooking up words and phrases and clauses." So, if we translate Jonah 1:1 literally, it would read like this: "*And* the word of the Lord came to Jonah." AND? Why is that there? This is 1:1! What comes before this? The answer is, a whole lot came before it. And a whole lot comes after it. God has been at work in the world since Genesis 1:1, and He was at work before that. All of our stories, like Jonah's, begin with a conjunction.

This is important for us today because of our inclination toward what C. S. Lewis called "chronological snobbery."[128] What he meant by that is our

---

[128] See, for instance, *Surprised by Joy,* Chapter 13.

46

tendency to value things simply because they are new, and to reject things simply because they are old. So, for instance when a pastor in the area told me that his church exists to reach young people and therefore they have no small groups for people over 40, I asked him, "How then will you obey the command in Titus for the older women to teach the younger women and the older men to teach the younger men?" This is why when I visit a church and sing only songs written in the last decade I want to ask, "Do you think that no one prior to the 21st Century ever had anything meaningful to say about God in song?" God is doing a great work in our generation and in this century, but we must be aware that God did not just begin doing a great work in these days. He has been doing a great work since the beginning and will continue it. Therefore, our story, like Jonah's, begins with "and" because God is eternal.

We also see that God is unlimited by space. He is omnipresent. In ancient times, people often had notions of gods as regional deities. These people worshiped this god in this place, while other people worshiped another god in another place. In many parts of the world, this is still the way people think. I had a Hindu priest tell me once that it was right for me to be Christian and for him to be Hindu, for Jesus was the God of Americans, but Ganesh, and Shiva, and Krishna and the others were the gods of the Indian people. The Israelites should have never believed that their God was limited by space, as if He only existed and could only be worshiped and served in Israel, but they often did. Jonah seems to have even considered this a possibility when later in the story he flees to Tarshish, thinking he can escape "the presence of the Lord." So, you can imagine how shocked he might have been when God's word came to him saying, "Arise and go to Nineveh." Why would the God of Israel want to send this Jewish prophet to Nineveh, a "great" city all the way over in modern-day Mosul, Iraq?

As you look at verse 1 in your Bibles, you will notice (at least in most English translations) that the word LORD is spelled with all capital letters. That maybe something you have seen many times and never considered the reason for it. This is a custom that began a long time ago of making a difference between various Hebrew divine titles. When it is all capital letters like this, the translators are indicating that they are translating the

47

Hebrew name of God, YHWH (which we pronounce, *Yahweh*). When it is just a capital L with lowercase "o-r-d", typically they are translating the word *Adonai*, which is a more general title of honor and reverence. *Adonai* is a title sometimes applied to men, similar to the old English custom of calling people "lord," but when it is used of men in the Bible, the translators will not capitalize the "L" at the beginning. So, you can do some Hebrew word study without ever learning the language simply by understanding how the English Bible you use handles these various words. Usually that will be explained in the front matter of your Bible.

This name, YHWH, is the covenant name by which God revealed Himself to His people in the days of Moses. This is the Jewish God, not the Assyrian god. But what Jonah might fail to comprehend is that his God is the only God there is! He is not the God of Israel only, but the God of the whole universe. And He is as present in Nineveh and in Tarshish as He is in Israel. And He can be served there, indeed He must be served there, as much as in Israel. Don't think that the Bible consists of an Old Testament that deals with God and Jews, and a New Testament that deals with Jesus and Gentiles. We see the Triune God working through His people to make Himself known to all nations through the entire Bible.

I wonder if a misunderstanding of God's omnipresence is what prompts some to say today, "Why should I care about people who live in places like Nepal when there is so much to be done for Christ in America?" Is this what prompts some churches to focus on one group of people to the exclusion of others in their ministry? Is this what prompts some to think that the only place they can serve the Lord is within the walls of the church building? Do we think God is a localized deity for our use and benefit only? Or are we convinced that He is the only true God, the God of the whole universe, as present and as worthy of worship and service in Nepal, Nigeria, or the planet of Neptune as He is in North America? He is unlimited by space. He is omnipresent.

Then notice also that God is unlimited in His knowledge. He is omniscient, all-knowing. Notice that He says to Jonah that the wickedness of Nineveh has "come up before" Him. He is aware of what they are doing in Nineveh. They cannot keep their sin a secret from God. He sees it. He knows it. He knows more about Nineveh than the Ninevites know. He knows more about Jonah than Jonah knows. And He knows more about you and me than we know about ourselves. Do we suppose that we can cling to "secret sins" in our lives? We are deceived. God knows. It "comes up before Him." He knows what is done when no one else is looking. He knows the secrets of our hearts and minds. And He knows everything about our past, our present, and our future.

Our text makes it clear that God is unlimited: unlimited by time in that He is eternal; unlimited by space in that He is omnipresent; unlimited in knowledge in that He is omniscient.

III. The Lord is holy.

The commission that the Lord gives Jonah is to arise and go to Nineveh. But God is not sending Him on vacation. He is sending Him on a mission to "cry against it for their wickedness has come up before" Him. Get that – not "preach to" or "talk about", but "cry *against*." This is confrontational preaching. He is to confront them about their wickedness. We are not told here what the wickedness of Nineveh consisted of, but the original audience of this story would have known full well. The historical records of the ancient world describe how Assyria's military would tear off the lips and hands of their victims, skin them alive, and amass piles of their victims' skulls as monuments to their own greatness. The prophet Nahum would later describe the city of Nineveh as a "bloody city," full of lies and pillage, saying, "For on whom has your evil not passed continually" (Nahum 3:1,19). And Israel had been the objects of much animosity from the Assyrians. Like the martyrs in the book of Revelation, the Israelites may have cried out, "How long O Lord?" How long would God put up with the wickedness of Nineveh? The answer comes here. O Nineveh, you may have felt as if you had free reign to do as you please in the earth for a long time, but the end is near. A day of reckoning is upon you. God is sending His prophet to you to announce to you that judgment is at hand, and you will answer for all the evil you have done.

Is that something we sometimes forget about the Lord? Do we forget sometimes that He is holy? When we see evil and wickedness all around us in the world, do we sometimes think that God is not paying attention? Do we want to cry out, "How long O Lord?" If we do not have faith that this

God is holy and He despises sin, then we will lose heart. The Psalmist, in Psalm 73, says that he nearly stumbled over the fact that the wicked prosper. He was envious of them being able to sin boldly and get away with it. It troubled him greatly, he says, until he went into the sanctuary of God. And it was then that he "perceived their end." Then he understood how they are "destroyed in a moment." The Lord is holy. He detests sin. And He has acted against it and He will act against it. And that is both a comfort and a warning to us.

It is a comfort when we feel the weight of this world's wickedness in its blunt and raw form. God is neither unaware nor unconcerned. He will act in His perfect time, though it may not be when we want it to be. But it is a warning as well. We mustn't be lulled into thinking that because God has not dealt severely with our own pet sins that He will not. He is not slow about keeping His promises, 2 Peter 3:9 says, but He is patient. He will keep His promise to judge the wicked, but for now He is patient, leaving a window open for us to come to repentance. But that window will not remain open forever, and we are deceived if we think it couldn't slam shut today. And the uncomfortable paradox between His holy determination to act against sin and His patience with sinners is brought into clearer focus when we consider one final point.

IV. The Lord is gracious.

When we consider the wickedness of Nineveh, we have to conclude that they deserve to bear the wrath of God in all of its fullness. They deserve the fate of Sodom and Gomorrah, which was consumed with fire and brimstone. That is what they will receive, in one form or another, unless they repent before the Lord. And that is what the Lord wants for them more than they realize. He says through Ezekiel (33:11), "I take no pleasure in the death of the wicked, but rather that the wicked turn from his way and live." He has left the window of opportunity open to them. He has delayed His wrath and allowed them to come to a turning point where they seek Him. But they haven't and now the end is near. Before the end comes, He gives them one final opportunity. Because He is gracious, He sends them His servant, Jonah. The prophet is sent with a message of warning that judgment is coming soon. And when they hear that message, they have a choice to make. They can harden their hearts in unbelief and be consumed in judgment, or they can repent and receive the mercy of this great God. He didn't have to do this, you know. He didn't have to warn them. God would have been completely just and holy to destroy them without advance notice. But He warned them because He is gracious. And just like Jonah, you too are God's gift of grace to a lost and dying world. You have been sent out under Christ's Great Commission with a message for all the world to hear.

The word of the Lord came to Jonah. But, centuries later, the Lord of the Word did something even more spectacular. The Gospel of John tells us that the Word became Flesh. God sent one greater than Jonah into the world. He came into the world Himself as one who is greater than Jonah: the incarnate God, Jesus Christ. Hebrews 1:1-2 says, "God, after He spoke long ago to the fathers in the prophets in many portions and in many ways, in these last days has spoken to us in His Son." He came with a message:

> For God so loved the world, that He gave His only begotten Son, that whoever believes in Him shall not perish, but have eternal life. For God did not send the Son into the world to judge the world, but that the world might be saved through Him. He who believes in Him is not judged; he who does not believe has been judged already, because he has not believed in the name of the only begotten Son of God.[129]

This sovereign and unlimited God is holy, and He must do something about the problem of a sinful human race. And because this holy God is gracious, He allowed a substitute to bear the wrath of judgment for us. Jesus Christ lived a life of perfect righteousness, yet in His death, He bore our sin and its penalty. And having conquered sin and death through His resurrection, He now offers us the great exchange – we can allow our sins to be dealt with in Christ and receive in return His righteousness as a covering. In so doing, God demonstrates Himself to be just (in the punishment of sin) and the Justifier, the One who makes sinners righteous (Romans 3:23-26).

---

[129] John 3:16-18

The Lord has made Himself known to us. We are not as blind men groping an elephant. He has revealed Himself to us as the Lord God who is sovereign, unlimited by time and space, unlimited in knowledge, perfectly holy, perfectly gracious. It is up to us now to respond. Will we choose to ignore what God has said and done and invite the judgment we deserve upon ourselves? Or will we allow Christ to be our sin-bearer and turn to Him in repentance and faith and be saved? We will discover in the pages ahead what Nineveh did. What is more important in this present moment is what we will do in response to the Lord of the Word who is revealed through the Word of the Lord.

II

The Dangers of Disobedience
Jonah 1:1-3

The word of the LORD came to Jonah the son of Amittai saying,
"Arise, go to Nineveh the great city and cry against it,
for their wickedness has come up before Me."
But Jonah rose up to flee to Tarshish from the presence of the LORD.
So he went down to Joppa, found a ship which was going to Tarshish,
paid the fare and went down into it to go with them
to Tarshish from the presence of the LORD.

In 1979, a then 22-year-old young man traveled with his pregnant wife and two young sons to the United States for a two-week journey. When one of the boys became sick, they saw a friendly doctor in Indianapolis who helped the child. The man traveled on to Los Angeles for some business meetings while his wife and children stayed in Indiana, visiting shopping malls and doing other normal "American" things. As the young family prepared to leave the States, seated in the departure lounge of an airport in Indiana, they noticed people staring strangely at them. Maybe it was her dress or his appearance that caught their attention. Some even took photographs of them seated there.[130] In her recollections of that visit to America, the wife never mentions being approached by any Christians who might have shared with this family the offer of eternal life that is found in Jesus Christ. Maybe it happened; probably it did not. But suppose it had happened. Suppose a Christian doctor had treated their ill son, and said before they left the office, "Now can I tell you about something far more important than physical healing?" Suppose someone in the shopping mall had approached her and said, "Has anyone ever shared with you the good news about Jesus?" Suppose that rather than staring and taking pictures of them in the airport, some Christian traveler had taken a seat beside of them

---

[130] Steve Coll, "Osama in America: The Final Answer." http://www.newyorker.com/online/blogs/stevecoll/2009/06/osama-in-america-the-final-answer.html. Accessed May 4, 2011.

and struck up a conversation that might have led to an offer of knowing Jesus Christ. We'll never know what might have become of the young man and his family had those circumstances transpired. Instead we know the horrific story of what did happen. We know that this young man became the leader of a global empire of terrorism. We know that he was the architect of countless acts of violence that amassed an incalculable number of human casualties. We know that on a Spring evening in 2011, President Barack Obama announced to America that this man had been shot and killed by Navy Seal Team Six in Abbottabad, Pakistan. And based on what we know of his life and what we know of the word of God, we may assume that he died without the hope of Jesus. And though we are grateful for the courage and commitment of all the military personnel who endured life-threatening conditions to bring his reign of terror to an end, we also know that Osama bin Laden's story could have been changed if a Christian had been courageous enough to tell him the good news about Jesus Christ.

I think we were all surprised to find out that bin Laden had been living in a rather well-developed city in Pakistan for some time. The news outlets were quick to ask the questions: Did the Pakistani government know where he was? If they knew where he was, why didn't they do anything? Let me ask you a different question: suppose we knew—we, the church of Jesus Christ. Suppose somehow we found out that Osama bin Laden was living in this building that some referred to as a mansion in Abbottabad. And suppose that someone suggested, "Why don't we head over to Abbottabad on a mission trip to share the gospel with bin Laden? If you are interested, sign up after the service today." Any takers?

You can now envision something of what went through the mind of the prophet Jonah when the Word of the Lord came to him saying, "Arise, go to Nineveh the great city and cry against it." Archeologists have discovered in the ruins of Nineveh and the other prominent cities of Assyria many evidences of the wickedness of that empire. Monuments depict and describe details that one historian calls "as gory and bloodcurdling a history as we know."[131] One Assyrian king boasted that he had flayed the

---

[131] Erika Bleibtreau, "Grisly Assyrian Record of Torture and Death," cited in James Bruckner, *Jonah, Nahum, Habakkuk, Zephaniah* (NIV Application Commentary; Grand Rapids: Zondervan, 2004), 28.

skin from many nobles, and built towers with decapitated skulls, and hung others from the trees. Boys and girls were burned alive. The king himself claims to have cut off arms and hands, noses, ears, and other extremities, and gouged out eyes.[132] And it was to these people that Jonah was called to go and preach a message for the Lord.

It was not unusual for God to give His prophets a message of judgment to proclaim against a wicked foreign nation. It was a bit unusual for Him to call the prophet to put in a personal appearance there. Yet this is what the Word of the Lord ordered Jonah to do. And Jonah did what we find no other prophet of God do in the entire Old Testament. The Lord said "Go!" and Jonah said, "No!" God's first command to Jonah was "Arise," [133] and the first word of Jonah's response is that he rose up. That's a good first step of obedience. But that is where his obedience ended. His "get up and go" got up and went, but he went in the wrong direction. Rather than beginning the 500 mile journey northeast to Nineveh (near modern day Mosul, Iraq), the Bible tells us that Jonah set out on a journey to Tarshish, on the far western coast of modern day Spain, some 2,000 miles due west. Jonah chose to disobey the Lord: a decision that would prove to be disastrous and dangerous.

So it is for us as well. When the Lord calls us to something, we cannot sit still. The Lord says "Arise," and we must. The Lord says "Go" and we must. But the decision is ours to make if we will move in the direction of obedience or disobedience. Like Jonah, we often choose disobedience, and when we do, we find as he did that it is a dangerous direction to journey. The detailed description of Jonah's defection demonstrates his decisive determination to go his own dangerous direction instead of the Lord's. And in it we see the dangers that lay in wait for us when we determine to travel a course of disobedience as well. So we ask, "Why is disobedience so dangerous?" And we find several answers to that question here in verse 3.

---

[132] Bruckner, 29.
[133] The word "Arise" (Hebrew: *qum*) does not appear in the NIV and some other newer English versions. It is hard to know why the translators opted to omit this word, but its omission here damages the ironic parallel between verses 2 and 3.

I. Disobedience believes an empty promise.

The sin of disobedience is both a theological problem and a moral one. At times, like the proverbial chicken and the egg, it is hard to tell which comes first. Sometimes, as Paul says in Romans 1, sinful people have *suppressed the truth in unrighteousness*, meaning that their desire to disobey God has caused them to reject truth about God, or else to believe a lie about God. So the moral error led to a theological error. But then there are times when the theological error comes first, and causes the moral error. This may have been the case when Adam and Eve sinned. They did not believe the promise of God which stated that in the day that they ate of the fruit, they would die. But they also believed the promise of Satan when he said, "You will surely not die! ... you will be like God."[134] Sometimes when we are tempted to disobey the Lord, we may think to ourselves, "God probably didn't mean what He said." Or we believe, "This is probably not really that big of a deal." Or we believe, "I can pull this off and get away with it." That would be a theological error, and once that theological error is made, the moral failure follows quickly after. We do what we want to do rather than what God wants us to do.

When Jonah was called to take the message of the Lord to the center of global terrorism, he didn't want to go. And he committed a theological error that led him into disobedience. He set out to flee "from the presence of the Lord." That phrase occurs twice in verse 3. Literally, we could render the Hebrew here "from the face of the Lord." Jonah thinks that there is some place he can go where God cannot find him and bother him with any more of these uncomfortable commands. That is a theological error. Disobedience beckons, saying, "Come over here, and you can hide from God." But it is an empty promise.

Surely, as a prophet of God, Jonah was familiar with the words of King David who had written centuries before in Psalm 139:7-10—

> *Where can I go from Your Spirit? Or where can I flee from Your presence? If I ascend to heaven, You are there; If I make my bed in*

---

[134] Genesis 2:17; 3:4-5

Sheol, behold, You are there. If I take the wings of the dawn, if I dwell in the remotest part of the sea, even there Your hand will lead me, and Your right hand will lay hold of me.

But at this moment, either Jonah chose not to believe that was true, resulting in his decision to disobey, or else his desire to disobey was so strong that he rewrote his theology to accommodate his sin. Had his sin simply been a moral one rather than a theological one, perhaps he could have stayed put in Israel and determined in his heart that he would not go to Nineveh, like a determined toddler who stamps his feet as if to say, "No, I will not do what you told me to, and I am going to stand right here and pout about it." But Jonah didn't do that. He arose, and he fled to Tarshish by way of Joppa, thinking (or at least hoping) that he could find some corner of the earth where he could hide from God. Interestingly, both Joppa and Tarshish were places where Jonah knew that he could go without encountering many Jewish people who would speak and remind him of this God who had called him. No temple, no priests, no prophets, few (if any) worshipers of Yahweh; he must have thought that these were places that the Lord was not overly concerned with. Here, he could blend in with crowds of pagans and escape the notice of God.

You and I laugh at that silly notion, don't we? Who on earth could think such a thing? I dare say that not only do we know many who think that, we ourselves have thought it repeatedly in our lives. When a Christian is determined to disobey God and enter into a sinful way of life, what is one of the first steps they often take? They begin to dissociate with the church. They begin to avoid contact with fellow believers. They make up excuses to justify their absence from the fellowship of believers, and they begin to surround themselves with others who give no thought to the moral decisions they are making. They stop reading the Bible and praying. They want nothing to do with anything or anyone that will remind them of the things of God. Maybe the thinking is, "If I am over here doing these things with these people, God won't notice." I would venture to say that there is not a person reading these words who hasn't entertained those thoughts at some moment, however brief, in his or her life. And I would also suggest that this is one contributing factor to the fact that in many churches, fifty or seventy-five percent of the members are not present on any given Sunday.

Why should a church take this matter seriously? Because the first step a person makes away from the Lord is often to step away from the place where His people gather, and this should concern us. It may well be that, as Richard Phillips has written, "like Jonah, the fact that they avoid godly company demonstrates the true state of their hearts."[135] They are drifting into the dangerous waters of disobedience, and we should care and reach out to rescue them before they drift away too far. Not only are they in error of "forsaking our own assembling together" (Hebrews 10:25), and removing themselves away from the place of ministry, discipleship, worship and fellowship; they may also be committing a theological error of trying to hide from the presence of the Lord. They need to be warned that this is not possible. It wasn't possible for Jonah, and it will not be for us. It is an empty promise, and believing it is one of the dangers of disobedience.

II. Disobedience travels a downward path.

I would imagine that most people, when they determine to disobey God, think they are taking a fast track to a higher plane of living. Disobeying God may appear to be the way up for a person: a ladder to climb that leads to a bigger salary, a better relationship with another person, nicer possessions, and the like. Jonah may be thinking that way. "If I go to Nineveh, who knows what will happen to me? If I stay here, God will not leave me alone. But if I go to Tarshish, I can start all over, be who I want to be, do what I want to do, settle down, get a good job, start a family, and have everything I want." But notice that the direction of every step Jonah takes in disobedience is described by the same word: "down." It occurs twice in verse 3. Jonah went *down* to Joppa, *down* into the ship. In verse 5, the same Hebrew word describes how he went *down* below deck to sleep. In 2:6, the same word is used when Jonah says, "I *descended* to the roots of the mountains." There, in the depths of the sea, Jonah was sinking deeper and deeper to the point of drowning and death. It seems obvious that the writer of the book of Jonah, whether it is Jonah himself or one of his close associates, uses this word repeatedly to warn us that if we choose to disobey God, the path we travel is one that leads down.

---

[135] Phillips, 217.

I visited the Grand Canyon in the Summer of 2011 when the Southern Baptist Convention was held in Phoenix. My family enjoys hiking in National Parks together, and we were looking forward to hiking the trails of the Canyon while we were in Arizona. I began to do some reading about Canyon hiking, and what I read caused the endeavor to lose some of its appeal. Standing atop the South Rim, the temperature may be a comfortable 75 degrees, and the journey looks so enticing. You start down the Bright Angel Trail to get a better look inside the Canyon. And the lure of the Canyon draws you deeper and deeper in, until you've hiked the 6 mile trail to the bottom. And you have seen amazing things, gotten some great photos to impress your Facebook friends. But with every step down, the temperature goes up. By the time you reach the floor of the canyon, it's 105 degrees. You are dehydrated and fatigued, and then you've got to hike back out, 6 miles, and the last mile or so is nearly vertical. Every summer, many people are pulled out of the canyon by rescuers, and some die, because they did not realize how dangerous it was to go that far down.[136]

The sin of disobedience is like this. We take a few steps in, and we want to go further, but every step takes us down, and the heat intensifies, and the conditions worsen, and the way out becomes more difficult. James Montgomery Boice says, "Any way that is away from [the Lord] is down. The way may look beautiful when we start. The seas may look peaceful and the ship attractive, but the way is still down."[137] The journey will take Jonah to the depths of the sea. And there he will cry out to the Lord to rescue him. And God will answer his prayer in an unexpected way. And it is only then that Jonah will move upward. In 2:6 he will say, "I descended to the roots of the mountains, ... but You have brought *up* my life from the pit, O Lord my God." The only way up once disobedience has taken us down so far is to turn to the Lord in repentance and plead with Him for a rescue. It is a dangerous journey down!

---

[136] In the interest of full disclosure, yes, we did hike a little ways down Bright Angel Trail, and part of the way down the Hermit Trail also. But I learned from what I had researched not to try to make it all the way down!
[137] James Montgomery Boice, *The Minor Prophets: Volume 1* (Grand Rapids: Baker, 1983), 267.

III. Disobedience pays a high price.

Make no mistake about it, obedience to the Lord is costly. Following Jesus throughout one's life may lead to costly sacrifice. Dietrich Bonhoeffer's famous book describes the painful *Cost of Discipleship*. But the cost of discipleship is never so great as *the cost of non-discipleship*. In verse 3, we read that Jonah went down to Joppa and found a ship that was going to Tarshish, and *he paid the fare*. You better believe he paid the fare! There are no free rides. We must remember that in the ancient world, as in many parts of the world today, money is something of a sophisticated innovation. I've visited villages in Africa where no one had any money, and no one needed money. If they had money, there was nothing around to spend it on. In the world in which Jonah lived, the economy operated largely without an exchange of currency. And a journey of this distance would have been costly. It likely cost more than Jonah could afford to pay. Some have speculated that Jonah may have had to sell his home and possessions to afford the price of this journey. But it was all worth it in his mind. This journey was going to get God off of his back for good. Once he was safely in Tarshish, a wealthy city with much industry to boast of, he could start over, rebuilding the life he wanted from scratch. There was only one problem with his plan. God knew something Jonah didn't know. He always does. God knew that Jonah wouldn't make it to Tarshish. Somewhere in the depths of the Mediterranean Sea, Jonah will be thrown overboard, and there will be no refund on the cost of his ticket. He will be back where he started from, with nothing to his name but a tragic story to tell.

Disobedience is costly, but then again, so is obedience. Surely Jonah would not have found a free ride to Nineveh either. But isn't it interesting that there was no mention of how Jonah would afford the journey to Nineveh? That is because when you go where God calls you to go and do what calls you to do, you can do so knowing that God will provide for you every step of the way. Recently I led five other church members on a mission trip that cost us $2,000 per person. No one on that team could have afforded that trip. But the question I asked this team to consider was not, "Can you afford it?" but rather, "Is God calling you to go?" And, for those who said yes, God provided abundantly. We even got radically detoured and incurred many additional expenses, but God had provided enough. We even had enough left over when we got home to send some back to bless some of the ministries with whom we had worked.

If you obey the Lord, He provides. And that is true for every aspect of life, not only international missions. Do you think you cannot tithe because you have bills to pay? It may well be that if you trust Him and obey, you will find that He provides in ways you never expected. There is always a cost to obey, but the Lord provides for it. There is a much higher cost to disobey, and you pay your own way. Donald Grey Barnhouse once said, "When you run away from the Lord you never get to where you are going, and you always pay your own fare. On the other hand, when you go the Lord's way you always get where you are going, and He pays the fare."[138]

You've seen those commercials from Southwest Airlines perhaps that feature the tagline, "Wanna get away?" Delta used to advertise with the motto, "Delta is ready when you are." If God is calling you to follow Him on the difficult path of obedience, you may want to get away. And Delta, or a ship at Joppa, or some method of escape will be there to take you where you want to go. But you may find that the cost of disobedience is far greater than the cost of obedience, and you may never make it to your final destination. This world is not a safe place to live. But if you are where the Lord wants you to be, doing what He wants you to, you can trust Him to protect and provide for you, and know that "your life is hidden with Christ in God."[139] If you think the cost of obedience is high, I assure you that it is nothing compared to the cost of disobedience. It is dangerous. And it pays a high price.

IV. Disobedience paints a vivid picture.

If you have ever received an email from me, you have about 65% of the information you need to hack into my email account. You know what site to go to, and you know what user name to enter. But what you don't have is the password. And the password exists to prove that the person logging in is really who he claims to be. Without it, you will be locked out. And

---

[138] Quoted in Boice, 268.
[139] Colossians 3:3.

there is a similar spiritual truth as well. You can visit the church, and call yourself a Christian, but you may be nothing more than a spiritual hacker. If you want to validate your identity as a Christian, you need the password. The password is *obedience*. Jesus said, "If you love Me, you will keep My commandments" (John 14:15). He said, "Why do you call Me, 'Lord, Lord,' and do not do what I say?" (Luke 6:46). You can have the right user name: "Christian." But do you have the password: "Obedience." Without it, you may find that you are locked out as the Lord says to you with fatal finality, "I never knew you. Depart from Me" (Matthew 7:23).[140]

Jonah was no rookie-prophet when this call came to him. Second Kings 14:25 tells us that he had prophesied in Israel concerning the reclaiming of ancient boundaries, and God brought it to pass under the hand of Jeroboam II. He was an experienced prophet, who had perhaps been a disciple of Elisha. He had a track record of faithfulness and success. But past spiritual accomplishments do not speak so loudly as a present pattern of obedience. How many people live in perpetual disobedience, deceived about their true spiritual condition? I believe firmly in the proposition that once a person is saved, he or she is always saved. But I am as firmly convinced by God's word that not everyone who claims to be saved really is. It is not past performance or past professions that matter so much as the present proof that one possesses saving faith. That proof is found in our obedience. God proves His people through their perseverance. And if Jonah's story ends here, I wouldn't give him a plug nickel for the prospects of his salvation. I don't even know what a plug nickel is, but I wouldn't give him one. If he truly knows the Lord, then we have to expect that this is not the end. He will get turned around and finish well, else he will die and leave us with life's most important question unanswered. You don't want to go out like that. I don't want my funeral sermon to be filled with unanswered questions. I want to know that my profession of faith in Christ was proven by my perseverance in the pursuit of godliness and obedience in my life.

Jonah is not indispensable to the plans of God. There are other prophets He can use. He can write Jonah off right here. When Esther was faced with the

---

[140] I have to credit an African pastor in Senegal, whose name I have forgotten, for this splendid little illustration.

difficult decision of taking a bold stand for the Lord, her righteous uncle Mordecai admonished her saying, "For if you remain silent at this time, relief and deliverance will arise for the Jews from another place and you and your father's house will perish."[141] In other words, your disobedience will not disrupt God's plans, but it might bring your own story to a tragic end. The same is true for Jonah, and for you and me. We cannot threaten God with our disobedience. He can just drop us in the ocean of judgment and let us perish there. Or He can break us and bring us back to Himself. And if we truly belong to Him, that is what He will do, for the sake of His own name. But the danger of disobedience is that it rips the veil away from our spiritual lives and exposes the vivid picture of who we really are in terms of our relationship with Christ. And for Jonah, right now, that is not a pretty picture. We'll have to wait and see how it turns out for him. But how will it turn out for you? What does your way of living say about your spiritual condition? Does your obedience display a picture of the glorious and gracious salvation you have received? Or does your disobedience portray a picture of one who is far away from the God who saves?

What a paradox Jonah presents to us! He has been called by the Lord to bring a message to a sinful people who will perish unless they turn to the Lord and cry out for salvation. But he disobeys. Aren't you glad that you aren't waiting for Jonah to bring you good news? Rather, rejoice today that the Lord Jesus referred to Himself as one who is greater than Jonah.[142] Sent by His Father to bring a warning of judgment and an offer of mercy to a wicked people, unlike Jonah, Jesus came, and He spoke, and He suffered, and He died to redeem us. And so the Apostle Paul can say in Philippians 2:5-8—

> *Have this attitude in yourselves which was also in Christ Jesus, who, although He existed in the form of God, did not regard equality with God a thing to be grasped , but emptied Himself, taking the form of a bond-servant, and being made in the likeness of men. Being found in appearance as a man, He humbled Himself by **becoming obedient** to the point of death, even death on a cross.*

---

[141] Esther 4:14
[142] Matthew 12:41

It is in the obedience of Christ that my disobedience, and yours and Jonah's disobedience, is dealt with. Our disobedience was placed on Him as He died. He bore the judgment we deserve. And He cleanses us and covers us in the garment of His perfect obedience when we turn to Him in repentance and faith. And He empowers us with His indwelling Spirit to live a life of obedience that demonstrates the genuineness of our faith. Turn to Him. Trust Him to save you. Walk in the obedience that He commands and empowers you to live. And tell His good news to the world! Disobedience is far too dangerous. All its promises are empty. Its price-tag is too high. It is a steep descent downward. And ultimately, our obedience or lack thereof make our spiritual condition evident to those around us.

III

Asleep in the Storm
Jonah 1:4-6

The LORD hurled a great wind on the sea and there was
a great storm on the sea so that the ship was about to break up.
Then the sailors became afraid and every man cried to his god,
and they threw the cargo which was in the ship into the sea to
lighten it for them. But Jonah had gone below into the hold of the ship,
lain down and fallen sound asleep. So the captain approached him
and said, "How is it that you are sleeping? Get up, call on your god.
Perhaps your god will be concerned about us so that we will not perish."

The early months of 2011 was a difficult time for air traffic controllers. By mid-April, seven of them had been reported to have fallen asleep on the job.[143] On the one hand, we may be inclined to say with some sympathy, "What's the big deal? Doesn't everyone get a little drowsy and maybe even catch a little nap in the office from time to time?" But on the other hand, not many of us are in jobs where a split-second of distracted attention could cost hundreds of lives and millions of dollars. That's kind of a big deal. In a moment of sleep, two planes could collide in the air or on the ground without even knowing that they are in danger because the controller whose job it was to alert and warn them was sleeping in the tower.

Remember what we have read in verses 1-3 of Jonah 1. The prophet had been called by God to take a warning to the great city of Nineveh. There was a disaster approaching, but Jonah refused to warn them. The speculations abound regarding why Jonah did this, and he will confess his

---

[143] Mike Ahlers, "Another Air Traffic Controller Suspended for Sleeping," http://articles.cnn.com/2011-04-16/travel/air.traffic.controller.asleep_1_regional-radar-facility-faa-administrator-randy-babbitt-faa-air-traffic-organization?_s=PM:TRAVEL . Accessed May 11, 2011.

motives in his own time here in the book, but we can easily guess that it has something to do with a hardened heart toward the pagan Gentile world and the mission of God to reach them with His mercy and grace. So, instead of obeying the Lord, Jonah went to Joppa and boarded a ship bound for Tarshish, and now he's gone below deck and fallen asleep. Interestingly, though he ran away from the mission of warning the unbelievers in Nineveh about the coming disaster, Jonah now finds himself surrounded by unbelievers on this ship, and they are facing their own disaster. Only, Jonah is ignorant of it because he is sound asleep. He can't warn them of what is coming, he can't help them through the crisis, he can't take part in the prayer meeting that is going on up on the top deck, because he is sleeping. The Septuagint, the Greek translation of the Hebrew Old Testament, suggests that Jonah was snoring! The Hebrew word that is originally used here to describe his sleep does not refer to a normal night's sleep. This is a very deep sleep. Jeremiah 51:39 uses this term to describe the sleep of one who has passed out from drunkenness. Saul slept in this kind of deep sleep and was not roused when David came in and took his spear and water jug from beside of his head.[144] In Judges 4:21, Sisera slept in this kind of exhausted sleep and did not awaken as Jael drove a tent spike through his temple and killed him. It was this kind of deep sleep that the Lord brought upon Adam when He performed the surgery of removing one of his ribs to create Eve. It is the sleep of exhaustion, the sleep of a drunken stupor, the sleep of anesthesia, that Jonah falls into in the innermost part of the ship. And while the prophet sleeps, the lives of others are at stake all around him.

We cannot help seeing a parallel with the state of the contemporary church. Exhausted from the busyness of so much less-important activity, intoxicated from drinking too much from the flasks of worldliness, anesthetized to the point of insensitivity to a lost and perishing world around us, the church sleeps while the storm rages. When the need for a clear word from the church has never been greater in the world, the only sound that is heard from the church is that of our snoring.

---

[144] 1 Samuel 26:12

When we were preparing for our move from Maryland back to North Carolina, we needed to tie up some loose ends down at Southeastern Seminary, so we spent the night with Donia's sister and her husband, who were living near the Seminary at the time. I vividly remember being snapped out of a deep sleep by the sound of the most obnoxious alarm clock I have ever heard. This ear shattering wake-up call comes out of this mysterious plastic animal that no one can tell if it is a dog or a cat. It is ugly, it is loud, and it is annoying. This alarm clock has become the stuff of legend in our family! But it is effective. It wakes everyone in the house up when it sounds the alarm. And in this text we find that God has His own alarm clocks to wake His sleeping people. He will not let Jonah sleep through this crisis, nor will He will allow His church to remain in a state of undisturbed slumber while a tempest ravages the world around us. He will sound His divine alarms to rouse us to action and remind us of the mission to which He has called us. Two of His alarms are seen in these three verses.

I. He targets us with the severe mercy of His providence.

Back in the early '90s, during the first Gulf War, we were all exposed to this new technology that our military was using called "smart bombs." On the evening news, we were able to see a black and white grainy video of a bomb go right into the smokestack of the targeted building. And I would speculate that we all reacted in amazement at the pinpoint precision and accuracy of this weapon. From miles away, it could spot its target and land in the exact spot it was aimed. This kind of accuracy and precision is, in fact, not a new development. Eight hundred years before Christ's birth, God was able to isolate His target and launch His weapon with even better accuracy than the latest military technology affords.

I've never sailed on the Mediterranean. Always wanted to, but I've never had the opportunity. I have been on a ship in the middle of the much smaller Black Sea before. Out in the midst of the Black Sea, you can stand on the deck and look in all directions and see nothing but water and sky. It makes you feel very small. Jonah was on board a ship in the middle of the Mediterranean, roughly six times larger than the Black Sea. It is a miniscule target on that vast blue sea. But God has pinpoint accuracy, and verse 4 tells us that He hurled a great wind right at this target and hit it.

Depending on your English version, you may read that the Lord "sent" this great wind onto the sea. No English version I know of leaves us to think that this storm just originated on its own. It was brought about directly by the hand of God. But to say that He "sent" the storm doesn't capture the full force of the Hebrew here. The NASB and ESV render the verb well when they say that the Lord *hurled* a great wind. It is the same Hebrew word that describes the throwing of a spear or a ball. It is to take aim and launch something. And that is what the Lord did. He set his sights on the ship that bore the sleeping disobedient prophet, and He fired this great wind directly at it. And He always hits His target.

Interestingly, the first to notice the severity of the storm is neither Jonah nor the sailors. The writer personifies the ship here in verse 4, as the Hebrew literally reads that it *threatened to break up*. You have to picture this ship announcing to its crew, "I'm about to come apart here!" And seeing the stress that the storm has placed upon the ship, the sailors quickly realize that their lives and livelihood are endangered. These guys have been through storms before, probably every time they are out at sea. But this storm has them fearful for their lives and calling out on every god they know of for rescue. They are so certain that this storm could be the death of them that they begin to sacrifice their livelihood in exchange for their lives. They begin throwing the cargo, literally the *stuff*, overboard to lighten the ship. This was a costly decision. That cargo was their business. It was the reason this ship existed, the reason these sailors had a job, their means of earning a living. But a life-threatening storm has a way of clarifying life's priorities. What mattered most at this moment in time was saving their necks more than saving their jobs. So, the cargo goes overboard.

This was a potentially disastrous storm. It threatened to destroy innocent lives and valuable goods. And it was thrown by the Lord. Why? It was because of His mercy. And we observe through this that the Lord's mercy sometimes takes severe manifestations. In this event, we see that the Lord, in His mercy will go to great lengths to prevent His people from making tragic shipwreck of their lives in disobedience to His will. Because God loves Nineveh, He will toss this ship all over the Mediterranean to wake up His sleeping prophet. Because God loves Jonah, He will not let him sleep his way to Tarshish. And because God loves the sailors on the deck, He will bring them to the point of desperation to see their need for Him. Had the sea remained calm and glassy, these sailors may have continued in the journey of their lives giving no thought to their need for God. The money is good, the work is steady, and all is well. They have gods they believe in, and they call on them when they need them, but without this severe storm they do not see that their gods are powerless to save them. And without this storm, Jonah can go on thinking that he has pulled one over on God, that he has slipped the bonds of God's presence and power. God loves Jonah too much to let him go on thinking that.

The only hope a lost soul has once they see their need for the Lord is to have someone present to share the good news of the Lord with them. And the sailors have just such a one as this. Only, at the moment, he is nearly comatose in the belly of the ship. But God has sent a mighty tempest as a divine alarm clock to rouse the sleepy prophet and awaken him to the reality that he can never escape the Lord or the calling God has placed on his life. He will arise, and he will speak for God to the pagans in Nineveh, but not before speaking first to the pagans on board this ship. God had targeted Jonah with the severe mercy of His providence by hurling this storm at the ship on which he was sleeping. And God will also do the same when we are running away from Him, sleeping on duty, and failing to be who He has called us to be and do what He has called us to do. The doors we are trying to walk through will be slammed in our face. The smooth waters will become choppy. God will orchestate sudden and expected changes in our circumstances to rouse us from our sleepy disobedience and awaken us to repentance and obedience. Is this bad news? Does it mean that God is zapping us with a lightning bolt of divine judgment? No, rather it is good news! It is His mercy at work, but sometimes His mercy is severe. He loves us too much to let us shipwreck ourselves in disobedience and spiritual laziness. So when this alarm of His providence sounds, when He sets aim at us and unleashes the storm, we should rejoice and give thanks because it is proof that we belong to Him. Be very concerned when you set your course for disobedience and find that God does not chase you down. Be very concerned when you have been lulled into spiritual sleepiness and find that God does not rattle you awake. Hebrews 12:7-8 says to the followers of Jesus, "God deals with you as with sons; for what son is there whom his father does not discipline? But if you are without discipline, of which all have become partakers, then you are illegitimate children and not sons." Are you "getting away with something"? That should cause you to tremble. For it may indicate that you have been deceived about your relationship with Christ. If you belong to Christ, you will be pursued and awakened by His providence because He loves you and has called you according to His own purpose. If you are not pursued and awakened, this suggests that you do not belong to Christ.

When Jonah sleeps during the storm, and when we do, we find that God rouses us to wakefulness by targeting us with the severe mercy of His providence. But this is not the only alarm God can use to wake us.

II. He rebukes us through the desperate pleas of the perishing.

Perhaps Jonah knew that if he hung around Israel, he'd encounter some prophet with keen insight into spiritual matters who would discern that he was in rebellion and rebuke him. Better, he thinks, to surround himself with unbelievers who won't care if he is living in obedience or not. But he thinks incorrectly. God can speak through unusual mouths to rebuke those who oppose His will. He spoke through Balaam's donkey[145] on one occasion, so choosing to speak through any human being, whether he or she is a believer or not, is no difficult task for Him.

As the men on deck realize that praying to their own gods is not helping them, it occurs to the captain that there is one man on the boat unaccounted for. He finds Jonah sleeping and his voice becomes an alarm to awaken Jonah from his sleep. His first statement to Jonah is, "How is it that you are sleeping?" This sailor has slept the better part of his life on reeling ships in rocking seas, but he can't fathom how anyone can sleep through this tempest! And then he speaks words that must be most unwelcome to Jonah. He says, "Get up, call on your god." Interestingly, the Hebrew

---

[145] Numbers 22:27-30

words he uses are the exact same words that God had spoken to Jonah. The Hebrew word translated as "Arise" in verse 2, God's initial command to Jonah, is the same word that the captain speaks to Jonah here: "Get up!" The second part of Jonah's commission in verse 2 was to "cry against" the city of Nineveh. But Jonah refused. Now this same word is repeated by the ship's captain. "Call on your god!" Arise and call! It must be a terrible case of deja vu for Jonah, who would have just as soon never heard those two words again. But God's plans for Jonah have not changed, and He will reissue His calling by any means necessary to wake the sleeping prophet and turn him back to the path of obedience.

Some read too much into the words of this captain. When he commands Jonah to call upon his god, it is not as if he has suddenly become convinced that Jonah must know the one true God of all the earth. Rather, being a polytheistic pagan who believes in the existence of many gods, this captain is simply crying out in desperation. Maybe Jonah knows about a god that the rest of the men don't know, and it wouldn't hurt to call on as many gods as possible in this crisis. There is not much confidence expressed by the captain when he says, "Perhaps your god will be concerned about us so that we will not perish." Their gods aren't coming through for them, but maybe Jonah's God can.

What the sailors don't know is that Jonah's God is the only God there is. The problem is that Jonah is not in the mood to talk to this God presently. He is trying to get away from Him. Whether the sailors realize it or not, the fact is that their only hope in the midst of this storm is for Jonah to get right with God. Otherwise they will all perish. So the desperate plea of the captain rouses Jonah from his slumber like an alarm, as if to say, "Look man, if you know of a god who can help us, now would be the time to talk to Him and tell us about Him." Don't miss the irony of this. Why did Jonah flee? Because he did not want to speak for his God to an audience of unbelieving pagans. It was fine with him if the people of Nineveh perished. They deserved it. But here he is, in the middle of his escape from that mission, surrounded by other unbelieving people who are begging him to speak to God and for God on their behalf, lest they perish.

All around us today are unbelievers who are being tossed about by storms on the sea of life. They are doing everything they know to do to survive the raging tempest. They are praying to gods who cannot hear and cannot save because they only exist in the figments of their imaginations. They are making radical decisions to try to fix the situation by their own strength and ingenuity, like sailors hurling the cargo overboard. But there is hope for them. There is good news for them in the midst of their storms. There is a God who can help them, who can save them if they turn to Him. As Paul said in Romans 10, "whoever will call on the name of the Lord will be saved." But he asks, "How then will they call on Him in whom they have not believed? How will they believe in Him whom they have not heard? And how will they hear without a preacher?"[146]

Carl Henry famously said, "The gospel is only good news if it gets there in time."[147] Before it is too late, is there someone who can tell them the good news of Jesus Christ? There is someone on that sinking ship on the stormy sea, but the only problem is that he is zonked out below deck! Somebody wake that guy up so they might be saved! And the same thing can be said concerning the church of Jesus Christ in our day. Is there anyone in this world filled with suffering and evil that can say a word of good news? Is there anyone around who can speak hope into this storm? Is there anyone who can make contact with a God who can save? The good news is that there is. It is the church of Jesus Christ and the Christians who comprise this church in the world. The bad news is that we are too much like Jonah! We are asleep while the storm rages. But God is waking us up with the desperate pleas of a perishing world, rousing us from our sleep and commanding us to get up and speak up! We must see this world going under in the storm and cry out to God for them. And we must cry out to them for Him!

When I came to know Jesus in 1992, I was eager to undergo a radical transformation. There were many things in my life that I wanted to change. Soon, God began to show me that there were *other* things that He wanted to change, and I wasn't so sure I was in agreement with Him about those

---

[146] Romans 10:13-14

[147] This quote is widely attributed to Henry, but I have been unable to locate an exact source for the statement.

things! But God didn't give up on me. He had sent storms my way, and somehow, like Jonah, I managed to hit the snooze button and stay asleep. But then He rebuked me through an unlikely source. One night, a very close friend of mine who was an unbeliever said to me, "You know, I remember when you used to call yourself an atheist. Now you call yourself a Christian. But the funny thing is, nothing has changed. The only difference I see is that now you call yourself by another name, and you have a Bible on your shelf. But you don't read it. You still do the same things you always did. From where I am sitting there is no difference in you and me." And then he said this, "Look, it seems to me that you either need to stop calling yourself a Christian, or start living like one." And I can tell you that those words did more to wake me up from my state of spiritual sleepiness than anything else that has ever happened to me. God spoke into my life through the mouth of an unbeliever, and He rebuked me. And though I wish that I could say that my friend has become a believer now, he hasn't. But I am so thankful that he was not afraid to say what he said to me on that night, because God used his words to change my life.

It seems to me that today the entire world is crying out with pleas of desperation. Tragedy, terror, disaster, and destruction fill the earth. And something inside of many people is saying, "I hope there is a God who can help me out there. I wish someone would tell me who He is." Many of those people have no one to turn to for that good news. They live among the peoples at the ends of the earth where Christ has not been named. We know who they are and where they live. And God has called us to go to them with the Gospel of Jesus Christ. But we have slept through the wake-up calls. He will keep calling until we wake up.

Others are perishing all around us. Frustrated, desperate, depressed and despairing, they put on a happy face and pretend they have it all together. But at night they lay their heads on a cold pillow and they pray to gods who are not there, and they wonder if anyone can really bring good news into their lives. They drive by a dozen churches in their daily commute. And they sit beside a handful of Christians at their workplace. They have Christians living across the street from them and next door to them. They have good reason to believe that we have a message they need to hear. But what do they hear from us? Snoring. The church is asleep in the storm. But

God will not let us sleep forever. If we truly belong to Him, we can expect that He will rouse us by the severe mercy of His providence or by the desperate pleas of the perishing.

I can't help noticing an interesting similarity between Jonah and Jesus here. Jonah is sleeping in the boat in the midst of a storm. His sleep is the slumber of callousness to the purpose of God. In the Gospels, we will read of an occasion when the Lord Jesus was asleep in a boat in the midst of a storm.[148] But His sleep is the slumber of confidence in the purpose of God. Like Jonah's sailing companions, the disciples of Jesus will wake Him from His sleep and say, "Don't you care that we are perishing?" And with a word, Jesus will speak and the storm will cease. For too long the church has been sleeping in a boat of our own while the sea rages with a tempest all around us. And the world wants to know if we care that they are perishing. If we do, we will point the world to Jesus, because He is the only one who can speak and calm the storm.

There is an awakening coming to all of His sleeping prophets. He will throw the storm at us to shake us from our beds. The desperate pleas of the perishing will grow so loud in our ears that we can no longer ignore their cries. If you have ears to hear, then you can hear them today. Will we hit the snooze button, roll back over, and drift back into dreamland, or will we wake up, repent, and recommit ourselves to the mission to which God has called us?

---

[148] Mark 4:35-41

IV

Discovering God's Will
Jonah 1:7

Each man said to his mate, "Come, let us cast lots
so we may learn on whose account this calamity has struck us."
So they cast lots and the lot fell on Jonah.

Margaret was a successful accountant and a faithful Christian woman in her late thirties. [149] Though she was good at her job, she found it somewhat unfulfilling and insignificant. One Sunday, a missionary came to speak at her church and challenged every member to consider how God might use each of their lives to fulfill His Great Commission. This struck Margaret deeply as she contemplated spending the next 25 years of her life crunching numbers in her present job. On Monday morning, the front page of the newspaper told of the devastation caused by a hurricane in the Marshall Islands. She was moved by the pictures that accompanied the article and felt compelled to pray for the people of the Marshall Islands. Before that day, she wasn't sure she could find the Marshall Islands on a map, but now it was heavy on her heart. During the day at work, she strolled into the breakroom and found one of her coworkers looking through vacation brochures from the office of the travel agency next door. She couldn't help noticing that one of the glossy leaflets advertised the stunning beauty of the Marshall Islands. She wondered if there might be some connection between all of these circumstances. As she returned to her desk, the receptionist buzzed her intercom and said that there was someone who would like to speak with her. The man walked in and introduced himself. He must have been surprised by her expression when he said that his name was Marshall. She left work early that day with a lot on her mind. Most of all, she was convinced that all of these things had occurred over

---

[149] A hypothetical case, adapted from a similar scenario in Bruce Waltke, *Finding the Will of God: A Pagan Notion?* (Grand Rapids: Eerdmans, 1995), 3-4. This book has been a tremendous help to me in my Christian life and in the preparation of this message.

the last twenty-four hours to clarify that God was calling her to be a missionary to the Marshall Islands. It seemed to her that God had clearly made His will known. But had He really, or was this just an unusual string of circumstances? How could she ever know for certain?

We would hope that, as Christians, we all desire to make wise decisions that honor God and that are in keeping with His will. When the decision comes down to deciding between good and evil, or apparently good and apparently bad, we have no problem knowing to choose the good. We don't always choose the good, but we know we should. Many times our decisions come down to good and good, and then we are perplexed. Should a young Christian attend Duke or the University of North Carolina? That may be a bad example of "good and good" if you are a Wake Forest or North Carolina State fan. Should she pursue a relationship with Jim or Tom? Should a person go on vacation to the Bahamas or on a mission trip to Kenya? What would God have us to do? This is when we begin to speak of "seeking" or "finding God's will" on the matter. And Christians set about trying to discover that will in any number of ways, and not all of them are valid. Some, like our hypothetical "Margaret," begin to see chains of connection between circumstances that would ordinarily appear random and coincidental. Others perhaps engage in some sort of ritual or mystical practice, while still others begin to look for signs. The process of making these decisions becomes paralyzing to us at times, as we fear failure (often in an unhealthy way) and we fear disappointing God and being "out of His will."

In Jonah 1:7, we find the sailors on the deck of the ship trying to determine the will of God. They are trying to figure out why it is that the storm has come upon them and what they can do to survive the storm. As veteran sailors, they have encountered storms before, but this one is like no other. So intense is this tempest that they rightly discern that there is a divine hand behind it. They have all cried out to every god they know, but there has been no relief. They have asked Jonah to pray to his god, but there is no record that he ever did. Unaided by the prophet, they begin to cast lots in hopes that the lot will lead them to the person who is responsible for the storm, and then they can begin sorting out what to do about it.

These sailors are not the last people who have ever tried to solve a divine mystery. In a given week, any of us may find ourselves wondering why something has happened, what God would have us to do, and how to make a right decision about a perplexing matter. We, like these sailors, need to get hold of God to discover His will and act upon it. But how will we do this? In our text we learn that there are some ways that will never work, some ways that may work sometimes, and one way that never fails to uncover God's will. We must keep in mind that for believers in the Lord Jesus Christ, God is our loving Father. He has promised to guide us and give us all good things. This means that we can rest assured that if we know Him by faith in Christ, then He is not hiding Himself or His will from us. Of course, we must also reckon with the fact that God may have purposes and plans that He will never reveal to us for reasons of His own choosing. As Bruce Waltke writes, "Simply because God has a plan does not mean that He necessarily has any intention of sharing it with you; as a matter of fact the message of Job is in part that the Lord in His sovereignty may allow terrible things to happen to you, and you may never know why."[150] But we can rest assured knowing that anything necessary for us to know about God and His will is going to be made known to His children. If earthly fathers know how to give good gifts to their children, how much more will our Father in Heaven give us what He knows that we need? He will not give His children serpents when they ask for fish, or stones when they ask for bread.[151] And when we find ourselves in need of knowing God's will, He makes it known. It is not a matter of "if He will," but "how He will."

I. There are ways of seeking God's will that will never work.

Every human culture in the world through all history has had some knowledge of a supreme divine being. And every culture where this belief is found has some "method" of discerning God's will. In ancient times, this practice of finding the divine will was known as "divination." Some eighty percent of all ancient writings that we currently possess offer details and prescriptions for determining the will of God.[152] In some of these cultures,

---

[150] Waltke, 15.
[151] Matthew 7:7-11
[152] Waltke, 26.

the practices have been rather bizarre by our sophisticated modern standards. One method involved tossing up arrows and observing how they land. The direction that the arrows pointed were thought to indicate the will of the deity. Another very common method was the study of the internal organs of a sacrificed animal. After cutting the animal open in a ritual, the vital organs were spilled on the ground, and the arrangement or specific features of certain organs were thought to communicate the will of the gods. One popular method involved the use of household idols. An offering would be made, some mantras or prayers recited, and then the inquirer would wait for some sign that the idol had heard and responded with a revelation. Ezekiel 21:21 speaks of all of these methods: "The King of Babylon stands at the parting of the way, at the head of the two ways, to use divination; he shakes the arrows, he consults the household idols, he looks at the liver."

Of course there are plenty of other methods that have been used through the centuries, some of which are still commonly practiced today. Studying the stars, astrology, is perhaps the most common of them. Every day countless people consult their horoscope and use it as a guide for their daily planning and decision making, giving no thought to the fact that they are using a pagan method of divination. The consulting of stars is stated throughout Scripture as being a practice on equal par with reading livers, consulting mediums and psychics, worshiping idols, and a number of other divination practices. But all of these methods, as well as others too numerous to name, have been forbidden for the people of God. The use of them is equated with "forsaking the Lord." In Deuteronomy 18, the Lord spoke through Moses to His people:

> *When you enter the land which the LORD your God gives you, you shall not learn to imitate the detestable things of those nations. There shall not be found among you anyone who makes his son or his daughter pass through the fire, one who uses divination, one who practices witchcraft, or one who interprets omens, or a sorcerer, or one who casts a spell, or a medium, or a spiritist, or one who calls up the dead. For whoever does these things is detestable to the LORD; and because of these detestable things the LORD your God will drive them out before you. You shall be*

blameless before the LORD your God. For those nations, which you
shall dispossess, listen to those who practice witchcraft and to
diviners, but as for you, the LORD your God has not allowed you to
do so.

For the Christian today, these methods of determining God's will are off-limits. They do not work. Now someone will take issue with that and say, "But I know of a situation in which it *did* work." I would respond by saying that if God considered these to be reliable methods of communicating His will, He would not have forbidden them. Remember, He is our Father and He longs to guide us in a way of life that pleases Him. If these methods enabled us to do that more effectively, He would have encouraged us to use them rather than forbidding them. So, will we allow an experience that we have had or that someone else we know has had trump God's revealed truth? If so, we are actually saying that we believe that God is evil, and has forbidden us from doing the things that actually lead us into a life of blessing. Rather, we must understand that He is good, and He wants us to know His will, and therefore He has forbidden us from the things that He will not use to make His will known.

We must not forget that Satan is active in the world, and one of his most predictable strategies for leading God's people astray is to persuade them to abandon the simplicity of trusting in God in exchange for subtle forms of idolatry. Satan is not out to make you a Satanist. He is perfectly content for you to be a Baptist that dabbles in idolatry rather than walking by faith with the Lord. Therefore, we should not be surprised if some of these methods have some "success rate." Satan can produce results that are sufficient to lead us astray, just as the Egyptian magicians were able to duplicate some of the miraculous signs that Moses and Aaron performed for Pharaoh.[153] They will be "successful" to the extent that they lead us to trust in them rather than in our Heavenly Father. Having accomplished that, they will only succeed in leading us into destruction.

Now, there are some methods that were employed at one time by God's people, with His approval, which are now obsolete. For instance, under the

---

[153] e.g., Exodus 7:8-13

priesthood of Israel, decisions were sometimes made by use of the Urim and the Thummim. In Exodus 28, we are told that the Urim and the Thummim were kept in the breastplate of the high priest and they were used to determine God's will on matters of national importance. Interestingly, we are never told what the Urim and Thummim were. Don't you want to know? Apparently God did not see fit to preserve a record of what they were. Perhaps He knows we would create idols from them. I can see it now: some Christian bookstore would have it packaged in a nice wooden box with silk lining. Your very own set of Urim and Thummim to make decisions with, kind of like the old Magic 8-Ball (anyone under 30 may not know what a Magic 8-Ball was; anyone under sixteen would understand what iCarly's Magic Meatball is—same thing!). But it is also interesting that this method was not fool-proof. In 1 Samuel 28:6, Saul inquired of the Lord, but even with the Urim and Thummim, no answer was given. So, while at one time, in the economy of God, it seems that the Urim and Thummim could be used to divine God's will, it cannot any longer, because it is lost to history under the providence of God. It is never mentioned again in Scripture after the Israelites returned from Babylon.

In our text we find another method that was used with some success throughout many generations, even among people outside of the covenant of God. This is the casting of lots. Though it took shape in a number of particular objects, the main idea in the casting of lots is akin to rolling dice, drawing straws, or flipping a coin. The belief among God's people and unbelievers alike was that God, or the gods as they may have believed, would superintend the roll of the dice to produce whatever outcome He desired. In fact we read in Proverbs 16:33, "The lot is cast into the lap, but its every decision is from the Lord." It seems that among all the methods of finding God's will, this was one of the most reliable methods available to humanity at one time. We find the use of lots used repeatedly and even commanded by God at times in the Old Testament. In the case of these sailors on the ship with Jonah, casting lots was used to determine "the guilty party."

It seems that, for a time, God endorsed and allowed the use of lots to determine His will in some situations. But it also seems that this method had a built-in expiration date. The last time in Scripture that we find a decision being made on the basis of lot-casting is in Acts 1:26, where lots were cast to choose a replacement apostle for Judas Iscariot. New Testament scholars often debate as to whether or not the early church acted rightly in doing this. It is a "descriptive" text, telling us "what happened," not a "prescriptive" text that tells us what we should do. There was no instruction from the Lord for the apostles to do this, but it seemed right to them and they cast lots and came up with Matthias. Interestingly, the New Testament does not record any further word about Matthias. However, in God's timing, He would select his own replacement apostle, a man named Saul, whom we know better as Paul. And throughout his ministry, Paul actually had to defend his claim to be an apostle perhaps because so many did not believe that he was God's choice. It may have been that people felt that God would not overrule the roll of the dice that had singled out Matthias. So it seems that by the time of Acts 1, the use of lots had expired as a reliable tool of determining God's will. They are never used in the New Testament after that. Therefore, for the Christian today seeking divine wisdom in making a decision, the casting of lots, the rolling of dice, the tossing of a coin, or any other random game of chance will not be effective in determining God's will. It worked for the sailors in Jonah's case, but it will not work for you and me today.

This is a somewhat selective survey of methods used in times past, some of which never worked for God's people to discover His will, others of which worked at one time, but will not work now.

II. There are ways of seeking God's will that work sometimes.

Throughout most of my life, I have had to learn to cope with cars that work *sometimes*. This has taught me the important lesson of being appreciative when it works, but having no expectation that it will work. It cranked this morning, and I am thankful that it did. The fact that it cranked this morning is no guarantee that it will crank tomorrow morning. That is not something I can just expect to happen. It works well when it works, but it only works sometimes. And the same can be said for certain methods of discovering God's will. Some of these may work sometimes to direct us to the right choices and decisions, and for that we give thanks to God for using them in that way. However, they must not be perceived to be infallible guides that we can turn to every time. We can't expect an accurate answer from them every time, because they only work *sometimes.*

In this text of Jonah, we find two means of discovering God's will which work sometimes. First, there is God's providence, His orchestration of our circumstances. Now, let me be clear: God's providence works *all the time,* but our understanding and perception of His providence is what doesn't always work. In the context of these verses in Jonah, a storm has arisen on the sea. The sailors surmise that the storm contains some message from a divine being, though they do not know which divine being, nor do they know what the message communicates. But, we need to give them credit for discerning that there is a divine message in the storm. And so it is in our lives. Circumstances arise that were choreographed by the providence of God to communicate His direction and guidance to us. For instance, you may wonder if it is God's will for you to adopt a child from Nepal. And when you go to inquire about doing that, at least at the time of this writing, you will be told that the United States government does not allow you to adopt a child from Nepal. The door of opportunity has been closed, and you don't even need to pray about it at the moment unless you are willing to move to Nepal or to a country where such adoptions are allowed. Circumstances have arisen to make that an easy decision. But we sometimes have difficulty interpreting what is going on in God's providence. There are times when God would lead us to overcome our circumstances, to change our course based on circumstances, or to persevere in spite of circumstances. So, at times circumstances are an indicator of God's providence in guiding us through a decision. At other times circumstances are unrelated or irrelevant to what God would guide us to do. Therefore, at best, circumstances only help us discover God's will sometimes.

We also find that there are times at which God guides us according to His will by speaking to us through other people. We see this in Jonah's life as the ship captain tells him in verse 6 to get up and call on his god. Now, from all earthly vantage points it looks as if this is just a panicked sailor trying to get out of a jam. Indeed, that may have been all that the sailor knew was going on. But, what we are often unaware of, what the captain himself may have been unaware of, and what Jonah likely was picking up on, is that the captain was unknowingly being used as a mouthpiece for God. What Jonah needed more than anything else in his life at that moment was to rise up and call on his God. Jonah had sought to distance himself from God, and it took an unbelieving sailor to beckon him to get right with God. And by the way, even though God spoke to Jonah through the captain, we still do not know that Jonah obeyed. The narrator does not record for us that Jonah ever called out to God until he was thrown overboard a few verses later.

I can recall conversations I have had in my lifetime in which later on, upon further reflection, I sensed God speaking to me through the mouth of that other person directing me according to His will. These messengers have not always even been believers. But they have been people whom God placed in the right place at the right time to say the right words to get my attention and direct me according to His path. I am quite sure that you have found the same thing in your own lives. But, here's the thing: it only works sometimes. Not everyone who speaks to us communicates God's will to us. Sometimes they are just words, human words, friendly words, even at times foolish words that happen to find their way into our ear canal. But at other times, God is using that friend, a parent or sibling, maybe even a child, or your teacher, or your pastor (I had to throw that one in!), that perfect stranger even, to speak His will into your life.

Because these things work *sometimes*, we have to be careful with them. We mustn't think that every turn of circumstance is intended to direct us according to God's will. We mustn't think that every time someone speaks to us that God is speaking through them. We can be thankful when it happens that way, but we cannot expect it to always happen that way. We can turn people into idols, whereby we are paralyzed to make any decisions apart from the input of a particular individual. This gives rise to a *guru* situation in our lives, and God would not have us elevate any human being to that status. We can also become lazy, sitting back and waiting on circumstances to dictate our actions and decisions rather than proactively thinking through things from a spiritual vantage point.

So, if there are some things that never work, and some things that sometimes work, is there not some way of discovering God's will that is always reliable? There is. And we have to go back to the very first verse of Jonah to find it.

III. There is only one way of discovering God's will that always works.

The word of the Lord came to Jonah. God spoke to Jonah in a number of ways. He spoke through the circumstance of the storm. He spoke through the words of the sailor. But do you realize that these were unnecessary? The storm and the sailor only repeated and reminded Jonah of what the Lord had initially spoken to him directly. It was because Jonah did not heed the unmediated word of the Lord that He resorted to speaking to him through other means. Had Jonah heeded the word of the Lord and obeyed His will, the sailors would not have been in the predicament of having to cast lots to determine His will!

Of course, Jonah is not the only person who refused to heed the word of the Lord and therefore had to discover God's will by other means. We often refer to "Gideon's fleece" to indicate some test we employ to discover God's will. But what is often overlooked is that God had spoken to Gideon directly, and then through the mouth of another person, and Gideon still did not believe, so he asked God for signs, not once but twice, involving his fleece. So the account in Judges 6 of Gideon's fleece is not intended to teach us to ask God for signs; it actually stands written to rebuke us when we are slow to believe what God has clearly spoken.

I am confident that in my own life and in the lives of so many others, the reason that we are perplexed about God's will and go to such great lengths of divination to discover it is that we have either not taken the time to discover for ourselves what God has spoken, or we have chosen not to believe what God has spoken. And how has God spoken in such clear and unmediated ways? Hebrews 1 tells us that God spoke in the past in many ways and in many portions by the prophets, but in these last days He has spoken to us through His Son. Jesus Christ is the incarnate, living Word of God. But how can you know anything about this Jesus? How can you hear Him speak or learn from Him how God would have you live a life that pleases Him? Thankfully, we have access to the Living Word of God via the written Word of God, our Bible. This book was written through the supernatural inspiration of the Holy Spirit, who also happens to reside within those who have received Jesus Christ by faith as Lord and Savior. So, when we open our Bibles, we are not reading lifeless words from a lifeless book. We are communicating with God Himself, who authored these words through inspiration, and who lives within us to guide us in our understanding and application of these words. How many other authors can you converse with while you read his or her book? But you can with God and His book! Paul says in 2 Timothy 3:16-17, "All Scripture is inspired by God and profitable for teaching, for reproof, for correction, for training in righteousness; so that the man of God may be adequate, equipped for every good work." John Frame has said that reading or listening to Scripture is "not merely a transaction between ourselves and a book, ... rather, in Scripture we meet God Himself. ... no experience offers a more profound closeness with God."[154]

If you would know God's will, it will require you to pursue Jesus Christ passionately. If you would pursue Jesus Christ passionately, it will require you to know the Bible thoroughly. God has inspired it for our benefit, that through it we might seek Him and find Him, and in so doing to find ourselves living in His will. The New Testament does not command us to seek God's will. Rather, in it we are commanded to seek God in the person of Jesus Christ, and to seek His Kingdom, and to *do* His will. If we will allow Him to speak into our lives through Scripture, and commit ourselves to heed this Word by the aid of the Holy Spirit, many of our perplexing decisions will be made for us. We may not read in the pages of Scripture which college we should attend, which job offer we should take, which person we should marry, or which kind of car we should purchase. But what we do read there will transform us into the kinds of people who can make those decisions out of the overflow of our love for Christ and our love for our neighbor. It has been well said that within the context of truly loving God with all of our heart, soul, mind, and strength, and genuinely loving our neighbor as ourselves (which I understand to mean "more than self" or "instead of self"), we can often do whatever it is we desire. A life like that is having its desires shaped by the hand of our Heavenly Father. We begin to want what He wants us to have, and therefore we can rest in

---

[154] John Frame, *Spiritual Formation* (Philadelphia: Westminster, 1981), 221.

the promise of Psalm 37:4: "Delight yourself in the Lord and He will give you the desires of your heart."

Jonah perhaps never realized how his refusal to heed God's Word would jeopardize his own life and the lives of so many others who would have been completely unaffected apart from his disobedience. This storm was unnecessary. The words of the captain did not need to be spoken. The lots never needed to be cast. God had spoken. That should have been enough to make the will of God clearly known. God has spoken to you and to me as well. We have His inscripturated Word pointing us to the incarnate Word, the Lord Jesus, and instructing us in how to live for His glory. Is *that* enough for us? Will we hear and believe and obey?

V

Fearing a Great Fear
Jonah 1:7-10

*Each man said to his mate, "Come, let us cast lots so we may learn
on whose account this calamity has struck us." So they cast lots
and the lot fell on Jonah. Then they said to him,
"Tell us, now! On whose account has this calamity struck us?
What is your occupation? And where do you come from?
What is your country? From what people are you?"
He said to them, "I am a Hebrew, and I fear the Lord God of heaven
who made the sea and the dry land." Then the men became extremely
frightened and they said to him, "How could you do this?"
For the men knew that he was fleeing from the presence of the Lord,
because he had told them.*

One of the most lovable characters on television in recent history has to
have been Monk, the obsessive-compulsive detective. In that television
series, Adrian Monk is a brilliant crime-solver who just happens to be
terrified of almost everything in the world. Thankfully most of us are not
like Monk, but all of us are afraid of something. The idea of a "fearless"
person is unrealistic. Fear is a part of our nature that scientists and
sociologists have concluded to be necessary for our survival. Fear is what
drives our "fight-or-flight" instinct, and that instinct may keep us alive in
some situations. Some of our fears are rational, while others are not. For
instance, many people have aichmophobia, a fear of needles. Others have
octophobia, a fear of the number "8." Some have glossophobia, a fear of
public speaking, while others have ergophobia, which is a fear of work. It
is perfectly rational to have emetophobia, the fear of vomiting; not so
rational to suffer from omphalophobia, the fear of belly-buttons. All of this
talk about these strange sounding fears may make someone uneasy who
suffers from phobophobia, the fear of fears. The list of phobias and the

number of people who suffer from them seems to be growing, but there is one fear that seems to be vanishing in the world today. We might call it "theophobia," or the fear of God. It certainly isn't a popular subject today.

Have we come to envision God as our easy-going pal who is never offended and is always on our side, no matter who we are or what we have done? Sometimes it is said that fear was a proper response to God in the Old Testament, where we read of His judgment and wrath, His anger and fury. But now, in the New Testament era, it is claimed that fear of the Lord should subside, because the God of the New Testament is a happier deity, who is all about love and joy and being our friend. There is only one problem with that view: it doesn't correspond to what the Bible actually teaches. We find descriptions of God's love and grace throughout the Old Testament, and we find descriptions of His wrath and judgment in the New. And we find admonitions to fear Him in the New and Old Testament alike. And those admonitions are addressed to believers and unbelievers alike. For instance, in 1 Peter 2:17, we read the very simple words: "Fear God." That is in the New Testament, and it is written to believers. Now some will say, "But doesn't the word 'fear' in the Bible mean something else, like serve, worship, or reverence?" You do not have to be a Greek scholar to see that the word translated "fear" in 1 Peter 2:17 is "phobeo," which ought to sound familiar to us, unless we have hellenologophobia, which is a fear of Greek words. If we have truly comprehended the magnitude of God's holiness and the depth of our own sinfulness, then we have no trouble wrapping our minds around the idea of fearing God. And wherever there is an aversion to talk of fearing God, I suspect that a misunderstanding of His holiness or our sinfulness is at the root of it.

In Paul's sweeping indictment of the human race found in Romans 3:10-18, he strings together a series of Old Testament quotations (get that, he is quoting the Old Testament in the New Testament) that describe the sinfulness of humanity. He opens by saying, "There is none righteous, not even one." And he concludes by saying, "There is no fear of God before their eyes." So, right there in the New Testament, we find Paul saying that one of the problems with sinful humanity is our lack of fear of the Lord. He is saying that is a bad thing. Certainly, as we look at the immorality, injustice, the evil, the suffering and the tyranny in the world, we feel it rising up within us – a strong desire to shout, "Is there no fear of God in the world?" And there is seemingly little. But more surprising perhaps is that world may often behold the church, with our high-profile scandals, rampant carnality and hypocrisy, and wonder amongst themselves, "Is there no fear of God in the church?" Both seem to be right. There is little fear of God in the world, and surprisingly little in the church. Have we stopped to consider that there may be a correlation between these realities? It may well be that if the church rightly understood what it means to fear the Lord, the world might come to fear Him and know Him also.

In our text today, we find some frightened sailors. Verses 4-5 speak of a great storm that the Lord sent upon the sea which was so intense that it caused these veteran mariners to be afraid. But as afraid as they were of the storm, it was not until later that they "became extremely frightened" (verse 10). The Hebrew expression found in verse 10 would be literally translated "they feared a great fear." The Hebrew language typically uses repetition to intensify an expression. So, when the storm came they were afraid, but now in verse 10 they are really-REALLY afraid. What was it that terrified them more than the storm? This great fear arose as Jonah opened up his mouth and spoke. The words spoken by Jonah brought a fear of the Lord upon these pagan polytheists, and that fear ultimately led them to worship the God of whom Jonah spoke. How did his words produce this effect? Can our words to a lost world have the same effect today? That is what we will consider as we look further into the text.

I. The world will come to fear the Lord as God's people identify themselves.

As children, many of us read the Grimm Brothers' fairy tale *Rumplestiltskin*. You may recall that in that story, the queen was threatened with the loss of her child unless she could guess the name of the mysterious little woodland creature. It was only at the last moment, because of the help of her servants, that she was able to guess that his name was Rumplestiltskin. We are often like that little creature, playing games with the world and challenging them to guess our true identity. We go about our business without telling others the truth of who we really are, namely that we are Christians, people who belong to God through faith in

Jesus Christ. It isn't that we mind them knowing, it's just that we would rather them guess. But they might as well come up with the name Rumplestiltskin as to come to the conclusion that we are Christians. The fact is that we are unable to live in such a way, and they are too uninformed to come up with the conclusion that we are Christians. We must make it known by both deed and word.

The sailors on the ship asked Jonah a series of questions in rapid-fire succession. And some of these questions had to do with his identity: "Where do you come from? What is your country? From what people are you?" And Jonah gives a brief response that answers all of those questions: "I am a Hebrew." These are the first recorded words of Jonah in the story. In a very brief form, the name "Hebrew" indicates where he came from, what his country is, and who his people are. But the name Hebrew also speaks much more than this. It identifies him as a descendent of Abraham, and a member of that famous people who were led out of Egypt and into the land of Canaan under the guidance of Moses and Joshua. Their reputation preceded them as neighboring nations heard of how their God had blessed them and worked through them in the world. In saying, "I am a Hebrew," Jonah was using short-hand to identify himself as one of those people whom Paul describes in Romans 9:4, saying that the Israelites are those "to whom belongs the adoption as sons, and the glory and the covenants and the giving of the Law and the temple service and the promises."

So, what are you telling the world about your identity? Are you making it known to those around you that you are a Christian? We are coming to realize today that this word, "Christian," is often abused and misunderstood, so we can no longer use "shorthand" as Jonah did. As we identify ourselves as Christians, we need to make clear that we are personally committed to following Jesus Christ as our Lord and trusting Him as our Savior; that we are adopted into the family of God; that God has revealed Himself to us in the person of Jesus Christ, and in the Gospel and the Word of God. We are living under the gracious promises of God that are ours through faith in Christ. As we make this known to those around us, we identify ourselves as citizens of His Kingdom, members of His family, and participants in His covenant. And this has an effect on those who hear us as we say these words. But it is not sufficient for us to merely identify ourselves in this way. If we would lead others to grasp the fear of the Lord, then we must go further.

II. The world will come to fear the Lord as God's people testify about Him.

A number of years ago, I was talking to some boys in a village in Kenya who were eager to try out their newly acquired English skills on a native speaker. After some basic greetings like, "Hello," and "How are you doing?" they asked me, "Do you like football?" I said, "Of course! All Americans like football." They looked puzzled and said, "We heard that Americans don't like football very much." I said, "Oh no! Football is probably America's favorite sport. I used to play football in the yard every day when I was a kid!" They said, "What position do you like to play?" And I said, "Well, I could always throw the ball very well, so usually my friends wanted me to be the quarterback." They looked confused. They said, "The only position in football that can throw a ball is the goal-keeper. What is a quarterback?" Suddenly, it occurred to me that we were talking about two different things. When I said "football," I meant "football." When they said "football," they meant "soccer." We had some good laughs about the confusion of that conversation. But it isn't hard to imagine that confusion over terminology could sometimes be more serious, and no laughing matter. And I fear that is what is happening often when we speak publicly about "God." We understand "God" to refer to one specific being, and the person we are speaking with may have an altogether different idea about who God is.

The sailors asked Jonah, "What is your occupation?" On the one hand we might say that he never got around to answering that question. On the other hand, it is possible that this is exactly the question he answered. No matter what it is that we do for a living, it is the occupation of the believer to worship and serve the living God. That is what we are to be "occupied" with, whether at work or at play, at home, at the office, or at church, in private and in public. So, when Jonah answered the question about his occupation, he said, "I fear the Lord God of heaven who made the sea and the dry land." Far from being a generic statement of belief in "the Man upstairs" or "the good Lord," this statement describes in great detail the God to whom Jonah had committed his life.

For starters, Jonah says, "I fear the LORD." We've already pointed out how our English Bibles use all capital letters when translating the Hebrew covenant name for God, YHWH (*Yahweh*). To call God by this name is to single Him out over every other deity in the world. This is the God who was worshiped by the Jewish people, but whose desire was to be worshiped by every nation on earth. He is the God of heaven, indicating that He alone is God, and that all other gods are false. He is not a deity who could be confined to a statue or a temple or an object. He dwells in Heaven, transcendent of this world and all that it contains. But He is not removed entirely from the world. He is transcendent, far off, but He is also imminent, close by. He created the sea and dry land, and He is at work in the world, as evidenced by the storm and by the ability of human beings to interact with Him in prayer and worship. Jonah's brief statement is an accurate testimony to who God is. It deals with specifics such as His name and His nature. And the sailors are moved by this testimony to fear the Lord that Jonah proclaims.

Some of you have lived long enough to see our society evolve not once but twice in regard to public discourse about God. Once upon a time in America, a person could talk about God openly, and most people would immediately associate the word "God" with the God of the Judeo-Christian tradition, the God of the Bible. But then, it became taboo to talk about God in public. The oft-repeated mantra of the latter 20th Century was that one should not discuss religion or politics in social settings. Now, however, the tide has turned again, and it is acceptable to talk about God in public, but there is a new twist. The word "God" no longer refers specifically to the God of the Bible. Now, when God is mentioned, the word could refer to countless deities that are worshiped in America. It is rather common to hear a celebrity mentioning God as they accept an award or an athlete giving thanks to God after a big game, but which God do they mean? No one knows for sure! So when we, the people of God who know Him through faith in Jesus Christ, speak about God, the world needs to hear specifics. Just as Jonah specifically defined God in his words to the sailors, we too must make it clear just who this God is whom we worship and serve. He is the one true and living God, the God of heaven, the creator of the earth and all that is in it, the righteous judge of the living and the dead who became a man in the person of Jesus Christ to bear our sins at the cross, the God who becomes a Father to those who call on Him to save them by faith in Christ.

Everyone has an idea about who God is. Those of us who know Him need to be specific as we testify about Him, so that whether the individual chooses to accept or reject Him, they know with whom they are dealing. And it may be that as we make Him known, those to whom we testify may find themselves coming to fear, and then to worship, the God we proclaim through the Gospel of Jesus Christ.

The sailors asked Jonah six questions in verses 8-10. Three of them dealt with his identity. He answered by saying, "I am a Hebrew." One dealt with his occupation. He answered in a profound way by referring to the God whom He worshiped. But the other two questions dealt with the immediate circumstances in which they found themselves. And Jonah's words on this matter were just as important.

III. The world will come to fear the Lord as God's people demonstrate the Gospel.

What is the world's primary criticism of the Christian church? It seems from conversations I have with people that their major critique is that the church is filled with hypocrites. This is staggering to me. A hypocrite is someone who claims to be one thing but proves to be another. And what the critics of the church mean is that the "church people" they know claim to be good people who have it all together, but don't actually live that way. And so the world is surprised that Christians sin, and that Christians struggle, and that Christians often don't seem to have it all together. If that is what the world has encountered, then they most certainly have met hypocrites, but I have to wonder if they have really met any Christians!

A Christian is not someone who claims to have it all together, to be a morally good person, or to be better than others. Of all people in the world, Christians are the most honest, because the true Christian, the one who has truly grasped the good news of the Gospel, should be the first to admit that our lives are train-wrecks that are being rescued by the grace of God and that we are desperate from one day to the next to experience the transforming power of Christ. We do not glory in our sin, and we do not make grace into a license for sin, but we glory in the cross because by it we are being rescued from our sin through an ongoing process that will not be completed until we see Jesus face-to-face.

The first question that the sailors asked Jonah in verse 8 was, "On whose account has this calamity struck us?" Though we do not read the exact words of his answer, we do see in verse 10 that Jonah "had told" the sailors that "he was fleeing from the presence of the Lord." This is important to notice. Jonah did not say, "Don't look at me! I'm a good person, I haven't done anything wrong." He confessed his own sin to these sailors and took responsibility for the consequences that his sin produced. In his confession, he acknowledged that God is gracious enough to use imperfect people to accomplish His purposes, and holy enough to discipline them when they sin. And notice that his confession was a contributing factor to the sailors "fearing a great fear."

Being Christ's witness before a lost world does not mean pretending that we have attained perfection or that we have it all together. It means being honest with the world about who we are, who God is, and how He mercifully reaches out to sinful people with the offer of redemption. It doesn't mean never falling. It means falling toward the cross when we fall. It means admitting that we still fall, but that we know how to be lifted up again by the power of Christ through repentance and confession. It means taking responsibility for our actions and their consequences because we know that God is holy, and that He takes our sin as seriously as anyone else's, and like a good Father, He disciplines us when we sin. Rather than pretending we have no sin, a testimony like this demonstrates the power of the gospel because it illustrates the truth that we never outgrow our need for grace, our dependence upon the Holy Spirit's power, and our desperation for the gospel in our daily lives. It proclaims that we have rightly comprehended the fear of the Lord, and it drives us in our daily living, our worship, our service, and our restoration when we fail Him. And when the world sees *this* in God's people, they will be more inclined to fear the Lord and worship Him as well. If God deals in this way with the sins of those who know Him, how much more so will He deal with those who do not know Him? Our lives become a living, breathing gospel message to the unbelieving world.

There is a final question asked of Jonah by the sailors in these verses. Once they have understood his identity as a Hebrew, God's name and God's nature, and the gospel of His holy and gracious work with sinful people, their fear of the Lord prompts them to ask Jonah, "How could you do this?" And Jonah never answers. There is no answer, no excuse or justification, for what he has done. He has taken full responsibility for his sin and its consequences, and has offered no "buts" in his confession. Often we are quick to offer excuses to justify what we have done and to minimize the sinfulness of our sin. Of course, we know that God sees through this, but the world sees through it as well. When a Christian sins, the world wants to know why. If you know this God, if you are one of His people, if you understand His holiness and grace, "how could you do this?" More persuasive than our attempts to justify ourselves is the honest admission that there is no good reason for what we have done. We have sinned against our God because at that moment in time, we lost sight of the gospel and indulged in our own sinful desires rather than pursuing His will. There are no excuses, and there can be no minimizing of it. We must simply own it, confess it, and carry it to the cross in repentance to find Christ's merciful forgiveness.

Phillip Cary has written that "the only reason why the word of Jonah the prophet is convincing is because he is such a screwup. There may be a lesson here for the people of God, who usually prefer to think that their witness to Him is convincing because they are such good people. ... there are important ways that our failures make our confession of faith credible."[155] In giving a transparent testimony of our need for the gospel, we make it clear that Christ has not come to call the righteous but the sinners to salvation. Those of us who have called on Him have found this

---

[155] Phillip Cary, *Jonah* (Brazos Theological Commentary on the Bible; Grand Rapids: Brazos, 2008), 64.

salvation, as can all others who hear our testimony and likewise turn to Him by faith and repentance.

Jesus left His church with a simple means of symbolizing our ongoing need for the gospel in our lives. The church is called often to take the bread and the cup of the Lord's Supper as a reminder that His broken body and shed blood is the sacrifice by which sinners are made righteous before God. If we say that we have no sin, then First John says that we deceive ourselves and make God out to be a liar and demonstrate that His true word is not in us. It is through this shed blood of Jesus Christ that we who are sinners are invited to receive salvation, the forgiveness of sins, and the promise of eternal life in Jesus Christ. The effect is immediate, but the fight is perpetual, until we are glorified in His presence. As we take the bread and the cup, as often as we do it, we do not testify that we are better than the rest of the world. Rather, we identify ourselves as a people who belong to the one true God through faith in Jesus Christ, a people who are desperate for grace, dependent on the truth of the Gospel, both saved and being saved from the penalty, the power, and the presence of sin in our lives. A theologically responsible church will regularly call its members to come to that table of the Lord and take up these symbolic elements as a continual reminder of our ongoing need for the Gospel of grace in our lives. In the partaking of the bread and the cup, we are reminded of who we are and who God is, and we are humbled before Him in fear, in worship, and in faith. Every time we do it, we are demonstrating visually to the unbelievers who happen to be present in those services the very same truths that we should demonstrate through our words and actions to the world each day of our lives.

VI

At the Crossroads of Repentance and Disobedience
Jonah 1:11-12

So they said to him, "What should we do to you that the sea may
become calm for us?"—for the sea was becoming increasingly stormy.
He said to them, "Pick me up and throw me into the sea.
Then the sea will become calm for you, for I know that
on account of me this great storm has come upon you."

In Victor Hugo's classic work *Les Miserables,* much of the story revolves
around the tension between the ex-convict Jean Valjean and Javert, the
stalwart police inspector. They met while Javert guarded the prison where
Valjean had served time. After Valjean's release, his life undergoes
significant positive change, in no small part due to the mercy that has been
shown to him by a village priest. In order to escape his haunting past,
Valjean assumes a new identity. Some time later, he crosses paths with
Javert again. Javert seems to bear some kind of grudge and is dead-set to
bring an end to Valjean's life of prosperity, freedom, and joy. Finally, at
long last, Valjean is in a position to vindicate himself by killing Inspector
Javert. He takes out his gun and fires it into the air, admonishing Javert to
flee. Later, when Javert has the opportunity to once again arrest Jean
Valjean, he is perplexed by a dilemma. Shall he do his duty, or shall he
show mercy to the one who has shown mercy to him? Unable to decide,
Javert takes his own life by throwing himself into the river. Javert becomes
for the reader a prototype of the one who has a heart so hard that mercy
itself cannot even shatter it. In a very real sense, Javert is like the prophet
Jonah.

At this point in the narrative, the sailors have determined by casting lots
that the storm which threatens to be the death of them all has arisen
because of Jonah. His confession under their interrogation has confirmed
that it is because he has disobeyed the Lord. All the while, the storm rages

on more and more intensely. Verse 11 says that it was "becoming increasingly stormy." In the Hebrew text, the wording is literally that the sea was walking and raging, evoking imagery of a violent beast on a rampage. And so, here in verse 11, they ask him, "What should we do to you that the sea may become calm for us?"

Throughout this study of Jonah, we have pointed out several times that we are often like this prophet—more like him that we want to admit. We run away from the Lord and from the difficult things He calls us to do, and because He is our loving Father, He disciplines us to bring us to repentance. Jonah finds himself here at the crossroads that we all encounter from time to time. Shall we continue in the path of disobedience, which will surely lead to more consequences and more danger, or shall we return to the Lord in humble repentance and obedience? The more we persist in disobedience, the harder our hearts become and the more difficult it becomes for us to turn around.

Ultimately, a stubborn refusal to return only indicates that we do not truly belong to God, for those who are His are proven by perseverance in righteousness and by His divine preservation of us. Not only will we eventually turn around if we are truly God's people, God will make it so for the sake of His own name and His own glory. That is why each crossroad is crucial. Every opportunity of repentance we ignore brings us one step closer to the dead-end of destruction. By looking at Jonah as he stands at this crossroad of the paths that lead to repentance or continued disobedience, we can learn from him, even from his mistakes, so that when we stand at the crossroad for ourselves, we may make the right turn that leads to life abundant, obedient, and eternal. The crossroad becomes a proving ground where our true spiritual condition is revealed.

I. The crossroad reveals the callousness of our hearts.

The question is simple enough: "What should we do to you that the sea may become calm for us?" The sailors have no interest at this point in continuing the journey. The cargo that they set out to deliver to Tarshish has been thrown overboard, the storm threatens to destroy the ship and bring death to them all. The answer is obviously not, "Press on ahead, men! Against all odds, let it be full speed ahead to Tarshish!" That option is not on the table anymore. Now, if Jonah's heart is right with God, there is only one appropriate answer here. The fitting thing for Jonah to say here is, "Guys, I have sinned by running away from God and His calling on my life, so let's turn this ship around and head back to shore, and drop me off at the nearest port to Nineveh that you can find so that I can fulfill what God has called me to do. Hand me an oar, or give me some job to do on the deck to make this happen as quickly as possible." A response like that would indicate that Jonah is not only aware of his sin (which he obviously is), but also that he has come to the end of himself and is now willing to obey what the Lord has called him to do. James Montgomery Boice has written, "I think that if Jonah had followed this course, not only would the storm have stopped, but they would have had the best wind back to Joppa imaginable."[156] But Jonah did not say this.

Rather than repenting and recommitting himself to a path of obedience, Jonah says, "Pick me up and throw me into the sea." Now, the thrust of what he says is lost on most of us because we know the rest of the story. We know that there is a great fish down there that is going to swallow him up, but Jonah doesn't know that yet. What he knows is that this sea is raging, and though it may become calm for the sailors, Jonah does not indicate any hope that it will suddenly become calm for him once he breaks the surface of the water. So, what is he getting at when he says, "Throw me overboard!"? Basically, it is a death wish. He is essentially saying, "I refuse to repent and obey, and it doesn't look like God is going to let me ride off into the sunset peacefully, so I might as well die right here in the middle of the sea." Here is a man who is so hard-hearted and so committed to pursuing the course of sinful disobedience that when it reaches its dead end, he would rather die than turn around.

Is there anything in our lives that we are clinging to, knowing that God is calling us to repent of it, which might lead us to this hard-hearted state of despair? Is there some sin that you would rather die than forsake? God, in His relentless pursuit of us and in His determination to make those who believe on Jesus become more like Jesus, will constantly be working to

---

[156] Boice, 277.

purify us of the things in our lives that are not pleasing to Him. This is the divine work of sanctification by which the Holy Spirit is transforming us into the image of Christ. He loves us enough to accept us as we are, with our sins; but He loves us too much to let us stay as we are, clinging to our sins. He will show us what He wants to change in us by conviction, by providence, and by the revelation of His Word. When we come to that crossroads, we reveal the true condition of our hearts. The great Puritan John Owen is known perhaps most for a single quotation:

Do you mortify;
do you make it your daily work;
be always at it while you live;
cease not a day from this work;
be killing sin or it will be killing you.[157]

Are we willing to kill the sin in our lives, or will we allow our sin to go on killing us? Any cherished sin that we cling to in our lives becomes to us like a friend or a lover. It is there for us when we think we need it; we can always turn to it for comfort and relief. But each time we do, our heart becomes harder toward God. Unremedied, this could end up proving that we have never truly turned to Christ at all, thus leading us in the path of eternal destruction. When we stand at the crossroads, with God offering us the opportunity to repent, we must be willing to let that dear friend die. Moreover, we must actively kill that old friend. This is why breaking an addiction or a bad habit or letting go of any sinful activity in our lives is so difficult, but also why it is so necessary. Persisting in that sin will harden us to the point where we, like Jonah, will choose death before repentance, and this is a terrifying decision for anyone who claims to be a follower of Jesus to make. For Jonah this means turning back from his pursuit of disobedience. He seems unwilling to do this, so he chooses death instead. For us, it will mean forsaking an addiction, a habit, a pattern of behavior or attitude or thinking. It will mean abandoning our own chosen path of life and returning to the path we know God has called us to.

---

[157] Kelly Kapic and Justin Taylor eds., *Overcoming Sin and Temptation: Three Classic Works by John Owen* (Wheaton, Ill.: Crossway, 2006), 50.

There are many people in the world whom God has called to serve Him in particular ways (as pastors, as missionaries, as preachers and teachers of His word, or servants in the church) who have chosen other things instead. God will bring you to the crossroads just as He did for Jonah. As Romans 2:4 says, "Or do you think lightly of the riches of His kindness and tolerance and patience, not knowing that the kindness of God leads you to repentance?" In God's merciful kindness, He has brought Jonah to the crossroads. Jonah has chosen his sin over repentance, and he has chosen death over the abundant and eternal life that God has offered him. In His kindness God will bring each of us to this crossroad as well, and what will we choose? Will we choose repentance, or will we think lightly of His kindness and tolerance and patience, harden our hearts even more, and pursue the path of death and destruction? The crossroad gives us an opportunity to discover and reveal the true condition of our hearts toward Him.

II. The crossroad reveals the cowardice in our lives.

The easiest decision to ever make in life is to maintain the status quo, to keep things as-is with no changes. Real change requires courage. None of us like change. Every material and immaterial thing in this world demonstrates a real and firm resistance to change. But change is necessary and is always happening all around us. God desires to change us: do we have the courage to allow Him to change us, or will we cowardly maintain the status quo? This is the conundrum Jonah finds himself in. He knows that repentance and obedience to the Lord will require courage, and it is a courage that he doesn't seem to possess. But notice that even in choosing death, he seems to lack courage as well. He is not embracing his fate as a committed martyr for a cause. If he were, he would have simply jumped overboard to his death. But like a coward, he puts the onus on the sailors, saying, "Pick me up and throw me into the sea, then the sea will become calm for you."

Some commentators have sought to paint Jonah with a more complimentary brush than I am using. They suggest that Jonah is saying a good thing here. They think that it is out of compassion for the sailors whose lives are at risk that he is voluntarily choosing a sacrificial death for their well-being. If that were the case, don't you think he would have jumped? By saying "Pick me up and throw me over," Jonah is saying, "Look, I know that I am probably not going to make it out of this alive, but frankly I don't really care if you live or die. So, if you want to live, then you better throw me in." No concern for their well-being or how his sin is endangering them, he puts them in a difficult predicament. They can take their chances, which appear to be very slim at the moment, or they can take action and put this man into what appears to be a certain death. By taking the cowardly way out, Jonah has forced all the doors of cowardly escape for the sailors to shut. Now, either decision they make will require courageous resolve. Because he refuses to take courageous responsibility, he forces them to do so.

We are likely too self-centered to recognize how our sin endangers others. We tend to only focus on ourselves, and take our chances maintaining the status quo because it is easy. When others confront us with our sin and how it is affecting them, we tend to think, "Well, big deal. If you want something to change here, you do what you need to do, but I'm not changing." That is cowardly and irresponsible. If there was any real compassion or courage in Jonah, he would take responsibility and act. If I am a sailor on that ship, I am saying to Jonah, "Turn yourself around or jump, Jonah! Don't just stand there while we suffer!" And this is what others are looking to us and thinking as our sin affects them with the overflow of consequences. "Come on man, either get right with God or just get this thing over with, but do something! Don't put us in this position of having to choose from two bad options!"

I don't think we fully comprehend the sinfulness of being a coward. We get that murder is a big deal. Idolatry, adultery and things like that, they are a really big deal. But being a coward is okay, isn't it? No, in fact, it is not okay. Cowardice is not a mark of the Christian, but rather is a sin of equal severity with murder, adultery, idolatry, and other acts of wickedness. God's word makes this clear in Revelation 21:7-8. After describing the glories of heaven, with the greatest glory being eternal life in the presence of God Himself, the Word of God states, "He who overcomes will inherit these things, and I will be his God and he will be My son." Get that – eternal life is for the *overcomer*. It takes courage to be an overcomer. The next verse, Revelation 21:8, says, "But for the *cowardly* and unbelieving and abominable and murderers and immoral persons and sorcerers and idolaters and all liars, their part will be in the lake that burns with fire and brimstone, which is the second death." So the Word of God says here that hell is a place for liars, idolaters, sorcerers, sexually immoral people, murderers, those who do abominable, detestable things, and yes, even for *cowards*. These are the marks of an unbeliever. Believers are courageous overcomers. Is Jonah a believer? "Surely he is!" we might say. After all, he is a prophet of God. Aren't all prophets believers? We might ask today, "Aren't all pastors, all preachers, all religious leaders in the Christian faith believers?" I shutter as I say that there are some who are perhaps not. How can we tell? What are the attributes that mark their lives? Do we find them to be courageous overcomers, or are they cowards? This is but one test that validates the genuineness of our faith in Christ.

For a number of years, we lived outside of Baltimore surrounded by Orioles fans. I'm going to tell you, being a Baltimore Orioles fan is hard work! You watch them, and you pull for them, but deep down, you just know they are going to blow it! It is gut-wrenching sometimes. For me, reading the book of Jonah is like that. I'm pulling for the guy; I really am. But I've read this book so many times, I know what's going to happen. I keep going back and rereading it and hoping it's going to turn out differently. I am cheering Jonah on from the sidelines, saying, "Come on Jonah! You can do this! If you are a true believer, then where is your courage? Let's see you overcome this disobedient bent in your life! Let's see if you have what it takes to come to the end of yourself and turn your life back over to the Lord and live in obedience to Him. You can do it!" But Jonah's response to all my cheering is always the same. And so I find myself kind of talking with him (I might need professional help!):

What's that you say, Jonah? You aren't going to change? You would rather just die? But you don't even have the courage to die, but instead you insist that someone else pull the trigger? Jonah, you are a coward. Are you a believer? Time will tell, for if you are, the Lord will not let you go out like this. You will either turn, or else the Lord will turn you for the sake of His own name and glory. But if you don't turn, and the Lord doesn't turn you, and you drown in the watery depths, then it would seem to indicate that you are not a true believer, for true believers are courageous overcomers, not cowards.

I know how that conversation goes, because I have had it with myself a few times in life. I've even been on the receiving end of a conversation like that with godly believers whom I love and respect.

Often when we want to discover the genuineness of someone's faith, we will ask a question like this: "If you die tonight, do you know for sure you will go to heaven?" That question is a good one, but the fact is that most of us feel pretty confident that we will not die tonight. Here's a better question: "If you survive the night and wake up tomorrow, do you have what it takes to be an overcomer? Do you have the courage to turn from that sin you are clinging to and follow Jesus?" That question more than any other will demonstrate the depth of our commitment to the Lord.

I am a firm believer that the words Jesus spoke are true. He said that everything that was written in the Scriptures points to Him (Luke 24:44-47). We read a passage like this, about a calloused and cowardly prophet who is teetering on the edge of eternal destruction, and ask, "How in the world does this point to Jesus?" Remember that Jesus identified Himself as One who is "greater than Jonah." You see, Jonah chooses death over repentance from his own sin, but is not willing to lay his own life down for his own sins in order to save others. Jesus is so much greater! He has no sin of His own; He lives a life of perfect obedience and righteousness. But, He lays His life down for the sins of the world—for my sins, and your sins, and Jonah's sins, and the sailors' sins—in order to save us all. In the cross that Jesus willingly embraced for us, He is plunged beneath the storm of God's judgment, carrying our sins with Him, so that the storm will become calm for us. As Jonah will emerge from the depths of the sea by way of the great fish that God sends to deliver Him, so Jesus will emerge from the depths of death by way of His resurrection, with victory over sin, and death, and hell. And so He is able to save all those rebels like Jonah, like you, and like me, who will recognize ourselves as sinners in need of a Savior, and turn to Him trusting Him to be that Savior and calling upon Him as the Lord over our lives. Have you received Him by faith as Savior and Lord? If not, then you should be warned that the storm of judgment for sin is brewing and it will take you under eternally. But if you trust in the One who has taken your sins under on your behalf, this gracious Lord Jesus, then you will be saved, forgiven, cleansed, made righteous, and granted life eternal and abundant.

If you have come to Christ for this salvation, then your life should be marked by an obedient walk with Him and the courage it takes to be an overcomer. If you know Him then He lives in you in the person of His Holy Spirit, and He is empowering you to live for Him. But if your life is characterized by callousness and cowardice, then perhaps you need to reexamine yourself and the genuineness of your commitment to Him. It may be that God has brought you to a crossroad and is offering you the opportunity, by His kindness, for repentance. Will you cling to sin, even if it means the death of you, or will you repent? Will you cowardly pursue the sinful status quo, or courageously overcome? Will you pursue your own course of life or follow His calling? Your response to Him will indicate the reality of your relationship with Him, gloriously for the better, or tragically for the worse.

VII

The Gospel According to Jonah
Jonah 1:13-16

*However, the men rowed desperately to return to land but they could not,
for the sea was becoming even stormier against them. Then they called
on the LORD and said, "We earnestly pray, O LORD, do not let us perish
on account of this man's life and do not put innocent blood on us; for You,
O LORD, have done as You have pleased." So they picked up Jonah, threw
him into the sea, and the sea stopped its raging. Then the men feared
the LORD greatly, and they offered a sacrifice to the LORD and made vows.*

I once had a professor who liked to surprise us with pop-quizzes. We
would walk into the room and find the map of Paul's Missionary Journeys
pulled down over the chalkboard and we knew that the map concealed
several questions that the professor was going to spring on us. These
quizzes almost always included at least one trick question that was
designed to point out our sloppy habits in studying the Bible. For instance,
I recall one quiz in which he asked, "How many wise men came to the
manger to worship Jesus?" Of course most of us were quick to answer
"Three." But he pointed out to us that the Bible calls them magi, not wise
men, and that we are never told how many there were, and that they did not
come to the manger, but to the "house," perhaps two to three years after
Jesus was born. On another occasion, the professor asked us, "How many
gospels are there in the Bible?" And most of us were quick to answer,
"Four." Of course, as usual, we were all wrong. The professor was quick to
admonish us that there is only ONE gospel in the Bible, and it is the
Gospel of Jesus Christ: the message of good news that Jesus Christ is God
Incarnate, who died for our sins, and is risen again for our salvation. I will
never forget how he drove the point into our minds, threatening us that we
must never refer to "the Gospel *of* Matthew," or "the Gospel *of* John," but
rather "the Gospel *According to* Matthew, *According to* Mark, *According*

to Luke, *According to* John," because the only Gospel is the Gospel *of* Jesus Christ.

This Gospel of Jesus Christ is found not only in those four books which we call *Gospels*; it is in actually found in every book of the Bible. So, on the one hand, I would say with my old professor, there is only one gospel. But in another sense, Charles Blanchard, who was the president of Wheaton College around the turn of the twentieth century, was also correct in his response when he was once asked how many gospels were in the Bible. He said, "Bless your soul, my dear brother, there are sixty-six. There is no portion of God's Word, New or Old Testament, which does not contain in one form or another, the good news."[158] Blanchard entitled his book on Jonah, *An Old Testament Gospel,* and such it is.

The Gospel is found throughout the Bible in many forms and fashions. It is narrated for us through the events of the life of Jesus in the four books we call Gospels; it is articulated with great clarity in the epistles; it is promised in advance in many of the prophetic books; it is foreshadowed with imagery and symbolism in other Old Testament books. And then there are cases such as we find in these verses in which the events and elements of a text provide a visual parallel to the truths of the Gospel.

In his sermon on this passage, the great preacher Charles Haddon Spurgeon begins by praising the sailors for their efforts to spare the life of Jonah by trying to row back to shore. He draws an analogy between this and the efforts of Christians to save the lost in the world, saying, "God give us Divine Grace, like these mariners, to row hard that if possible we may bring the ship to land laboring that none around us may be left to perish."[159] But then Spurgeon shifts gears, saying, "I shall not, however, dwell upon that aspect of the text. Our Savior selected Jonah as one of His peculiar types." In referring to Jonah as a "type," Spurgeon means that Jesus pointed to Jonah as an Old Testament character who, by either comparison or contrast, foreshadowed His life and mission of salvation.

[158] Charles A. Blanchard, *An Old Testament Gospel* (Chicago: Bible Institute Colportage Association, 1918), 17.
[159] Charles Haddon Spurgeon, "Labor in Vain." Sermon no. 567, May 1, 1864. http://www.spurgeongems.org/vols10-12/chs567.pdf Accessed June 28, 2011.

Jesus said on at least two separate occasions to those who sought signs from Him, "An evil and adulterous generation seeks after a sign; and a sign will not be given it, except the sign of Jonah."[160] Spurgeon says, "We believe, therefore, that we are not erring if we translate the details of the history of Jonah into spiritual illustrations of man's experience and action with regard to Christ and His Gospel."[161] Spurgeon is not advocating that we interpret this or any other passage of Scripture by using allegory or heavily layered symbolism. Rather, he is appealing to the Lord Jesus Himself, who said that this story points to Him. And Spurgeon sees in this text, as do I, a great parallel between the experience of the people on board this storm-tossed ship and the eternal truths of the Gospel of Jesus Christ. And so, if we can see the parallels, we will see here in this text a Gospel According to Jonah. The elements of it are as true and clear as any which we read in the Gospels or Epistles of the New Testament.

I. The Gospel informs us that self-effort is insufficient to save us.

In *Mere Christianity*, C. S. Lewis writes that "human beings, all over the earth, have this curious idea that they ought to behave in a certain way, and cannot really get rid of it."[162] It's true, isn't it? All people everywhere, no matter what they say they believe, truly live like they are aware that there is a standard of right and wrong. Those standards vary sometimes, but by and large, they overlap with one another. People throughout the world and throughout history have understood in their very nature that there are certain things they should do and certain things they should not do. But Lewis goes on to say that in spite of this universal awareness that people ought to behave in a certain way, "they do not in fact behave in that way."[163] Now of course, what Lewis is driving at here is that doctrine that we refer to as "depravity." Depravity refers to the universal human condition of sinfulness. God has revealed enough of Himself in creation and human nature to make every human being aware that God exists and that He has a standard of right and wrong. Paul says this in Romans 1, and says that by and large people have not yielded themselves to this truth but

---

[160] Matthew 16:4. See also Matthew 12:39-41; Luke 11:29-30.
[161] Spurgeon.
[162] C. S. Lewis, *Mere Christianity* (New York: Harper Collins, 2001), 8.
[163] Ibid.

have suppressed it in unrighteousness (Romans 1:18). In other words, we have sinned in order to hide from our sin.

Whenever the realization comes to the human heart and mind that we have committed some sin that is deserving of judgment from a holy God, we immediately sense the need to *do something* to make it right. So, in nearly ever religion of the world, people are taught that if you want to be forgiven, to have God's approval, to make it to paradise, or whatever other happy state that one desires to be in, you must do this and that, and not do these other things. Nearly every religion teaches this; *nearly*, but not all. There is one glaring exception to the religions of the world in this regard, and that is Christianity. Only true Christianity proclaims to the world that you *cannot DO anything* to earn forgiveness, to earn favor with God, or to earn heaven.

Let's turn our attention to the sailors on board the ship with Jonah. Sin has caused them to be in a torrential storm which threatens to capsize and dismantle the ship, and to bring them all to a watery grave. Granted, in this story, the issue at the root of this storm is Jonah's sin: his rebellious attempt to run away from the call and presence of the Lord. But, are these sailors not sinners also? Indeed they are, and they know it. That is why, once Jonah reveals that the God who created the heavens and the earth is bringing judgment upon him for his sin, they fear this God all the more. If He would act in this way toward one of His own people, and a prophet no less, how much more will He deal with these pagans who have never given Him a single thought in their lives? So aware are they of their own culpability before the holy and sovereign God of the universe that when Jonah commands them to throw him overboard, they refuse to out of fear of compounding their own sin! But like all sinners, they know that they must do something! So they begin rowing desperately. The Hebrew text indicates that they were "digging" into the water with their oars, trying to make it back to dry land. They want to be saved, and in their minds the only way for this to happen is to work hard for it. But the sailors found that in spite of all their rowing, the sea became increasingly stormy. God would not allow them to be deluded into thinking that they were making any real progress toward safety and refuge. The harder they rowed, the more the storm raged. Ultimately, three words summarize the effort: "they could not."

These same three words can be written over every attempt to earn forgiveness, to earn God's favor, to earn salvation and eternal life by self-effort: "they could not." Attempts to improve oneself morally are never ill-advised, but they are insufficient to save a sinner from his sins. They can prevent him or her from future sin, but they cannot atone for past sins. Religious activity is all well and good, unless one thinks that by attending church enough times, saying enough prayers, and doing enough good deeds one has bribed God into overlooking one's sins. Many have tried. Many bad people have tried their hand at being "good enough." But the storm is not stilled. The sea rages on and continues to threaten them with eternal destruction. Try as they may to work hard to earn God's favor, the words of this text become a haunting epitaph for them: *they could not.*

Paul could not make it any clearer than what he has said in Ephesians 2:8-9—

- *For by grace you have been saved* - That means you cannot do anything to earn salvation; it is given to you freely by God, by His grace, which by definition means that you do not deserve it

- *through faith; and that not of yourselves, it is the gift of God* – That means that you receive this gift of God's grace by faith (by believing, by trusting) in Him, through the Lord Jesus Christ and His saving work in His life and death and resurrection. But the faith is not something you *do*. Paul indicates here that you cannot manufacture this kind of faith in yourself. God gives it to you.

- *not as a result of works, so that no one may boast* – And so here it is, plainly stated: you cannot be saved as a result of your own works or self-effort. If you could then you would have something to boast about. "Look how good I am! What a good job I did rowing this ship safely into harbor!" But you cannot. Works cannot save.

So, the gospel teaches us what the storm teaches the sailors, namely, that self-effort is insufficient to save. And if this were all that the gospel proclaimed to us, then it would be no gospel at all. The word "gospel" means "good news," and this appears to be very bad news. We are all sinners deserving of judgment, but we can do nothing to save ourselves. That sounds bad. But the good news is that salvation is possible, just not this way. God's way of salvation is a better way, thankfully. It cannot be earned or deserved by self-effort, but it can be received freely as a gift of His grace because of what He has done for us, and that is seen in parallel with the second movement of this passage.

II. The Gospel informs us that salvation comes by a sacrificial substitute.

There are several commendable qualities about the sailors on board the ship with Jonah. They do not want to see Jonah die. They do not want him thrown overboard into the stormy sea, and they are reluctant to believe that his death will lead to their life. They seem to have more of an understanding of the value of human life than Jonah ever displays in this entire book. And so, they resort to trying to save themselves, and to save Jonah even, by their own efforts, but they cannot. But the words that Jonah has spoken to them are absolutely true. If they are to live through the storm, Jonah has to die. This storm is all about God dealing with Jonah for his sin. And though he is willing to acknowledge his sin, he is not willing to turn from his sin. You have to understand that God has no interest in allowing these sailors to make it safely back to shore where they might deposit a still hard-hearted Jonah on the banks. If his heart has not changed, then he will only run away again or find some other way to express his disobedience. No, for Jonah, apart from a full repentance, there is only one way out, and that is death.

The Bible makes this principle clear from the very moment that sin enters into human experience: the wages of sin is death.[164] And Jonah's sin is deserving of death under the righteous judgment of God. If Jonah doesn't die for his own sin here, then all of these men will die, and each one will bring his own sins before the judgment seat of God. God's righteous

---

[164] Genesis 2:17; Romans 5:12; 6:23

judgment will be satisfied, one way or another. The only hope for these sailors is for them to allow Jonah to die so that they might be saved. As soon as the sailors accepted that fact and threw Jonah overboard, notice what happened: "the sea stopped its raging." They were saved because God's righteous judgment was satisfied and sin met its deadly end.

You do not have to be a seminary-trained theologian to see the parallel between this story and a greater story. Spurgeon says, "Here is Jonah. Leave out the fact that he was sinful and he becomes an eminent type of Christ."[165] Jonah says in verse 12, "Pick me up and throw me into the sea. Then the sea will become calm for you, for I know that on account of me this great storm has come upon you." Jonah is getting what he deserves for his sin. But Jesus is the One who is greater than Jonah. The message of Jesus for the world is, "I have been picked up and thrown beneath the flood of My Father's wrath so that this sea of judgment may become calm for you. It is on account of *you* that this great storm has come upon *Me*." The wages of sin *is* death. But Jesus had no sin of His own to warrant a death such as He died. Rather, He died the death He died as a substitute, a sacrifice offered in our place, bearing not His own sins, but my sins and yours, so that we may be saved. Jonah boarded the ship bound for Tarshish because of his disobedience to the will of God. Jesus boarded the ship of human experience because of His obedience to the will of His Father.

God's righteous judgment against sin must be satisfied, but if every man bears his own sin then all will perish eternally. God, out of His great love and mercy, established a principle from the beginning of accepting a sacrificial substitute for sin. And it was ultimately fulfilled in the sacrifice of His Son. The sailors look upon Jonah as he says, "The only hope you have is for me to die." They do not want to think of it! It is a horrible option to consider, but it is their only hope. In the same way, the Lord Jesus speaks to the world saying, "The only hope you have is for Me to die." We don't want to think of it! It is offensive for us to look at the cross and think that our sins deserve that. We want to think that we can be good enough, that we can row the boat hard enough in the right direction to save ourselves without such a bloody sacrifice. Every time we watch a film

---

[165] Spurgeon.

about the life of Jesus, or see a drama in which His story is portrayed, we come to that brutal scene depicting the cross, and we watch men take hammers and nails and begin to torture the Lord Jesus, brutally nailing Him to the cross, and we want to cry out, "Stop it! Don't do this! There must be some mistake! There must be some other way!" This seems horrible to us, and it is. But this horror of Jesus dying to save us is our only hope, and we mustn't stop it. We must embrace it, we must allow Him to bear the cross for us, for only if He does will we be saved.

God's attributes are perfect and infinite. In His perfect, infinite justice and righteousness, sin must be punished with its due penalty of death. But in God's perfect and infinite love, mercy, and grace, He is willing for the sinless substitute to die in our place bearing our sins that humanity may be saved. And as Jesus is plunged beneath the storm of judgment on our behalf, the sea of God's wrath becomes calm for those who call upon Him in faith and trust Him to save them. Salvation is only possible by the death of a sacrificial substitute, and Jesus is the only one who can do it. Will you be forgiven? Then Jesus must die for you. Will you be made righteous before a holy God? Then Jesus must die for you. Will you receive the promise of eternal life? Then Jesus must die for you. He is your only hope.

Now we turn our attention to another great parallel here in this Gospel according to Jonah.

III. The Gospel informs us that salvation has a transforming effect on those who experience it.

When we meet these sailors initially, they are not religious or spiritual men. They are men going about their business giving no thought to the things of God. But when the storm comes, their inherent knowledge of spiritual realities begins to show through. Verse 5 says that every man cried to his god. They are idol worshipers who know nothing about the one true God. But Jonah speaks to them of this God: His name is Yahweh; He made the sea and the dry land; He is holy and must punish sin; He is gracious and saves those who call upon His name. And the witness of Jonah is used by the power of the Holy Spirit to produce a reverential fear in their hearts for this one true God. They believed the message that Jonah spoke, and they received salvation at the hand of Jonah's God. As they do, notice their response: *they feared the Lord greatly, and they offered a sacrifice to the Lord, and made vows.* Literally, in the Hebrew text, their response is intensified with repetition: *they feared the Lord with a great fear; they sacrificed a sacrifice to the Lord; they vowed vows.*

These truths of God's word must be heard clearly and carefully: We are saved by faith and not works, but the faith that saves is a faith that demonstrates itself through works. The works do not bring salvation into our lives, but the salvation brings the works into our lives. We do not trust our works to save us, we trust Jesus to save us. And once Jesus saves us, we work to bring Him glory. We are not saved by what we do for God, but we are saved in order to do something for God. This is what Paul says in that great salvation text in Ephesians 2:8-10:

> For by grace you have been saved through faith; and that not of yourselves, it is the gift of God; not as a result of works, so that no one may boast. For we are His workmanship, created in Christ Jesus for good works, which God prepared beforehand so that we would walk in them.

And what are the works that salvation produces in our lives? They are the same as those we see the sailors performing here in verse 16: Fear, sacrifice, and vows. Translated into the Christian perspective, our fear of the Lord is a humble submission to Him *as Lord,* as the King and Master of our lives. We live in the awareness that our lives do not belong ultimately to ourselves but to Him. As 1 Corinthians 6:19-20 says, "You are not your own ... you have been bought with a price: therefore glorify God in your body." What is a sacrifice but an act of supreme worship? In the Old Testament, to sacrifice was to bring an animal before the Lord in recognition of your sin, God's holiness, and God's grace. We no longer bring sacrificial victims before the Lord, but we come in an act of supreme worship before the One who *is* the ultimate sacrificial victim. The sacrifice for our sins is Jesus, and we worship Him in recognition of our sin, and God's holiness, and God's grace, exalting Him and glorifying Him for our great salvation. We present ourselves to Him as a living sacrifice in our worship (Romans 12:1-2). And what is a vow but a commitment to a life of

114

service to the Lord? We make vows unto the Lord, acknowledging that God is worthy of more than lip service; He deserves our life service.

Our vow is this: "God, take my life and use it for your glory. I am Yours, You are the King. Call me as You wish to serve You, only empower me and fill me and go with me in it, and I will do it." These are not the vows that we might associate with what is commonly called a "foxhole conversion." Those are the foolish vows that are offered beneath a blanket of bombs and bullets by which fearful people say, "God, get me out of this and I will do anything for you." Notice that the sailors are not in the foxhole. The storm is no longer raging. They are not bartering with God for redemption. They have already been saved, and they are saying, "Oh God, You are great and glorious, and Your salvation is great and glorious, and You are worthy of nothing less than every moment of my existence. I am Your servant forever, Lord." This fear of the Lord, this worship of the Lord, this service of the Lord, is the grateful response of a soul that has been genuinely, graciously, and gloriously saved.

Is there a Gospel According to Jonah? Yes indeed. And it is the same gospel that is found in Isaiah, and Genesis, and Malachi, and Matthew, and John, and Acts, and Romans, and Revelation. It is the Gospel of Jesus Christ, and it informs us that we cannot work hard enough to save ourselves from our sins; that our only hope is in the death of Jesus Christ as a sacrificial substitute; and that true saving faith in Jesus has a transforming effect on all who call upon Him by faith. In Acts 4:12, the Apostle Peter announced the good news that "there is salvation." Praise God there is a salvation for sinners! And Peter made it very clear that this salvation is "found in no one else for there is no other name under heaven given among men by which we must be saved." There is no other name, and no other gospel, but the name and the gospel of Jesus Christ. All of Scripture, yes even Jonah, testifies to this good news. Believe this gospel. Experience this gospel. Proclaim this gospel.

VIII

Studying Theology in A School of Fish
Jonah 1:17

And the LORD appointed a great fish to swallow Jonah,
and Jonah was in the stomach of the fish three days and three nights.

Ask any toddler in any Sunday School class in any church in America what the book of the Jonah is all about, and you will likely hear that it is about a man who got swallowed by a whale. If you walk down the church hallway to the adult Sunday School department and ask the same question, you may be surprised to get the same answer. I remember when I first received a Bible – I was 18 years old and hadn't set foot in a church more than half a dozen times in my life. I looked at the table of contents and saw there, "JONAH." I said to myself, "I know that one! That's the story about the guy who got swallowed by a whale." I don't know how I knew that. Somehow the folklore of this story had crept into my memory bank, and I knew that. But when I started reading it, I remember thinking, "Where's the whale?" And then I came to this verse and found the whale, but it wasn't a whale; it was a fish. When I finished reading Jonah the first time, I remember thinking, "That's odd, it really is not about a guy getting swallowed by a whale (or even a fish) after all." In fact, the fish only shows up by name in three verses of the book of Jonah. The book is about so much more than this fish.

For a century and a half now, critics of the Bible have scoffed at this episode in Jonah's prophetic career and said, "I can't believe in a Bible that tells stories about people getting swallowed by a whale, a fish, whatever, and living to tell about it. That cannot happen, so the Bible isn't true." And in saying this, they're supposed to be saying something that sounds intelligent. But this is actually not an intelligent statement. The person who makes a claim like this has not studied to come to this conclusion. Rather, they have decided that they refuse to believe in miracles, and therefore everything in the Bible that is presented as a miracle is rejected without any consideration whatsoever. This is intellectual equivalent to someone deciding to believe that the moon is made of green cheese and dismissing any contrary notion without being willing to give a fair and honest consideration to the idea. While we Christians are often labeled as being narrow-minded, it seems that this shoe perhaps fits the foot of the scoffing unbeliever better.

One common Christian response to claims such as these has been to provide anecdotes and evidences that would "prove" to the unbeliever that such miraculous events were not so hard to believe. So, for instance when it comes to Jonah, there is this story that has been told and retold countless times, and it continues to be told in evangelical literature today. According to this story, there was a British sailor on a whaling ship off the coast of South America who was swallowed by a whale and later found alive inside its belly. "Aha!" we say, "So there, you see, it can happen!" But the only problem with that is that all attempts to validate any portion of the now infamous story have failed.[166] Therefore when Christians today resort to this kind of "sledgehammer apologetics," and particularly when we use information that is of questionable validity, it really doesn't help our case. In fact, it hurts our case in (at least) two ways. First, when we use spurious folklore, such as we receive in forwarded emails and other media, we give the impression to the world that we cannot do business with cold, hard facts. But, the truth is that we can, and we should. There are many evidences and arguments that are truthful, valid, and persuasive. Where these are used humbly by a Christian witness, the Holy Spirit often uses them to usher an unbeliever closer to the point of salvation. The second way that the "sledgehammer" approach hurts our cause is that, by telling stories such as these "modern-day Jonah" fish tales, we are actually

---

[166] Most notably, see Edward B. Davis, "A Whale of a Tale: Fundamentalist Fish Stories" in *Perspectives on Science and the Christian Faith,* 43, ed. J. W. Hass, Jr. [Ipswich, Mass.: American Scientific Affiliation, 1991], 224-237. http://www.asa3.org/ASA/PSCF/1991 /PSCF12-91Davis.html. In a fascinating response to this article, Jerry Bergman says, "Davis gave us our miracle back." http://www.asa3.org/ASA/PSCF/1992/PSCF6-92Bergman 2.html. Accessed October 24, 2011.

undervaluing the power and glory of God that the miracles themselves intend to proclaim.

If something recorded in the Bible was truly a miracle, then you should not expect to read about the same phenomenon recurring repeatedly in the daily news. Miracles occur at moments of specific revelation, and they are rare by definition. As Douglas Stuart writes, "A miracle is a divine act beyond human replication or explanation."[167] It is foolish for us to say to the world, "Oh sure Jonah could get swallowed by a whale and live to tell about it. See, it's happened dozens of times!" In saying that, we are actually short-selling God. The glory of God that is displayed in a miracle is intensified by the fact that this has *NOT* happened dozens of times, nor should we expect it to.

For some time now, the debate around this passage has focused on whether or not there exists a sea creature that could swallow a man, and in whose stomach a man could survive for such a time, and whether or not such a creature is to be found in the Mediterranean Sea. When I was in the middle of preparing this particular study, a church member brought me the June 2011 issue of *Smithsonian* which features a fascinating cover story on the whale shark (*Rhincodon typus*). I had the privilege of seeing these magnificent creatures at the Georgia Aquarium some years ago before both of their specimens died. They are quite extraordinary creatures. The largest fish in the sea, whale sharks can grow to 45 feet or more in length and weigh many tons. Pictures in that article show human beings swimming side-by-side with the enormous fish, and certainly it appears that a human could easily be swallowed by one. I will be the first to admit, I do not know that it is possible. But to engage in a debate about the precise breed of fish or any other issue of this sort is to greatly miss the point here in the book of Jonah. After all, since the fish is only mentioned three times here in the text, and no details are given concerning the nature of the fish, we must assume that the writer of this narrative did not consider these specifics important to his story. Desmond Alexander explains, "The author's portrayal of this most peculiar event is very low key; it has

---

[167] Stuart, 474.

certainly not been included in order to heighten the dramatic quality of the narrative. This being so, why should the author have invented it, if it did not really happen?"[168]

John Walton's observation on this point deserves repeating: "it is useless to discuss the gullet sizes and geographical habitats of dozens of species of whales, or the chemical content of mammalian digestive juices and their projected effect on human epidermis over prolonged periods. If we wanted to discuss this sort of thing, we would have to begin with first things first, and ask whether or not God could talk to man, as he did in Jonah 1:1."[169] If a critic is determined to reject the Bible on the basis of its supernatural content, he need not wait to get to this point in the Bible to do so, nor even to this point in the book of Jonah.

This whole discussion reminds me of a story I heard once about two men who were arguing about the truthfulness of the Bible. The critic said to the believer, "Do you mean that you believe that story of Jonah and the whale?" And the believer said, "I do." And the critic said, "How can you know this to be true when there are so many details that we do not know?" The believer said, "I believe it by faith, and one day in heaven I will ask Jonah about those details." The critic responded, "What if you get to heaven and find that Jonah is not there?" And the believer said, "Well, in that case, I guess you can find him and ask him."

If you just take verse 17 alone, ask yourself, "What is the subject of this sentence?" The subject is not the fish but the Lord. And that simple observation is enough to indicate to us that the point here is not about the fish that the Lord appointed but rather about the Lord who appointed the fish. If we come away from this with a better understanding of marine biology but with no better understanding of biblical theology, then we have failed and our error bears potentially eternal consequences. It is far better for the fish to teach us something about God, than for God to teach us something about the fish. That is, after all, why God appointed this fish: so

---

[168] Desmond Alexander, David Baker, and Bruce Waltke, *Obadiah, Jonah, Micah* (Tyndale Old Testament Commentaries 23a; Downers Grove, Ill.: Intervarsity Press, 1988), 111-112.
[169] Cited in Page, 215.

that He might teach Jonah a lesson about Himself. R. T. Kendall has said, "The belly of a fish is not a happy place to live, but it is a good place to learn."[170] We might use a play on words here to say that God has chosen to teach Jonah theology in a school of fish. Charles Blanchard entitles his sermon on this verse "Fish University." Though Jonah was likely a student in Elisha's great school of the prophets, in his futile attempts to run away from the Lord he found himself at "the place where God intended to complete his education."[171] And the theological lessons that God teaches Jonah about Himself in this school of fish are the same ones that He desires to teach us as we read this account here in His word. Some of these lessons have come up multiple times already within Jonah, but we benefit from the repetition because of the importance of these truths.

I. Lesson #1: God is sovereign

If you watch the late nightly news, the things you see there have the potential to cause you to lose sleep: crime, crises, catastrophes in our city and all over the world. It can all be rather stressful and depressing unless, of course, you believe in a sovereign God. When we speak of God's sovereignty, we are referring to His ultimate authority over all that takes place in creation. We do not believe in a God who created the universe and then took a permanent vacation. The famous deists of the Enlightenment period spoke often of God, but the god they referred to was one who had brought the world into being with the precision of a skilled clockmaker. And like the clockmaker, the deist god wound the thing up and then took his hands off of it. This is not the God of the Bible. The God of the Bible rules, meaning that He is the creator and judge of all that He has made; but He also reigns, meaning that He is intricately involved in the workings of what He has made. Nothing is going on here in the world that He doesn't know about, that He hasn't either caused or allowed to happen for some reason, that He is unable to control, and that He is powerless to do something about.

---

[170] Ibid., 241.
[171] Blanchard, 56-57.

If you believe in this kind of God, you will probably save a lot of money at the pharmacy. A firm conviction that God is sovereign goes a long way to eliminating, or at least moderating, anxiety, depression, insomnia, and probably a host of other maladies as well. Is this not what Paul is driving at in Philippians 4:6-7 where he says, "Be anxious for nothing"? We might say, "Paul haven't you read the paper? Don't you watch the news? Didn't you hear that report? How can we not be anxious?" Ah, but Paul says instead of being anxious, "in everything by prayer and supplication with thanksgiving let your requests be made known to God. And the peace of God, which surpasses all comprehension, will guard your hearts and your minds in Christ Jesus." When you pray, you are acknowledging that you believe in a God who is sovereign over your circumstances and has the ability to work in your circumstances, and indeed is already at work in your circumstances. I'm starting to feel better already!

We see God's sovereignty here in Jonah 1:17 as He *appoints* a great fish to swallow Jonah. Prior to this, it certainly appears that Jonah has met his end. He is going to drown in the depths of the Mediterranean Sea. But God is in control here. It was God who sovereignly called Jonah to go to Nineveh. Jonah didn't sign up for that job; God called him. It was God who threw a violent storm upon the sea in order to halt the prophet from his attempt to flee. That storm didn't arise because of a random occurrence in the atmosphere or because someone did a rain dance. God brought that storm about in His sovereignty. It was God who sovereignly caused the toss of the lots to point to Jonah as the guilty party on the ship. Left to random chance, those lots could have pointed to anyone on deck, but God was in control of the lots. When Jonah was thrown overboard, God caused the sea to become calm. It was no chemical reaction caused by the oil of Jonah's skin mixing with the salty sea water. It was the sovereignty of God. And as Jonah goes down beneath the waves, down to the depths, entwined in bands of kelp and sinking like a stone toward his death, it was God who sovereignly appointed a fish to come and swallow him.

It is an interesting phenomenon in the book of Jonah, how God sovereignly appoints things for use in His service. He appointed a prophet. He appointed a storm. He appointed a fish. He will appoint a plant. He will appoint a worm. He will appoint a scorching wind. And of all these things, the only one to put up a fight was the prophet. All the others complied with His sovereign will. Whatever kind of creature this was, a whale, a shark, or any other (the Hebrew could refer to any large creature of the sea), God had placed it exactly where He wanted it to be to do exactly what He wanted it to do. And what God wanted the fish to do was to swallow Jonah and keep him alive for three days and three nights in his belly and deposit (or literally in the Hebrew, *vomit*) him out on the shore. There Jonah, having learned a great lesson in the sovereignty of God, would commence to obediently carry out the orders that God had given him in Jonah 1:2.

A lesson in God's sovereignty does much to motivate us toward obedience as well. We are not going to outrun Him, and if necessary He has the power and authority to deputize all creation into His service to arrest us and redirect us on the path of obediently serving Him. When we know this, we are more likely to think twice about pursuing a course of disobedience. Are you running from God? Are you trying to get away from Him or from what He has called you to do? You must know that if He is determined to use you, He will not let you escape. You may find yourself in the jaws of a sovereignly appointed agent that God is using to redirect you.

Moreover, you may find yourself splashing about today in fear of drowning in some circumstance that has arisen either because of your own doings, someone else's choices, or some unknown circumstance. God would have you know that He is sovereign! There are no limitations on His ability to come to your aid or to appoint some element of creation, another person, a turn of events, and if it is necessary, yes, even a great fish, to rescue you and deliver you if He so desires. And so, you can save your energy from all that flailing about, and drop anchor in the doctrine of His sovereignty. You can trust that if He desires to rescue you, He is certainly *able* to do so.

Jonah learned this lesson, and we must also. But when we look at how Jonah learned this, we may be taken by surprise. After all, it would be perfectly just for God to allow Jonah an undignified burial at sea considering his great sin. But that is not what happens. The great fish teaches Jonah and us another lesson about who God is.

II. Lesson #2: God is merciful

Among those who reject that the events of Jonah ever happened are some biblical scholars who believe that this book of Scripture is a parable or allegory. They believe that Jonah represents Israel, and the fish represents Babylon, the empire that "swallowed up" the Southern Kingdom of Judah in 586 BC and deported the people to modern day Iraq. Despite the popularity of this theory, it is loaded with problems. For example, if Jonah represents Israel, then it is not accurate to say that "Israel" was swallowed up by Babylon, for the name "Israel" at that time referred to the Northern Kingdom, which had been swallowed up already (some 140 years earlier) by the Assyrians. And since Assyria already figures into the story by its chief city Nineveh, it makes no sense for it to be symbolically represented by the sea creature. More relevant to our discussion here is the purpose behind God's appointment of this fish. The Babylonian captivity was also appointed by the sovereignty of God, but His purpose in that event was judgment (call it punishment or discipline) for the idolatry of Judah (the Southern Kingdom) and their abandonment of God's covenant with them. This fish that swallowed Jonah was not appointed for the punishment, discipline, or judgment of the prophet. The fish is a life-saving vessel sent by God to rescue Jonah. So, the allegorical or parabolic interpretations of the book seem to create more problems than they solve.

If we go with a non-historical interpretation we miss out on this wonderful picture of mercy. Jonah does not deserve to be rescued. He has abandoned God's calling on his life and run away, or attempted to run away, from even the presence of God. But God does not rescue Jonah because Jonah is worthy. He rescues Jonah because He is a God of mercy. And that is the same reason He has rescued us from our sins in the salvation that Jesus Christ offers. It is not because we deserve it, but it is because God is merciful.

It is often helpful to remind ourselves of the definition of three important terms when it comes to God's dealings with humanity. First is the concept of justice. This means that people get what they deserve. If Jonah gets justice here, then he drowns in the sea. The second concept is mercy, which means that God withholds the negative consequence that is deserved. By not allowing Jonah to sink and die, God spares him from a fate that he rightly deserves. The third concept is grace. It means that God not only withholds the negative consequence that is deserved, but moreover grants some positive benefit that is not deserved. My pastor used to illustrate these concepts with a story of his son riding his bicycle. [172] A parent may tell a child he or she is not to ride a bicycle on the major street, and if the child disobeys, then the bicycle might be taken away for a month. But suppose when the child is caught out on the major street, the parent comes home and says, "Now you know the rules and broke them, so you now you deserve for the bike to be taken away for a month." That is justice. But then the parent says, "I am only going to take the bike away for a week." That is mercy. And then a little while later the same afternoon the parent says to the child, "How about you and I go out for some ice cream?" That is grace.

When it comes to Jonah, and to you and me and every other human being, God has said that the wages of sin is death, which leads to an eternal separation from God. But for Jonah, God sent a fish to save him from those consequences. And in God's mercy, He has not sent us a fish, but His Son, Jesus Christ. God has incarnated Himself in human flesh to take our death upon Himself. In His mercy, He has spared us from what we deserve. And in His grace, God gives Jonah another opportunity, a recommissioning into His service, which we will see later in the book. For us, God has graciously given forgiveness of sin, a covering in His own righteousness, the indwelling presence of His Spirit, and eternal life with Him in heaven. So we must never complain that we did not get what we deserve from God. We should thank Him that instead, we have received mercy and grace.

Now, here is the irony of Jonah's situation. Why did he run away? God had sent him to Nineveh to preach a message of justice: "Cry against it, for their wickedness has come up before Me" (1:2). The content of the message is seen in 3:4, "Yet forty days and Nineveh will be overthrown." The message is that God is going to bring justice to Nineveh. But Jonah knows enough about the ways of God to know that these messages always

---

[172] C. Mark Corts, *Making Sense of Your Faith* (Winston-Salem, NC: ShareLife, 1997), 14-15.

have an underlying "unless" clause. God's justice is never detached from His mercy and grace. Jonah knows that in preaching that message, God is offering them an opportunity to repent and receive a merciful pardon and a gracious salvation. And Jonah cannot bear the thought of pagan sinners receiving something better than they deserve from God, so he refuses to go to Nineveh to preach that. But in so doing, Jonah proves that he is no better that Nineveh. His sins are equally as great as theirs. He has rejected God just as they have. And so God has sent the fish to teach Jonah that he needs mercy as much as Nineveh does. Jonah offers no complaint that God is willing to save the likes of himself. And by this, he comes to understand that if God can save him when he doesn't deserve it, then He can save the Ninevites too. If Jonah has experienced this mercy, how can he not share it with others?

Oh, how often are we just like Jonah? We look down on others in utter contempt, thinking in the depths of our hearts that God should have nothing to do with the likes of them! But do we not realize that we are equally sinful, equally deserving of a justice filled with wrath, and equally desperate for a Savior who is rich in mercy? Once we have truly seen our sins as God sees them, we will say with the Apostle Paul, "It is a trustworthy statement, deserving full acceptance, that Christ Jesus came into the world to save sinners, among whom I am foremost of all" (1 Tim 1:15). When I come to realize that no person's sins are greater than mine, when I hate my own sin worse than I hate the sin of any other person, then I come to realize that if God is merciful enough to save a sinner like myself, then there is no one whom He cannot save, and no one with whom I should not offer the riches of His mercy. Contemporary Christian writers are offering theory upon theory of why the church in our generation is in such a radical decline. In my opinion, we need look no further than this. We have forgotten that we are redeemed by mercy, and that apart from that saving mercy, we are no better than the multitudes who are perishing around us. God will have us to learn of His mercy, even if He has to take us to the school of fish to learn it. Jonah received an advanced degree there, and God will likewise enroll us if that is what it takes for us to learn that He is merciful to save sinners, and we better be thankful that He is, for in this is our only hope.

Before Jonah can graduate from the school of fish, he has one final course to pass.

III. Lesson #3: God is faithful.

The concept of faithfulness has fallen on hard times. Faithfulness has to do with promises kept. Yet, all around us, we see one example after another of *unfaithfulness.* Marriage vows are broken, campaign promises are forgotten, and promises, commitments, and agreements are discarded in exchange for the pursuit of selfish desires. Things that should be ever present reminders of the idea of faithfulness are disappearing from our landscape. We should not be surprised to find fallen human beings unfaithful to their word. But we should not look to them and think that this is therefore acceptable. Rather, we should look beyond fallen humanity to a holy God who has kept every promise He ever made and who has, or will in time, bring about all that He has spoken.

God's faithfulness to His own promises is seen here in multiple layers. On one layer, the fish represents God's faithfulness to Jonah. On another, the fish indicates God's faithfulness to Nineveh. But in another, and far more important sense as we will see, this fish is a reminder of God's faithfulness to us.

First, we see here that God proves His faithfulness to Jonah as a participant in His covenant. We Baptists are fond of an old saying: "Once saved, always saved." But there is always a nagging question in the backs of our minds, "Yeah, but what about so-and-so, who did this-and-that?" I believe that Jonah and the fish are a sufficient explanation for all of this. My firm conviction based on the tapestry of all of Scripture is that no one who is saved will ever become unsaved. However, I am also convicted of the truth that not all who claim to be saved genuinely are. And God's way of proving the real from the artificial is through perseverance and preservation. Put plainly, what this means is that all who have genuinely been saved, or to speak in terms of Jonah's situation, those who have a genuine covenant relationship with God, will persevere in a course of godly living. This does not mean that they never sin, but it means that when they do, they will repent and return to the Lord, either by their own choosing or by God's sovereign intervention. This is not about you choosing to be saved or to stay saved. This is about God faithfully keeping a promise. Now, if God had allowed Jonah to drown, which would have been perfectly just in light of Jonah's sins, God would have violated His own faithfulness to preserve those who truly belong to Him by faith. Because it was God, and not Jonah, who had established this covenant relationship by His grace, then Jonah could not undo it. God will keep the covenant, even though Jonah appears to have no desire to keep it. By rescuing Jonah, God proves His faithfulness to His covenant with Jonah. He demonstrates that Jonah's salvation is ultimately not dependent on what Jonah does or doesn't do, but on what God promises. The eternal security of our salvation is not about our ability to hold on to God or to keep the promise we have made to Him. It is about God's ability to hold onto us and to keep the promises He has made to those whom He saves.

On an altogether different level, the fish that swallowed Jonah speaks of God's promises concerning Nineveh, or more generally, His promises concerning all the nations, including Israel. We are well familiar with the language of Israel being "God's chosen people." But the point of Israel being God's chosen people was never that Israel alone would know and worship God. God chose Israel for the purpose of making Him known to the rest of the world. And God warned Israel that should they ever violate the covenant that He had established with them, He would raise up other nations to chastise them and drive them back to faithfulness. And this is the reality of what is going on with this fish. Because Israel had not proclaimed this one true God to the nations, but rather had begun to chase after the idols of the nations, God was going to raise up another nation to discipline them. In His sovereignty, He chose to use Assyria. But He would not use Assyria without first dealing with their sins. So God's desire to save Jonah and send him to Nineveh is a means of sparing Assyria from judgment so that He might use Assyria to bring judgment upon Israel. All of this illustrates for us the truth that is seen on nearly every page of the Bible: God desires to be known, and worshiped, and obeyed by people of every nation, every tribe, and every tongue on the earth. But those nations will not obey a God they do not worship; they cannot worship a God whom they do not know; and they cannot know a God who has never been preached to them. So, God is using this fish to spare Jonah, that He might use Jonah to spare Nineveh, that His saving grace might be experienced and matchless name might be glorified in the language of the Assyrian people.

God is still desirous of the worship of the nearly 6,700 people groups of the world who remain unreached, including approximately 3,600 people groups who have little or no access to the Gospel. They live in the most difficult and terrifying places on the earth. But God would have His truth reach them, and He desires to use you and me to make it happen. Run if you will, but you will not outrun the Lord nor His appointed fish.

Finally, Jonah in the belly of this fish speaks to us of God's faithfulness to us—we who have come to know God by faith in Jesus Christ. When the religious leaders of Jesus' day demanded that He give them a sign to prove that He was who He said He was, He said, "An evil and adulterous generation craves for a sign; and yet no sign will be given to it but the sign of Jonah the prophet; for just as Jonah was three days and three nights in the belly of the sea monster, so will the Son of Man be three days and three nights in the heart of the earth" (Matthew 12:38-40). And of course, by this, Jesus was referring to His death on the cross for our sins, His burial, and His resurrection on the third day. This is the culminating event in redemptive history, the event to which all that has been written in the Word of God decisively points. From the first promise of redemption in Genesis 3:15, through all of the institutions of priesthood and temple and sacrifice, to the prophecies and prophetic acts of the Old Testament, human history sprinted forward to that singular event. God had promised time and time again, in many forms and fashions, in varying degrees of specificity, in word and deed and imagery, that He would save sinners. In Jesus Christ, He made good on His word. He is faithful, and as Jesus says, just as Jonah's experience in the belly of the fish proved that God is sovereign, and merciful, and faithful to His promise and purpose, so Jesus is the sign of these same things to the world. Do you seek a sign to prove that Jesus is a Savior to sinners? Then look to the cross, and then to the empty tomb, for He said that this is the only sign you will receive. God has kept His word, and salvation for sinners has been accomplished in Jesus Christ for all who turn to Him in faith in repentance. If you have, then you can rest in the certainty of His promise knowing that He is faithful to keep you in the salvation to which He has called you. If you have not, then the call is for you to do so with all urgency. Turn to this One who is greater than Jonah and call upon Him to save you in His sovereign mercy, according to His unfailing faithfulness to His promise.

Jonah learned a theology lesson in the school of fish that should have been unforgettable. We'll have to wait and see if it really was for him. God desires to teach us the same truths, and He will go to unstoppable lengths to drive the point home. He is sovereign, He is merciful, He is faithful.

IX

Reminders on Prayer
Jonah 2:1-2

*Then Jonah prayed to the LORD his God from the stomach of the fish,
and he said, "I called out of my distress to the LORD, And He answered me.
I cried for help from the depth of Sheol; You heard my voice."*

Late in his life, the theologian Carl Henry was asked to reflect on his long life and ministry and consider what he might have done differently. Henry purportedly replied that he would "spend more time in prayer and seek to reach out in a more earnest way to non-Christians."[173] I suppose that most of us would confess that we have likewise not invested ourselves in prayer and in the sharing of the good news of Jesus to the extent that we could have. I don't know any Christian who complains that he or she has spent *too much* time witnessing and praying! But when we come to Jonah, we find a man who doesn't seem to want to do much of either. When God calls him to carry a message to Nineveh, he doesn't do it. When the ship captain urges him to pray to his God, he doesn't do it. In fact, throughout the entire book thus far, we have not seen Jonah praying at all. He did not pray about his response to God's call; he did not pray about his attempted journey to Tarshish; he didn't pray when the storm came; he didn't pray before he was thrown overboard. But now as he sinks like a stone toward the floor of the Mediterranean Sea, coming closer and closer to death with every passing second, he turns to the Lord in prayer.

It doesn't seem that he had simply forgotten to pray before this time. It seems more likely that he refused to pray because he was trying to flee from the presence of the Lord. To pray is to enter the presence of the Lord, and that was the last place the disobedient prophet wanted to be. Intimacy

---

[173] I received this quote anecdotally and have been seeking an exact citation for it.

with Him is not something we desire to cultivate while we simultaneously seek the indulgence of our carnal desires. Then at other times, due to pride, spiritual laziness or simply to forgetfulness, we find ourselves sliding into a pattern of prayerlessness. But God has a way of reminding us of our need for Him and our need to commune with Him in prayer. We need a continual reminder of the great privilege we have in prayer, and the desperate dependence we have upon the presence and power of God that is available to us through prayer. There are very few passages in this small book of Jonah in which the prophet serves as a model of any kind for us. Like many other characters in Scripture, Jonah is a negative example: one whose mistakes and failures serve as warnings and lessons for us. But here is a rare case in which Jonah does the right thing. God has reminded him of his need for prayer, and he prays. And the reminders that Jonah received concerning prayer are the same ones that we ourselves need to receive as well.

I. God has a way of reminding us when to pray.

Michael Jordan became a superstar in the 1982 NCAA Championship game when his jump shot in the final fifteen seconds gave North Carolina a victory over Georgetown. Those of us who grew up watching him play have many lasting images in our minds of Jordan throwing up a last second shot to clinch a win as the buzzer sounded. Time and time again, everyone in the game of basketball was reminded that it was never too late in the game to put the ball in Jordan's hands. As good as Jordan was in coming through in the clutch, one fan's blog records that Jordan missed as many buzzer-beaters as he made. He was 9 for 18 with 24 seconds or less on the clock when the game was on the line.[174] So, even though we think that Jordan is the guy we want to give the ball to in the final second, he is just likely to miss the shot as he is to make it.

Jonah is reminded here that there is someone with a better record in the clutch than Michael Jordan. God's record of coming through when everything is on the line is perfect. Jonah learns that it is never too late to

---

[174] "Michael Jordan: Game Winning Shots." http://chasing23.com/michael-jordan-game-winning-shots/ Accessed July 14, 2011.

pray. Have we learned that? Though we are often too forgetful, too lazy, or too reluctant to pray, God has a way of reminding us that it is never too late.

In Jonah 1:15 we read that the sailors threw Jonah into the sea, and in 1:17 we read that the Lord appointed a fish to swallow him. But we are not told how much time elapsed between those two events. When Jonah hits the water, the pace of the narrative in Jonah becomes like a slow motion dramatic scene in a movie. It is safe to assume that it wasn't days, and unlikely hours. We don't know, however, if there were seconds or minutes that elapsed between the time Jonah entered the sea and the time Jonah entered the fish. We do know that it was long enough for him to pray. In the opening words of Chapter 2 we read, "Then Jonah prayed to the Lord his God from the stomach of the fish." This is the first time in the whole book that we have seen Jonah in prayer. But it is not the first time he has prayed. In this prayer from inside the belly of the fish, he is recounting how God answered another prayer he prayed while he was drowning in the sea. He will go on to mention how the waves passed over him and seaweed wrapped around his head. He will recount how he descended to the roots of the mountains, which is likely a reference to the floor of the sea. He describes his physical condition as one of distress, fainting away.

That he believed death was near is evident in that he says, "I cried for help from the depth of Sheol." The New American Standard and English Standard versions have transliterated the Hebrew term, giving us the proper noun of Sheol here, while the King James attempts to translate the word with "hell," and the NIV uses "grave." It is easy to see from this survey of English translations how this common Hebrew term has caused much confusion among Christians as to its precise meaning. There is a sense in which all of these attempts to render the term into English are correct.

In an unpublished faculty lecture from Southeastern Baptist Theological Seminary, Dr. Allen Moseley suggests that the Hebrew word *Sheol* occurs in the Old Testament with two common meanings.[175] First, for both the righteous and unrighteous, *Sheol* can simply mean death, the end of earthly life. Hence, it is sometimes translated in English Bibles with the sense of "the grave." Second, Moseley suggests that when *Sheol* is used in reference to the destiny of the unrighteous, it has a much more precise meaning. For them, *Sheol* is equal to the place of eternal torment, or hell. In Jonah's case, it seems likely that he is using the term in the former sense, meaning "death," or "the grave."

As he sinks deeper and deeper toward the bottom of the sea, his conscious thought is that death is inevitable. In desperation at the very door of death Jonah prayed a prayer that we do not have the privilege to read here. But we know that God answered this prayer by appointing a great fish to swallow the prophet and spare his life. From the belly of the fish, Jonah gives praise to God for such a great salvation, saying, "I called out of my distress to the Lord, and He answered me. I cried for help from the depth of Sheol; You heard my voice." For Jonah, as long as any ounce of life remained in him, it was not too late to pray, no matter how desperate the circumstance.

Sometimes, we are in a situation like Jonah was. In our stubborn rebellion, we have deliberately forsaken prayer because we do not want to think about God while we indulge in sin. But when sin's calamity and consequences begin to overwhelm us, we desperately cry out to God for a rescue that we are well aware that we do not deserve. And so many times, believers have found that our God, who is abounding in mercy and rich with an abundance of grace, comes through in the clutch to rescue us. At other times, we have neglected prayer not because of willful disobedience but because of spiritual laziness. We get caught up in the flow of things and find ourselves being swept away by the currents of the fallen world in which we live, forgetting that there is a God who can rescue us. At other times, mainly because of our delusions of pride, we think we can handle a situation by ourselves without God's help. We massage our minds with

---

[175] Allen Moseley, "Sheol and Differentiated Destinies in the Old Testament." Unpublished faculty lecture delivered in the Southeastern Baptist Theological Seminary Chapel, Fall 2005.

platitudes like, "God won't give me more than I can handle,"[176] and we try to muster the strength to face our hardships in our own strength. But when we find ourselves spiraling into great distress and misery, with death or disaster coming into view, we cry out to God in desperation and learn that no situation is ever beyond God's help.

It is never too late to cry out to Him in prayer as long as there is life within us. If only we could learn that it is also never too early! Had Jonah prayed and sought the Lord sooner, how much suffering could he have avoided? The same is true for us. When we forget that it is never too early to pray, God is faithful. He has a way of reminding us that it is also never too late to pray.

II. God has a way of reminding us how to pray.

I will never forget the feeling of absolute horror that came over me one Sunday shortly after I came to know the Lord. My best friend whom God used to bring me to faith in Jesus was an usher in our church and one day he asked me to fill in for another usher who was absent. I was eager to serve, so I jumped right in. As we stood up front with the plates ready to collect the offering, the music director looked down at us and said, "Russ, lead us in prayer." I attribute it to the power of God that I didn't faint or vomit on the spot. I managed to mumble something vaguely generic and insincere, quickly said the Amen, and managed to get back to my seat without losing consciousness. In my nervousness, the only thought in my mind was that all these people were going to hear my prayer! I was very self-conscious to use the right words and say the right things. But God has taught me through the intervening years that the most important thing to remember when we pray is that we are talking to Him. It is the Lord who hears our voice when we pray, and who hears the prayer of our hearts even more clearly than the prayer of our mouths.

---

[176] This statement seems to me to overstate what "I" can handle. In my flesh, I can't handle much! Jesus said apart from Him I can do nothing (John 15:5). So, I think it is more helpful for us to say that God will not give us more than He can handle in, with, and through us. That seems to be what Scripture teaches (Philippians 4:13; 1 Corinthians 10:13, et al.).

The point is easy to miss here in the text, but it is found in verse 2 when Jonah says, "You heard my voice." While that seems rather unextraordinary at first glance, there are two wondrous things about that statement. First, is it not just an absolute marvel of grace that the holy God of the universe, who created all that exists and sustains it perpetually by His active providence, would even care what we humans have to say? David wrote in Psalm 8:4, "What is man that You take thought of him, and the son of man that You care for him?" This is perhaps the most merciful miracle of all when it comes to prayer, that God would actually hear the voice of a sinful human being!

There is something else extraordinary in Jonah's statement that the Lord heard his voice. Where is Jonah praying when he says that the Lord heard his voice? He is drowning in the depths of the sea. Have you ever tried to talk under water? The sounds are barely audible, and thoroughly incoherent. You cannot have a conversation with someone underwater! They cannot hear your voice. It's just bubbles. But God can hear our voices even when no one else can. Isn't that amazing?

There's a great scene in the movie *Patton* in which General Patton gives the chaplain one hour to write a prayer for him to pray in order to stop the bad weather that is affecting his troops. The chaplain leaves the general in a somewhat fearful state, wondering if he can come up with just the right words in such a short time. Well, imagine how Jonah must feel! He doesn't have an hour. He has seconds—or less! There's no time to come up with just the right words, no time to rehearse it, to practice the enunciation and diction. This prayer is nothing more than bubbles rising to the surface of the water with a mumble. But when he prayed it, the Lord heard his voice. And the Lord reminded him that He is not impressed with flowery language eloquently spoken. The Lord hears the voice of the one who prays with sincerity in his heart, regardless of the volume or vocabulary of his mouth.

Have you ever found yourself in a situation where you needed to pray, but the words just wouldn't come? This can be frustrating and discouraging to us, only further leading us down into the valley of desperation. But there are some truths that can help us through these moments. The follower of

Jesus Christ has precious promises for us when we struggle in prayer. Romans 8:26 tells us that "the Spirit also helps our weakness; for we do not know how to pray as we should, but the Spirit Himself intercedes for us with groanings too deep for words." This comforts us to know that the Holy Spirit is giving words to the burdens of our hearts if we will just be still before the Lord in an attitude of prayer. And if this were not enough, Hebrews 7:25 tells us that the Lord Jesus Himself is making intercession for us before the Father. So lest we think that God is interested in our words alone, we are reminded that the Father is hearing the very words of His Spirit and His Son as we bow before Him in humble prayer.

This is why, for centuries, Christians have found comfort in their time of desperate prayer when words do not come, by simply uttering a prayer that has come to be known as "The Jesus Prayer." In the early 18th Century, a monk called Nicodemus of the Holy Mountain wrote: "Prayer of the heart … consists principally of a person placing his mind within the heart and, without speaking with his mouth, but only with inner words spoken in the heart, saying this brief and single prayer, 'Lord Jesus Christ, Son of God, have mercy on me'," a sinner.[177] In those moments when the heart senses the need for prayer but the mouth refuses to utter the words, if we fix our minds on these words and utter them aloud or in silence, or as it were, with bubbles from the depths of the sea, we have confidence that our voice will be heard in heaven. It is not because this is some magic formula that unlocks the gates of heaven, like saying "Open Sesame" or "Abra Cadabra." It is because these words express a truth that is always reflective of our hearts and lives. It confesses who Christ is: "Lord Jesus Christ, Son of God." It confesses who we are: "a sinner." And it requests, regardless of our specific need, the general need that any sinner standing in the presence of a holy God has: "have mercy on me." We do not know what words Jonah sought to form in the voiceless vacuum of the deep, but we know that these words would have been appropriate in his situation. He was indeed a sinner, as are we all, and desperately in need of mercy from on high.

---

[177] Frederica Mathewes-Green, *The Illumined Heart,* (Brewster, Mass.: Paraclete, 2001), 70. While Mathews-Green does not include the words "a sinner" in the quotation, most forms of the prayer include the words.

So God has a way of reminding us how to pray. When the words won't come, we trust in the intercession of the Spirit who puts words to our burdened hearts, and they reach the Father's ears by way of the intercession of the Risen Lord Jesus, and mercy is found there. This is a great reminder for us when there are no words. But, there is another reminder here to help us even with the words.

III. God has a way of reminding us what to pray.

Often when I travel to another country, one of my greatest fears is that I will not know how to communicate with the people. Usually I know that I will have an interpreter, or at least someone who understands English enough for me to say what I need to say. Still, what if there is an emergency? What if we get lost? What if we need to find a restroom? And so before every trip I take, I purchase a phrase book of common expressions to look up and find the words I need when I need them. Once when I was in Senegal, a man was speaking French to me. I looked in my phrase book and found how to say, "I don't speak French very well." *Je ne parle pas tres bien Francais.* That sounds smooth. Too bad I couldn't say it that way. I said something that sounded like "Jay nay par-lay tress buyin' Frances." And the guy just shook his head, looked me in the eye, and said, "Yeah, I can tell!"

Now, thankfully, when it comes to praying, we don't have to learn a new language. Muslims are taught that Arabic is the language of God. The Quran is only considered authoritative when it is read in Arabic, and Muslims pray five times a day memorized prayers in Arabic, even when they do not know the language. Now, we know that God speaks the language of every tribe and nation, and He can be spoken to with the language of every people as well, and even without language at all. But what do we say to God when we pray? God has given us a phrase book of sorts to use, not to mindlessly recite in vain repetition, but to inform us as we pray. That phrase book is called the Bible. As we read it and absorb it, its truths, its vocabulary, its categories of thought, its patterns, and its rhythms take root in our hearts and minds and inform our prayers. The same happened with Jonah.

While we don't know the words that Jonah prayed with silent bubbles as he was drowning, once he was safe inside the confines of the fish's belly, we have a written transcript of the prayer he prayed. And the words may sound familiar to us. Every phrase of this prayer that comprises the entirety of Chapter 2 finds parallel expression in the book of Psalms. In verse 2 alone, there are echoes of at least five different Psalms. Most notably, we see the similarity between Jonah's prayer and Psalm 18:5-6, which reads: *"The cords of Sheol surrounded me; the snares of death confronted me. In my distress I called upon the Lord, and cried to my God for help; He heard my voice out of His temple, and my cry for help before Him came into His ears."* You can walk through the rest of the verses in Jonah 2 and find similar parallels.

Jonah would have been reading the Psalms all of his life. David's psalms had been written in the years surrounding 1000 BC, so they had been used by God's people in prayer and worship for some 200 years or more by Jonah's time. Many of these psalms, and in some cases all of them, had been committed to memory by many Israelites. And by singing them in worship and praying the words of the Psalms, the people of God learned to use God's own words to speak to Him about the things that concerned their lives. And this serves a reminder to us that when we pray God's Word can help us formulate what we pray. It can even happen without our conscious effort. The words of the Bible become lodged in our hearts and mind, and just as God has spoken them to us in our hearing and reading, so we begin to speak them back to Him in prayer. Jonah was reminded of these truths of God's Word as he began to utter this prayer from inside the fish, and we are likewise reminded of the value of committing Scripture to memory. The more God's word fills our hearts, the less we will struggle with what to pray as we approach the throne of grace. We can take confidence that our words will be heard in heaven, for that is where our words have come from.

IV. God has a way of reminding why it is possible to pray.

Several years ago, a friend of mine who is a traveling evangelist left his mobile phone in my car. I knew that his phone had stored in its memory the personal phone numbers of some of the most prominent preachers, pastors, and Christian musicians in America. As I looked at that phone, I had this thought that I could use that phone to contact any one of them. With the push of a button on that phone I could ring the cell phone of a Grammy Award winning artist, or the vacation home of a pastor of a 10,000 member church. But I also knew that once the call was connected, I would not have gotten far with a conversation, for I did not have a personal relationship with them like my friend did. My call would have been considered a most unwelcome intrusion.

There is a similar truth when it comes to prayer. Communication with God requires a relationship with God, lest our prayer be something of an unwelcome intrusion in His presence. But Jonah could pray to the Lord, Yahweh, the one true God of the universe, because (as verse 1 says) this was the Lord *his* God. It would be hard to overstate how important that single word "his" is in the text. The Lord is God, but He is also *his* God, Jonah's God. The word *his* indicates that Jonah, in spite of his sin, was still involved in a personal relationship with the Lord. He has tried to run away from the Lord, but has found that the relationship that enables him to pray to his God is one that rests firmly in the hands of God. God had initiated it, and God was preserving it. And because of that, the voice of Jonah would always be welcome in heaven's throne room.

You may wonder, "Will my prayer be heard in heaven?" Maybe you've never given that question any thought. Your assumption might have always been that God hears everyone's prayer. Well, certainly God is not hard of hearing, and He is everywhere at all times, so He *can* hear every prayer that gets prayed, but the issue is more than just whether He *can* hear it. We all know the difference between hearing and listening. When you go to church and sit in a worship service, everyone can *hear* the preacher. Not everyone is *listening* to the preacher. Listening has something to do with being attentive to what is being said. Similar to that distinction, there is a sense in which God is *able to hear* the prayers of anyone in the world, but He gives *His attentive ear* to those who have a relationship with Him. Some of you live in the reality of that relationship every day of your lives. But others perhaps did not know such a thing was possible. It is, and you don't have to go seeking it. That's a good thing, for Romans 3:11 says that there is none who seeks for God. Rather, God is the great seeker who has come seeking after us.

Jesus said that no one comes to the Father except through Him (John 14:6). This is true of salvation; it is true of worship; and it is true of prayer. Because of His death on the cross, in which He died as our substitute to atone for our sins, and His glorious resurrection from the dead, it is now possible for sinful people (such as we are) to have a personal relationship with God. We are invited to turn from our sins and place our faith and trust in Jesus to save us, that we might be forgiven and have that relationship that God desires to have with us. He wants to be "your God," as He was Jonah's God, and Jesus is the one who makes that possible. If you never have before, it would be my prayer that even this very day, you would turn to Him by faith and receive Him. Then you may look toward heaven and know that the Lord is your God, and when you cry out to Him in your distress, you will know that He hears your voice and attends to your prayer.

X

When God's People Sin
Jonah 2:3-4

"For You had cast me into the deep, Into the heart of the seas, and the current engulfed me. All Your breakers and billows passed over me. So I said, 'I have been expelled from Your sight. Nevertheless I will look again toward Your holy temple.'"

For many Christians, the promise found in Romans 8:28 is cherished as a personal favorite. It says, "And we know that God causes all things to work together for good to those who love God, to those who are called according to His purpose." What a great comfort it is to know that whatever comes our way is being used by the hand of God to bring good into our lives! This promise does *not* assure us that all things *are good*, but rather that God is using all the things that are going on in our lives, the good things and the bad things, to bring good to us. This is not a promise that can be claimed by every person. It is for those who "love God" and "are called according to His purpose." This means those who have a personal relationship with God through faith in Jesus Christ.

Often people cling to this promise expecting that, in return for every unpleasant circumstance they endure, there will be some identifiable good that comes to them in equal measure. Because of that understanding, many are discouraged and disappointed because they have not yet seen any good come into their lives that makes the bad that they experienced "worth it." But the larger context of Romans 8 helps us understand that God is promising a *specific* good to His people. In Romans 8:29, we read, "For those whom He foreknew, He also predestined to become conformed to the image of His Son." This means that the ultimate good that God is working in our lives, the purpose for which He has called us into salvation and which He relentlessly works to bring about for us through sanctification, is that we become conformed to the image of Jesus. God is using all the things in our lives, the good things and the bad things alike, to make us more like Christ. He has declared us to be righteous and covered us in the righteousness of Jesus (justification), and He is determined to make our lives reflect that righteousness by persistently shaping us through all that we encounter and experience in life (sanctification). We will not be fully conformed into the image of Christ until we are face-to-face with Him in glory. John writes in 1 John 3:2, "We know that when He appears, we will be like Him, because we will see Him just as He is." Until then, the process is incomplete, and God will be faithful to continue working all things together to that good end. As Philippians 1:6 says, "He who began a good work in you will perfect it until the day of Christ Jesus."

Gordon MacDonald, in his excellent book *Ordering Your Private World*, compares the process of our sanctification with clearing a field. He describes how he and his wife set out to build a house, but before they could, they had to clear the land. First, the large boulders had to go, then the smaller stones, then came the seemingly endless task of removing the smallest stones and pebbles. MacDonald says that his process of spiritual maturity has taken shape like that. Immediately after he came to know Jesus, he says that God began to remove the boulders—the glaring and obvious sins in his life. But then, he says that Christ began to work on the smaller stones—things he'd never noticed before in his life because they were hidden by the enormous boulders. Then, he says, "I reached that point … where Christ and I were dealing with stones and pebbles. They are too numerous to imagine, and as far as I can see, for the rest of my days on earth I will be working with the many stones and pebbles in my life." And occasionally, while we deal with these stones and pebbles, we uncover larger stones and boulders that we were unaware of, and God begins to deal with those as well.[178] And this is the good that God is always at work performing in the lives of His people. He is removing all that is present in our lives that does not conform to the image of Jesus. In short, because we are sinners by nature and by choice, God is always at work dealing with our sin.

---

[178] Gordon MacDonald, *Ordering Your Private World* (Nashville: Nelson, 1985), 152-153.

Now, when we come to Jonah, we meet a man who knew God and had served Him faithfully for many years. But when the challenging call came to Jonah to deliver God's message to the city of Nineveh, the home of the Assyrian people who were despised by Israel, Jonah fled in disobedience. Perhaps Jonah had thought that he was beyond the boulder-clearing stage of his spiritual life, but with this divine call to Nineveh an enormous boulder was unearthed in his soul. And try as Jonah may to run away from it, God was determined to clear it from the field and bring him to repentance. And God is determined to do the same for each of us as well. If we are followers of Jesus, then God will relentlessly work all the things of our lives, our sins and our successes alike, together for His good purpose of making us more like Jesus. It is no secret that God's people sin. All of us are aware of that in our own souls. But what Jonah seemed unaware of, and what we are often unaware of, is the lengths that God will go to when His people sin to transform them into a reflection of His own righteousness.

Our text here is a portion of the prayer that Jonah prayed from inside the belly of a fish—the great fish that God appointed to swallow the prophet and spare his life. And as Jonah reflects on the saving mercy of God in this miraculous event, he sees God's hand at work in what he has experienced, dealing with him and his sin in severe mercy. As we consider the words that Jonah expresses in this prayer, we should likewise consider how God deals with us and with our sin.

I. When God's people sin, He deals with us by fatherly discipline.

Most people love a good mystery. Many of the most popular television series, movies, and books have involved a suspense-filled quest to determine "who-done-it." The best mystery writers know how to spring a last-second twist of plot on the reader. All the while you have been thinking that you knew who the guilty party was, but on the last page or in the final scene the plot twists and you see that someone else you didn't suspect actually did it. Well, Jonah's story does not quite unfold like one of those mysteries, but when Jonah prays, he rightly identifies the real "who-done-it" behind all that has transpired.

Before coming to this verse of Jonah, if you had been asked, "Who cast Jonah into the deep?" most of us would have answered, "the sailors." And we even have a proof-text in Jonah 1:15. "*They* picked up Jonah, threw him into the sea." Sounds like an open-and-shut case, doesn't it? But this is actually only partly correct. Jonah is now able to see clearly that the hand of God was at work in his circumstances. "*You* had cast me into the deep," he acknowledges in his prayer. As if having breakers and billows to pass over his head wasn't bad enough, Jonah acknowledges to the Lord that these are "*Your* breakers and billows." The wind and waves belong to the God who made them, and He has made them to be His instruments of discipline toward His wayward prophet.

The role of the sailors was a secondary one. The primary force at work in Jonah's situation is God Himself. As Wayne Grudem writes, "Scripture simultaneously affirms that the men threw Jonah into the sea and that God threw him into the sea. ... What Scripture reveals to us, and what Jonah himself realized, was that God was bringing about His plan through the willing choices of real human beings."[179] The sailors' action to throw Jonah overboard was something God brought about and used for His purpose of disciplining his prophet for his sin.

We might look at Jonah's predicament the way that many have done, in a predominantly negative light. The nineteenth century Scottish preacher Hugh Martin wrote, "God had clothed Himself towards Jonah in all the insignia of a judge—an incensed judge. ... His God was indeed pursuing him as an enemy."[180] But, it seems that the very fact that God did not let Jonah perish beneath the waves, sparing him mercifully with the divinely appointed fish, indicates that this was not merely the work of an angry and vengeful Judge. Rather, this was the work of a loving Father who disciplines His children when they sin against Him.

Hebrews 12:5-11 helps us understand what God is doing in His fatherly discipline of us:

---

[179] Wayne Grudem, *Systematic Theology* (Grand Rapids: Zondervan,), 326.
[180] Hugh Martin, *Jonah* (Geneva Series of Commentaries; Carlisle, Penn.: Banner of Truth, 1958), 195.

> *My son, do not regard lightly the discipline of the LORD, nor faint when you are reproved by Him, for those whom the LORD loves He disciplines, and He scourges every son whom He receives. It is for discipline that you endure; God deals with you as with sons; for what son is there whom his father does not discipline? But if you are without discipline, of which all have become partakers, then you are illegitimate children and not sons. Furthermore, we had earthly fathers to discipline us, and we respected them; shall we not much rather be subject to the Father of spirits, and live? For they disciplined us for a short time as seemed best to them, but He disciplines us for our good, so that we may share His holiness. All discipline for the moment seems not to be joyful, but sorrowful; yet to those who have been trained by it, afterwards it yields the peaceful fruit of righteousness.*

Here again, as in Romans 8, we see that God—our loving Father—has a purpose in all that He causes or allows in our lives. That purpose is "for our good, so that we may share His holiness." And discipline is always difficult, but it is never intended for our ruin. It is out of the Father's great love for His children that He disciplines them. It is not enjoyable to experience. It is painful, even sorrowful as Hebrews says. But, when we are trained by it, it yields the peaceful fruit of righteousness.

So, when we sin (not *if,* but *when*), our Father loves us enough to pursue us and to intervene in our situation with fatherly discipline. He may throw us into the deep and bring His breakers and billows over our heads, but it is for His good purpose of shaping us into the holy and righteous image of Jesus. And we must be thankful for this discipline when it comes, for it is evidence of God's love for us, God's faithfulness to us and to His purpose in our lives, and proof that we truly belong to Him. We should never fear getting *caught* in sin more than we fear *getting away with it*! It is a terrifying thing to sin and get away with it! If God, who sees all that is done in secret and knows everything perfectly about us, allows us to go undisciplined when we sin, then the alarming reality should dawn upon us that we do not truly belong to Him. We are, in that case, as Hebrews says, "illegitimate children and not sons." So, as sons, we welcome the discipline of our Father, knowing that by it He is dealing with us and our sin in a way that leads to our good, and to His good purpose of making us more like Jesus.

II. When God's people sin, He allows us to experience sin's consequences.

Regardless of your educational background, we have all likely learned much of what we know in the same way. Call it the "School of Hard Knocks" if you will. If a person hasn't been educated there, he or she has not been well-educated, regardless of their diplomas or degrees. Often, for many reasons, a parent or grandparent will seek to protect a child by insulating them from the consequences of their actions. And this child grows up in most cases to be spoiled, irresponsible, and immature. Good parents know that consequences are valuable teachers in life. As our perfect Father, God often deals with us and with our sin by allowing us to experience the hard consequences.

In verse 4, Jonah acknowledges in his prayer, "I have been expelled from Your sight." The verb is passive; God is still the primary cause at work in situation. God has, in essence, kicked Jonah out of His presence. But in so doing, God was simply allowing Jonah to get what he wanted. Remember back in 1:3 that when God called Jonah to go to Nineveh, Jonah "rose up to flee to Tarshish *from the presence of the Lord.*" In verse 10, Jonah confessed to the sailors that he "was fleeing from the presence of the Lord." Jonah wanted to get out of God's presence, so God kicked him out. Jonah got what he wanted, and it had the destructive potential of being the worst thing that ever happened to him.

Of course, we know that since God is omnipresent (He is everywhere at all times) there is nowhere one can go on earth to be truly out of His presence. In fact, the only place where one can truly be said to be "out of God's presence" is in hell. And Jonah had perhaps come close enough to feel the heat, to see the darkness, and to sense the horror of what it would mean to truly be barred forever from God's presence. So, He cried out to God for mercy.

Often when we don't get what we want in life, we may think that God does not love us. But in reality, His love for us may be the reason He is withholding what we want. What we want may bring with it the consequence of disaster. In Romans 1, when Paul describes the wrath that God is unleashing from heaven against the ungodly and unrighteous, three times he states that God is judging these people by "giving them over" to their own desires, their own degrading passions, and their own depraved minds. God is judging them with wrath by giving them what they want. In giving them what they want, God is showing them the folly and the destructive nature of sin. And many of those who taste the bitterness of those consequences find themselves, like Jonah, repenting over their rebellion against the Lord and returning to Him with a cry for help.

Have you been there? Have you desired to have something so desperately that you rebelled from the Lord in order to obtain it? Have you longed to be released from what you think are His restrictive cords? It might be that God will grant your wishes. It might be that God will let you have what you want. He might, for a season, let you experience what life would be like without His presence surrounding you. David sang to the Lord in Psalm 16:11, "You will make known to me the path of life; In Your presence is fullness of joy; In Your right hand there are pleasures forever." But often we have abandoned the path of life and chosen the path of destruction. We find ourselves withdrawing from the presence of the Lord. We thought we were seeking joy and pleasure, but those are only ultimately found in the presence of the Lord—in His right hand. And from the depths of despair, we cry out to God for redemption. And when His merciful rescue comes, we have come through the school of hard knocks with a real education. We have learned by the consequences we have experienced that sin's promises are empty and its allure is fleeting. While sin may offer pleasures for a season (Hebrews 11:25), in God's presence there is fullness of joy and pleasure forevermore. And in teaching us that lesson, God is working out His good purposes in our lives, even through the unpleasant consequences of our sin.

III. When God's people sin, He leads us toward hope.

In the Fall of 2006, a politician that many Americans were unfamiliar with published a book entitled *The Audacity of Hope* and it instantly became a bestseller. And two years later, the American people elected that man who had the audacity to talk about hope as President of the United States. We do not know how the history books will remember Barack Obama as a President, but I think that generations to come will look back on his election as a reflection of the hunger for hope that is found in every human heart, and the willingness of people to follow someone who promises to get them there. These promises often go unfulfilled because they are based only on empty rhetoric, unfounded optimism and wishful thinking. Politicians are often accused of breaking campaign promises, but the problem is usually that they were making promises that they had no power to deliver. The biblical idea of hope has to do with more than just wishful thinking. It is a confident expectancy in the power and the promises of God. It is a certainty that what God has promised *is* going to happen because He is able to make it so.

As we read verse 4, we find a man who is transported from horror to hope. After describing all that God has done to discipline him and to make him experience the consequences of his sin, Jonah's tone takes a sudden and unexpected twist. "I have been expelled from Your sight. *Nevertheless, I will look again toward Your holy temple.*" Notice his confidence: he does not say, "Oh, how I wish that I might look again toward Your holy temple!" No there is hope in his heart as he says, "I *will* look again toward Your holy temple." Here is a man who has been dealt with by the severe mercy of the Lord, and through discipline and the school of hard knocks, has come to embrace hope—hope that is fixed upon the Lord Himself.

Jonah's hope is found in what God has revealed about Himself in His word. In Jonah 4:2, the prophet will say to the Lord, "I knew that You are a gracious and compassionate God, slow to anger and abundant in lovingkindness, and one who relents concerning calamity." How did Jonah know that about God? Jonah knew his Bible! This very description of God occurs repeatedly throughout the Old Testament, particularly in the portions that were already in existence by Jonah's time. The first occurrence of this statement is found in Exodus 34:6-7. In the midst of giving His law to Israel, God declared Himself to be "The LORD, the LORD God, compassionate and gracious, slow to anger, and abounding in lovingkindness and truth; who keeps lovingkindness for thousands, who forgives iniquity, transgression and sin." God had proven Himself faithful time and time again in His dealings with His people when they sinned against Him. And here is a broken man, a backslidden prophet, holding God at His very own word. He has been disciplined by the Lord's fatherly love. He has tasted the bitterness of his sin's consequences. And turning to the Lord in confession and repentance, he is confident that God will be faithful to His nature and to His promise. Jonah will be forgiven and restored, and he will live to once again ascend the Temple Mount to offer sacrifices of worship to his God.

If Jonah, who only possessed about a third of the revelation of God's Word that we possess, had the audacity to find this kind of hope in the Lord, then how much more confident should we be? Not only do we possess the entirety of God's written word, we have God's word incarnate in the person of the Lord Jesus Christ as the surety of all that He has promised. When we, who belong to God by faith in Christ, sin against our Lord, we can take hope in the promises of His word. He disciplines us like a loving Father. He does not withhold our consequences from us. But He is working all of this together for His good purpose of making us holy, transforming us into the likeness of Jesus. And our certainty, our audacious hope, is based entirely upon Jesus Christ. Paul said in 2 Corinthians 1:20, "As many are the promises of God, in Him they are yes; therefore also through Him is our Amen." For this Jesus has truly taken our sins upon Himself in His death on the cross. He bore the wrath of the Righteous Judge for every sin we have committed, past, present, and future. God has dealt with our sin fully and finally in Jesus. On the cross, Jesus cried out, "My God, My God, why have You forsaken Me?" He was expelled from the Father's sight, carrying our sin away. And yet, it was His confident expectation, His audacious hope, that death was not the end for Himself. And because of Him, it is not the end for us. Jesus would look again upon His Father's holy temple. He would not simply return to the Jerusalem temple where a priest makes sacrifices. He had *become* the Priest, and the Sacrifice, and the Temple. He promised those of His generation, *"Destroy this temple, and in three days I will raise it up"* (John 2:19). Looking back on that statement, John wrote, "He was speaking of the temple of His body. So when He was raised from the dead, His disciples remembered that He said this; and they believed the Scripture and the word which Jesus had spoken."

149

It is this crucified and risen Jesus who is the anchor of our hope.[181] When we sin against our Lord, He disciplines us. He allows us to experience our consequences. But He does not deal with us in such a way to destroy us. He deals with us in such a way to bring us to hope—to the confident expectation that every word He has promised will come to pass. And the Gospel that saved us and made us to become God's people is the sure reminder that guards our hearts and minds when we sin. This good news announces that Jesus came into the world to save sinners, and that God will relentlessly work in our lives for His good purpose of making us holy. And when we sin, though for a season we experience the unpleasant consequences of our sin and the loving discipline of our Father, we are led by the Gospel into the hope that we will be brought into His presence by the blood of Christ and we will look not only to His temple, but we will look upon His face.

First John 3:1-3 says it best:

> *See how great a love the Father has bestowed on us, that we would be called children of God; and such we are. For this reason the world does not know us, because it did not know Him. Beloved, now we are children of God, and it has not appeared as yet what we will be. We know that when He appears, we will be like Him, because we will see Him just as He is. And everyone who has this hope fixed on Him purifies himself, just as He is pure.*

If you do not know Jesus, then you do not have this hope. Ephesians 2:12 describes those who are separated from Christ as being "without hope and without God in the world." That is a dangerous place to be, a place of hopeless despair. But the Gospel offers you hope. Turn from your sin and call upon Jesus to save you if you never have before. Your sins have been dealt with in His death, and His resurrection is the surety of your salvation. His righteousness is your covering, and our Heavenly Father will transform you into His image by the power of the indwelling Holy Spirit. To turn away from Him is to discard the only real hope we have in exchange for the hollow and false hopes of wishful thinking.

---

[181] Hebrews 6:19-20.

XI

The Way Up
Jonah 2:5-7

"Water encompassed me to the point of death.
The great deep engulfed me, weeds were wrapped around my head.
I descended to the roots of the mountains. The earth with its bars
was around me forever, but You have brought up my life
from the pit, O LORD my God. While I was fainting away,
I remembered the LORD, and my prayer came to You,
into Your holy temple."

In the cockpit of every airplane is an instrument known as the "attitude indicator," also referred to as the "artificial horizon." This gyroscopic device tells the pilot whether he is climbing or descending, flying straight or banking into a turn. Even in broad daylight, one could be descending or climbing at a slight degree of incline without realizing it, so this instrument is essential. A typical artificial horizon is round, and the lower half of the circle is brown or black, indicating the ground, and the upper half is blue or white, indicating the sky.

A retired Air Force MP who had served in Vietnam once told me a story about what could go wrong if you ignore the artificial horizon indicator. One night, he said, a pilot was making an approach in a fighter jet to their base. It was one of those really dark nights when you can barely see your hand in front of your face. As the pilot was nearing the runway, the tower notified him that he was flying too fast and too low on his approach. The pilot seemed unconcerned because he said he didn't even see the runway lights, but he commented about how bright the stars were that night. Folks in the tower were confused, because they couldn't even see any stars in the sky. Suddenly, they realized that the pilot was flying upside down. The stars he thought he was seeing over his head were actually the runway lights. When they informed the pilot of this, he took a glance at the artificial horizon and realized his mistake. Panic struck the pilot, and he pulled his ejection handles. The canopy blasted off and his seat was thrust out of the aircraft. The explosive blast propelled the pilot directly into the ground below and he was killed.

There are situations in life in which it is of severe importance that we know the difference between the way up and the way down. As important as that difference is for a pilot to recognize, it is even more important when it comes to our spiritual lives. As Jonah would discover through his own ordeal, there are many steps one can take that lead downward, but there is only one way up. The downward path is one that leads us away from the Lord, while the upward path brings us closer to Him. So far, nearly every step Jonah had taken was downward. In Jonah 2:5-7, we see that he had descended nearly as low as he could go, and it was there that Jonah found the way up before it was too late.

We have all known Christians who have experienced what we commonly call "backsliding." Many of us have experienced this for ourselves. Backsliding occurs when a follower of Jesus makes a series of bad choices: neglecting spiritual disciplines, committing blatant acts of sin, distancing oneself from the accountability of Christian fellowship, avoiding God's word. The way of the backslider is one that leads down. In some Christian circles, it is believed that one can backslide so far as to actually lose one's salvation. When we take the whole counsel of God's Word into consideration, however, we become convinced that it is impossible for a true child of God to ever lose his or her salvation. Among the many passages of Scripture that assure us of this, we could cite John 10:27-29, in which Jesus says:

> *My sheep hear My voice, and I know them, and they follow Me; and I give eternal life to them, and they will never perish; and no one will snatch them out of My hand. My Father, who has given them to Me, is greater than all; and no one is able to snatch them out of the Father's hand.*

So, from what Jesus is saying here, we understand that a true follower of Jesus can never perish. His hold on those who are His is stronger than anything that we can do or anything that can be done to us. Therefore, while the true believer may backslide, he or she will, before it is too late, return to following Christ faithfully. But what of those who do not return before it is too late? Have they lost their salvation? No, according to what we read in God's word, we would understand that person to have never truly been a follower of Christ in the first place. They died lost because they never were saved. And for this reason, it is of the utmost importance for us to realize, after descending spiritually into whatever state of backsliddenness that we find ourselves, that there is a way up, but there is *only one* way up. Jonah discovered this. From his experiences, we too can learn this lesson. This is of infinite significance for ourselves, but also for those whom we know and encounter who are backslidden, that we may show them the way up. So, what is the way up?

I. We must realize the desperation of our condition.

In the summer of 2011, a 10-year-old girl was playing around in the shallow water of the ocean at Topsail Beach, North Carolina, when something grabbed her leg and pulled her down. She was in pain, but thought it was just someone playing around with her under the water. When a pool of blood began develop around her, her mother and a friend pulled her out of the water to discover a wide open gash in her leg. At the hospital, doctors removed a shark's tooth from her leg and told the family it was the worst bite they had seen. They had given no thought to the possibility that an afternoon of fun on the beach could be so dangerous and potentially deadly.[182] Several other shark bite stories along the North Carolina coast emerged over a short period of time after that news broke, leading some to believe that tourism in the area could be affected. But the reality of the matter is that swimming in the ocean always carries risks. Sharks can bite, jellyfish can sting, undertows and riptides can sweep a person under; you can even lacerate a foot on a broken seashell. But it is easy to ignore the dangers when you are having a good time. And that is

---

[182] Ramon Herrera, "Shark bites girl at North Topsail Beach." http://www.wwaytv3.com/2011/06/30/first-3-shark-bites-girl-north-topsail-beach. Accessed August 4, 2011.

the risk of backsliddenness as well. A person can be going along thinking that all is well in the midst of their fun and games and not realize the deadly dangers that encircle them.

In the opening verses of Jonah, God called the prophet to carry a message to one of Assyria's most prominent cities, saying, "Arise, go to Nineveh." In 1:3, we read that Jonah "rose up," and that is the last move that Jonah made in an upward direction. He did not arise to obey, but he "rose up to flee to Tarshish from the presence of the Lord." And every subsequent step Jonah took was downward. Notice in 1:3 that Jonah went *down* to Joppa. He went *down* into the ship. In 1:5, Jonah had gone *below* into the hold of the ship, lain *down* and fallen sound asleep. When the Lord sent the storm to halt Jonah's downward progress, he still did not return in repentance to the Lord, and so he went further down. The sailors threw him *down* into the sea. He describes the sea as *the deep* (2:3), and now in 2:6, he says that he *descended* to the roots of the mountains. He was *down* on the very floor of the Mediterranean Sea. His life hangs in the balance as he describes his condition as being "encompassed" by water "to the point of death." He was engulfed by the great deep. Seaweed was wrapped around his head. He saw his condition as desperate. In 2:2 he mentions the "depth of Sheol," which for a Hebrew person would mean the very throes of death. And here in 2:6 he says, "the earth with its bars was around me forever." That statement has given rise to numerous interpretations, but all of them agree that the situation Jonah describes here is one of inescapable desperation. He is in a situation in which he can do nothing to improve his condition. It is severe. Apart from God's intervention, he will be forced to lay in the bed which he has made by his own disobedience. And from that bed he will never rise unless the Lord rescues him.

Like Jonah, we may have come up against something unappealing in God's Word or some uncomfortable call that He has placed on our lives. In response, we disobey. Foolishly thinking that we may be improving our lives by disregarding God's word or disobeying His call, we are unaware that the steps we take are downward. As long as we think everything is okay, that things aren't really that bad, or that God will let us slide out of this, we are deceived. Backsliding might be common, but it is not "normal" for a Christian, and it is not okay. It is a big deal. It is dangerous. It is deadly. It is destructive. The way up from such a condition begins by realizing the desperation of the situation.

II. We must return to the Lord in repentance.

Several years ago, my father-in-law gave my wife a wonderful gift for Christmas: a GPS device. She has never been really good with directions. The best illustration of that probably comes from a time when she and a friend decided to take a trip to the beach. Several hours into the trip, it occurred to my wife that she did not usually travel through mountains in order to get to the beach. They had set out on the interstate traveling west instead of east. Realizing their error, they turned the car around and began traveling in the opposite direction. Now, let's suppose that they never made that U-turn. Eventually, they would have come to a beach. In about forty hours of driving time, they would have set foot on the sandy beaches of California, rather than the beaches of North Carolina, which should have only been about a four hour drive. Thankfully they saw the need to turn the car around, and they had the opportunity to make that U-turn.

When we speak of repentance, we are talking about a spiritual U-turn. It is the decisive turning from the direction of moving away from the Lord in sin to moving toward Him in faith and obedience. Thankfully, the Lord speaks to us from His word and the conviction of the Holy Spirit to make us aware of our need to turn around, and He gives us the opportunity in His grace to make this spiritual U-turn. All of us will sin, and all of us will experience seasons of compounded sin where one bad decision leads to another. But it does not have to be a fatal and final tragedy if we make the spiritual U-turn of repentance.

Jonah did this, and he recounts it in verse 7. After his long and downward spiral into destruction, he comes to rest on the floor of the sea. As his life was fainting away, he says, "I remembered the Lord." When we talk about remembering something, usually we mean that we have forgotten something, and then it returns to our minds. This is not the way the word is used in the Old Testament. The Hebrew concept of remembrance doesn't stand always in direct opposition to forgetting. In the account of Noah in Genesis 8, we read that "God remembered Noah." We mustn't think that

God ever forgot about Noah. Frank Page comments that the Hebrew term commonly used for "remember" in the Old Testament means "to act on the basis of knowledge."[183] When God "remembered" Noah, it means that God acted on the basis of what He knew about Noah and his situation in the ark. The same is true of Jonah. It is clear from the entire context of this book that Jonah never forgot about the Lord. He simply refused to act on what he knew to be true about God. But as he finds himself in the relentless grip of death, he sees the folly of his course of actions, and he turns again toward the Lord in repentance and acts on the truth that he knows about the Lord.

How did Jonah act toward the Lord on the basis of this knowledge? In his dying nanoseconds, he prayed. We do not know the exact words that he said, but the main thrust of it is recorded for us in 2:2—"*I called out of my distress to the Lord, ... I cried for help from the depth of Sheol.*" And that prayer that Jonah prayed came before the Lord. Jonah says, "My prayer came to You into Your holy temple." It is not necessary to think that Jonah means here the actual temple in Jerusalem, as if to suggest that his cry could be heard all the way from there. In fact, King David could speak of his prayers being heard by God in His temple when the Jerusalem temple had not even been built yet.[184] To speak of the Lord in His temple is to speak of the dwelling place of the Lord, whether an actual building is being referred to or not.

In John's Gospel, the eternal and divine Word of God is said to have "become flesh and dwelt among us" in the person of Jesus Christ. In the Greek text, the wording is literally that this Word became flesh and "tabernacled" among us. Jesus referred to His body as the temple of the Lord, the dwelling place of God. And on the basis of that temple being torn down and rebuilt in the death, burial, and resurrection of Jesus Christ, we can have confidence that our prayers come before the dwelling place of God. As long as life remains in us, though it may be fainting away, our prayer of repentance can rise to God in His temple through the Lord Jesus Christ where it is heard and answered.

---

[183] Page, 250.
[184] 2 Samuel 22:7

Our good news, the Gospel of Jesus Christ, is not that Jesus came to make good people better. The Gospel is that Jesus came to save sinners. That is what we are, and our constant struggle with sin does not come to an end the moment we come to faith in Him. When we were unbelievers, the Gospel came to us in our sinful state and beckoned us to turn from our sin in repentance and believe on the Lord Jesus Christ. And when we have done that and been saved by God's grace in Christ, our need for the Gospel does not go away. The believer needs the Gospel as much as the unbeliever, for that same call to repent and trust in Christ is as essential for us to live for Christ as it is for the unbeliever to turn to Him. As long as we ignore our need for repentance and refuse to remember the Lord and call upon Him, we continue to progress downward. The way up begins with realizing the desperation of our situation and returning to the Lord in repentance.

III. We must recognize the work of God's hand.

Survival experts sometimes give unrealistic advice. For instance, to prevent drowning, we will read that the most important thing is to not panic and flail and flop around. I imagine that no one has ever consciously thought about that advice when they were drowning. Anyone who realizes that he or she is drowning is going to panic and they are going to flail and flop. The best chance of survival in those situations is to be rescued by someone else. C. S. Lewis writes in *Mere Christianity*, "If I am drowning in a rapid river, a man who still has one foot on the bank may give me a hand which saves my life." Now, Lewis says, "Ought I to shout back (between my gasps), 'No, it's not fair! You have an advantage! You're keeping one foot on the bank'?" Lewis says this "advantage" that the man with one foot on the bank has "is the only reason why he can be of any use to me." And then he says these words which cut like a dagger into our proud hearts: "To what will you look for help if you will not look to that which is stronger than yourself?"[185]

Jonah has gone down, down, down. Death draws nearer with every passing second. His situation is desperate. Now, at the bottom of the sea, Jonah

---

[185] C. S. Lewis, *Mere Christianity*, 59.

realizes that there is nothing he can do to save himself. If he will not call out to God for help, then there is no help to be found! And so he calls out to God in a prayer of repentance, and it is at that moment that he says, "You have brought up my life from the pit O Lord my God." The "pit" was a common Hebrew expression used to describe death. The way up from such depths is not to *climb* but to be *lifted*. This is the first upward movement since Jonah "rose up" to flee from the Lord. God lifted Jonah *up* from that low point by way of a divinely appointed fish which swallowed him to rescue him (1:17).

Jonah recognized that it was the hand of God at work in rescuing and saving him, and without that saving hand he would be dead. The prayer of Jonah here in Chapter 2 is recorded from inside the belly of that fish. Surely, his environment is not comfortable. I imagine it smells bad, it is likely very hot, and he is likely surrounded by all manners of disgusting things. Uncomfortable as it is, Jonah is safe there inside the fish, having been lifted up by the grace of God from his desperate situation.

In verse 10, we will read that the Lord commanded the fish, and it vomited Jonah up onto the dry land. Imagine that with me. I was at the beach on vacation recently, and as I sat there watching the waves come and go, I thought about this text and what it might be like to see an enormous fish come there to the water's edge, open its mouth and vomit a living man out on to the sand. Suppose you were to see such a thing as that! Now, you watch that man begin to shake himself off: his skin looking leprous from the effects of the stomach acid of the great fish; he stinks to the high heavens; his clothing is tattered, and his hair is disheveled. Now suppose that man looks at you lounging in your beach chair, and he says, "Wow! Can you believe what I did? I am really something! I saved myself from drowning by crawling inside that big fish's mouth and keeping myself alive in his stomach! Have you ever seen the likes of me?"

I played that scenario through my mind as I sat on the beach, and I just started laughing out loud. How ridiculous! Jonah has done nothing to save himself. He couldn't! His rescue has been accomplished entirely by the grace of God! Apart from grace, the Lord would have been entirely just in letting him drown and decompose at the bottom of the sea because of his sinful disobedience. But in His grace, the Lord lifted Jonah up even though he didn't deserve it and could do nothing to help himself. This is not a case of God helping those who help themselves! There are such times when God won't do for you what He expects you to do for yourself, but there are some things you just cannot do. Saving yourself and restoring yourself to God is something that neither Jonah nor any of us can do for ourselves. Jonah can't take any credit for any of this. All of the credit, all of the glory of it, goes to God Himself, whose hand has lifted Jonah from his pitiful state. Jonah recognizes this as he says to the Lord, "You have brought up my life from the pit."

If you find yourself like Jonah, drifting down, down, down, you must recognize that there is only one way up. You won't bring yourself out of this. You can't do anything to rescue yourself. Your only hope is in the strong hand of God to lift you up. You must realize how desperate your situation is, and return to the Lord in repentance, calling out to Him for mercy and trusting that He is able to lift you up from the depths to which have fallen.

Do you have a friend or loved one who is backslidden? What advice are you giving them? "Stop this, do this, don't do that, start doing things this way!" You might as well cry out to a drowning man, "Stop drowning and swim for goodness sake!" It is impossible. The counsel we must give is rooted in the Gospel of Jesus Christ! Realize how deadly your sin is and cry out to God in repentance for His mercy and trust His power to rescue you! The good news by which God saves us is the good news that secures us to Him and restores us into right relationship with Him.

Jesus Christ took our sins upon Himself and carried them beneath the sea of God's wrath on our behalf. On the cross as He died, He descended to the depths of judgment for our sake. The earth, with its bars, was around Him forever, or so it appeared as the stone was sealed over His tomb. But God the Father has brought His life up from the pit, and with Him He has brought up the lives of all who trust in Him. In Jonah's day, believers called out to God on the basis of all that He had promised. Today, all those promises have come to pass in Jesus. Because of His sinless life, His sacrificial death, and His glorious resurrection, sinners can be redeemed from the pit of sin and death and enter into a personal relationship by which we can speak of God as "O Lord *my* God." Perhaps someone reading these words has never called out to Jesus to save them. If that person is you, my prayer is that you would see the desperation of your situation, call out to God in repentance and faith, and trust the promise of His Gospel to save you. Among those of us who have been saved, we are never out of danger of spiritual decline. Like Jonah, deliberate sin, neglect of spiritual disciplines, or withdrawal from Christian fellowship can lead us down, down, down into a miserable, backslidden state. And in that moment, the only way up is the same good news we first believed. Realize the desperation of your condition. Continued spiritual decline may be more severe than we imagine for it may indicate that we have never truly been saved! But the way up is the same in either case. Turn to the Lord in repentance, and call out to Him to lift you up from the pit, and trust that He can. If you will be rescued, He must! He is able if you call out to Him in true repentance and faith.

In Revelation 2, we read the words of Jesus to His church in Ephesus. The entire church had backslidden. He says, "I have this against you, that you have left your first love." And so the counsel of the Lord is just what we have seen here in Jonah's situation: "remember from where you have fallen, and repent and do the deeds you did at first." When we remember from where we have fallen, that close and intimate fellowship we once knew as we walked in the light of the Lord, we see how severe our situation is. When we repent, we return to the Lord with a fresh recommitment to Him, serving Him with the deeds that we once did in the past. And we find ourselves being pulled up by His mercy and grace. Imagine what the world would look like if all the churches of Jesus Christ would experience this kind of revival? May it begin in us today! But it cannot begin in *us* as a whole until it begins in each of us as individuals. So, before we pray, "Lord, begin this in us," we must be willing to pray, "Begin this in me, O Lord my God! Lift me from my backsliding and restore me to you. I have been sinking down, down, down. O Lord my God, lift me up as I return to You!"

XII

Clinging to Idols, Forfeiting Grace
Jonah 2:8

"Those who regard vain idols forsake their faithfulness"

It was nearly midnight when we crossed the border on foot from one South Asian country into another. Once we were past the border station, nine of us and all of our luggage were piled into a pickup truck to head toward our hotel. As the lights of the border station faded quickly behind us, we were engulfed in darkness: no streetlights; no houselights; no shop lights; just darkness. The first light I remember seeing was glowing faintly red in the distance ahead. As we drew nearer, the red lights grew brighter, and as we passed by we could see the gigantic statue of a red, almost human-formed idol standing at the entrance to a Hindu temple. I felt like we were looking into the gates of hell itself, with Satan standing guard at the front door. Of course, over the next two weeks we would see many temples and many idols, and many expressions of idol worship, but seeing that one so soon after we entered the country was enough to alert us all that we were encountering spiritual forces of darkness in a way that some of us had never experienced. Several times during our journey, I was reminded of the account of Paul's visit to Athens when his "spirit was being provoked within him as he was observing the city full of idols" (Acts 17:16).

Now, of course, when we think of idols and idol worship, we tend to think of people who look different from us, who live in far away places and speak strange languages, bowing down before crude statues in a hut or golden statues in a magnificent temple. And certainly, that sort of idolatry is as rampant in the world today as it ever has been. But have we paused to consider that our society is filled with idols of its own? Tim Keller writes in his book *Counterfeit Gods:*

> *We may not physically kneel before the statue of Aphrodite, but many young women today are driven into depression and eating disorders by an obsessive concern over their body image. We may not actually burn incense to Artemis, but when money and career are raised to cosmic proportions, we perform a kind of child sacrifice, neglecting family and community to achieve a higher place in business and gain more wealth and prestige.*[186]

Of course, we could list countless other examples of contemporary idols that are worshiped in America today. In fact, as Keller says, "Anything can be an idol, and everything has been an idol. ... *Any*thing in life can serve as an idol, a God-alternative, a counterfeit god."[187]

In the First Commandment, the Lord said, "I am the LORD your God ... You shall have no other gods before me" (Exodus 20:2-3). In the Second Commandment, He said, "You shall not make for yourself an idol, or any likeness of what is in heaven above or on the earth beneath or in the water under the earth. You shall not worship them or serve them." (Exodus 20:4-5). Notice that carefully: God clearly forbids us from worshiping or serving any likeness of what is in heaven, or what is on earth, or what is in the sea. That means *everything* in the whole of existence. Our worship and our service are to be reserved for the Lord Himself, and Him alone. Anything other than that is idolatry. It could be argued that the remaining eight Commandments are violated only after we violate the first two.

John Calvin famously wrote nearly 500 years ago that, "man's nature, so to speak, is a perpetual factory of idols."[188] We find this to be true in Scripture and in our experience. There seem to be no limits on what human beings will attach a pseudo-religious devotion, rendering worship and service in idolatrous ways. These idols are not always tangible or visible. In Ezekiel 14:3, we read of men who have "set up idols in their hearts." So, though we may not see any statues or images, altars or temples, we must investigate our hearts to find if any idols have been established there.

---

[186] Timothy Keller, *Counterfeit Gods* (New York: Dutton, 2009), xii.
[187] Ibid., xvi.
[188] John Calvin, *Institutes of the Christian Religion*, ed. John T. McNeill, trans. Ford Lewis Battles (Philadelphia: Westminster, 1960), 1:108.

In Jonah 2:8, we read a statement couched in Jonah's prayer from inside the belly of the fish that speaks to idol worship. We might pause to consider what in the world this statement has to do with anything else in the book of Jonah. Jonah had fled from God's calling because he did not want to take a message of warning to a city which was known for its rampant idolatry. In his journey to get away from God, he had crossed paths with a group of sailors who were just as idolatrous as those in Nineveh. As the storm raged, they were calling out to a spectrum of false deities for relief to no avail. As Jonah spoke to them about His God, from Whom he was attempting to flee, they were gloriously converted to the worship of the one true God. And as Jonah sank to the depths of the Mediterranean Sea, I believe that Jonah became aware of idols in his own heart. He had chosen to serve himself and his own interests rather than the Lord. His sense of faithfulness to his country had trumped his sense of faithfulness to God. His own prejudices, his own safety, and his own pleasure were the objects of his complete devotion. But as death drew nearer while he was sinking, it seems that Jonah became aware that he was just as idolatrous as those sailors had been and just as idolatrous as Nineveh was. Verses 8 and 9 become a prayer of repentance for Jonah as he forsakes his own idolatry and recommits himself to the worship and service of the Lord. When he confesses in verse 9, "Salvation is from the Lord," he seems to recognize that he could no longer protest the Lord's intention to save idol-worshipers in His grace and mercy, for he had received such a great salvation in the midst of his idolatry as well.

Like Jonah, each of us must come to realize our own tendency to establish idols in our hearts, and we must recognize our need for the salvation that comes from the Lord in His sovereign grace. When we experience that grace, we are moved with compassion toward the multitudes of people in the world who are also enslaved to idols. We consider those desperate South Asian people who march in and out of that grotesque temple to make offerings before the glowing red statue. We consider the West Africans who make sacrifices beneath the branches of their village's sacred tree. And we consider a multitude of educated and enlightened Americans and Westerners who likewise make offerings and sacrifices of worship to other idols that have been erected in their hearts and in our culture. In this brief verse, Jonah 2:8, there are two key ideas that we must understand about idolatry.

I. We must understand the act of idolatry.

Since the middle of the 19th Century, anthropologists, sociologists, psychologists, and other specialists have attempted to explain the undeniable fact that religious ideas and practices are found in every human culture. Today, the most common assumption is that idolatry, the worship of images or objects found in creation, was the most primitive and crude form of religion. It is widely believed that as humans evolved, religious beliefs underwent changes to more sophisticated forms, culminating in the development of monotheistic religion—the belief and worship of one transcendent divine being. And since those who hold this view believe that evolution is continuing, they believe that eventually, human beings will abandon even monotheism and move on to a system of belief that does not include any notions of deities or a spiritual realm at all. But the actual historical evidence seems to fall more in line with what we would expect as we take the Bible as our guide. It seems that all human cultures have a religion that has not *evolved* but *devolved* from monotheism or something close to it into a sophisticated structure of many gods, many rituals, and an elaborate hierarchy of priests, shamans, medicine men, or the like. That makes sense given that every human culture descends from the family of Noah. Every culture and nation and people had its start with a patriarch who knew the truth of God because he would have learned it from Noah or his three sons. Over time, rather than maintaining faith in this one true God, people turned instead to idols.[189]

In the Bible, we find that even Israel itself is a case study in this. Abraham was converted from an idolatrous background to faith in the one true God. But by the time his descendants had been in Egypt for 400 years, this God was all but a forgotten memory to them. So God spoke through Moses to remind the people of who He was, and He led them out by His mighty signs and wonders. Make no mistake that when Israel passed through the

---

[189] The case for "original monotheism" is well advanced by Winfried Corduan in *Neighboring Faiths* (Downers Grove, Ill.: InterVarsity, 1998).

waters of the Red Sea, they were thoroughgoing monotheists. But, when Moses went up on Mount Sinai for forty days, the people grew impatient waiting for his return, and they said to Aaron, "Make us a god!" And so Aaron made an idol of gold and declared to the people, "This is your god, O Israel, who brought you up from the land of Egypt." Now, this was most certainly *NOT* the God who brought them out of Egypt! But the people longed for something they could see and touch to worship. And throughout the rest of Israel's history prior to the Babylonian Captivity, Israel repeatedly abandoned their faithfulness to God in exchange for seasons of idolatry. When Jonah was called to Nineveh, the Northern Kingdom of Israel was on the brink of divine judgment for their idolatry. Part of Jonah's reluctance to go to Nineveh may have sprung from his suspicion that if God spared Assyria, He would use them to annihilate Israel. And in time, history would prove that this hunch was correct.

Idolatry enters into the experience of modern people in much the same way, and none of us are exempt. Jonah describes idolatry here as *regarding vain idols*. To *regard* an idol in this way is to place one's trust in it, to make sacrifices to it, to elevate it above all else. In other words, we begin to worship it. The very words Jonah uses in verse 9 to describe his recommitment to the Lord (sacrifice, thanksgiving, vows) are the things that people begin to do in regard to their idols. But where does it start?

Idolatry begins when we get in our minds the wrong idea of heaven. I don't mean the wrong idea of the place we go when we die, but a wrong idea of the ultimate attainment, the ultimate satisfaction, the ultimate glory. God created us with yearnings that only He can satisfy and with a desire to behold something that is uniquely found in Him. That is what heaven is. The most glorious thing about heaven is that not that we get heaven, but that *in heaven* we get *God Himself*; we see Him face-to-face and dwell in His glorious presence there. Idolatry begins when we lose sight of this and begin to think that our ultimate longings and desires can be satisfied somewhere else, with something or someone else. Whatever that is, it becomes a fake-heaven in our minds. You want to know what fake-heaven looks like? Just browse the magazine stands in the stores. Fake-heaven is a beautiful face, a nice body, an exotic beach, a fast car, a winning team, a nicer house, a newer gadget, mastery of a game or a skill, and so on. And we look at those glossy images and we think, "Ah. If only I had that! Life would be complete if I looked like that, or if my spouse looked like that, or if I had that house, or if I could live in that place, or if I could do that, or if I could own that thing," and so on.

Now, if there is a fake-heaven, then there is a fake-hell. And fake-hell looks like the opposite of fake-heaven. Fake-hell can be being fat, being ugly, being alone, being un-cool, being dumb, being unsuccessful, not having the things you want, and so-on. So, a person has the wrong idea of heaven and the wrong idea of hell, and that's where the idol comes in. The idol is a fake-god that a person begins to trust to save them from fake-hell and take them to fake-heaven. You can call them "functional saviors." So, to save them from fat-hell, a person may put their faith in a diet or an exercise regime. To save them from ugly-hell, a person will trust in a cosmetic, a surgery, or a wardrobe. To save them from dumb-hell, a person may trust in an education, or in some books or ideas. To save them from single-hell, the person may begin to trust in a person or a particular method of attracting a mate. To save them from poor-hell, the person trusts in money, or investments, or their career. We could go on and on, but the point is that the functional savior, the fake-god, begins to become the object of a person's trust and faith to get them what they want and save them from what they dread.

This is exactly how idolatry has taken shape throughout human history. For example, when people worshiped fertility gods, it was because they had an idea that the ultimate fulfillment in life came in having children, and the greatest fear was being barren. So, someone says they know of a deity that promises to give children to people, and they begin to trust, to worship, and to serve it. The same thing happens today when someone think that success is the ultimate meaning of life. They fear failure to the extent that they begin to worship their career, their education, or their money, in order to get success and avoid failure. That is but one example of how modern idolatry is the same as it has always been.

So, who is an idolater? Is it someone who bows before a statue with a sacrifice? Sometimes it is, but sometimes it is me and you, or any other person in the world. It may be that today, some of us will be ensnared by idolatry without even knowing it. So how do we discover the idols in our lives? Ask yourself questions like this: What do I long for most passionately? What do I care about most deeply? What do I think about most often? What am I most motivated and driven by? What do I give myself most fully to? Where do I run for comfort? What am I most afraid of? What do I complain about the most? What angers or frustrates me most? How do I define myself to others? What do I brag about the most? What do I want more than anything else? What have I sacrificed the most for? Whose approval do I seek more than anyone else's? What do I treasure the most?

Do you see how these questions expose the idols in our lives? Do you see how the Bible would instruct our lives in all of these areas? Our deepest longings should be for the Lord Himself! Our greatest motivation should be His glory! Our greatest comfort should be His fatherly love! Our greatest sacrifice should be for His Kingdom! His approval of us should be infinitely more important than that of any other! Our greatest fear should be being separated from Him! Our boasting, our identity, and our treasure should be wrapped up in our relationship with Him! And when God, His kingdom, His gospel, His saving work in Jesus Christ, begin to be replaced as the answers to our great questions, they are replaced by idols.

God loves us too much to allow us to find satisfaction in something that is not Him. Heaven is too precious and too glorious for us to find fulfillment and glory in any fake-heaven. Hell is too dreadful for us to think that, when we have escaped fake-hell, we have attained the ultimate deliverance. The real God wants you to have the real joy of real heaven and to escape the real horror of real hell. And that brings us to the tragic consequence of idolatry.

II. We must understand the consequence of idolatry.

At this point, someone may wonder, "Is it *always* idolatry to want or to have something?" I mean, education is good, good health is a good thing, marriage is good, and money is good, isn't it? Of course it is! The problem is how we attach ourselves to the good things, and we allow a *good*-thing to become a *god*-thing. We begin to focus more on the good gifts of God rather than God Himself, who is the giver of good gifts. We begin to worship the creation more than the creator, as Paul says in Romans 1. But the problem is that these are *vain idols*. The phrase here in Jonah has been translated by some as *empty nothings*. They cannot deliver. Oh sure, they may be able to take you from being poor to being rich, or from being fat to being thin, or from being dumb to being smart, but they fail to deliver the satisfaction that they promised. The world is full of people who have gotten what they wanted, escaped what they feared, and yet still found that they were unsatisfied. It has all been an *empty nothing*. And we are left in the despair and discouragement of having wasted our time, our money, our relationships, and in the end our lives, on something that cannot and will not satisfy.

Jonah has learned through his ordeal that *"those who regard vain idols"* have forsaken something. But what did they forsake? The New American Standard Bible (NASB) says that they have forsaken *"their faithfulness."* This would seem to imply that they have failed to be faithful to the Lord, and obviously this is true. If you are using other English translations, they may read somewhat differently. The King James Version (KJV) says that they forsake "their own mercy." The English Standard Version (ESV) says that they "forsake their hope of steadfast love." The New International Version (NIV) says that they "forfeit the grace that could be theirs." In these translations, the emphasis is not on what the idolater fails to *do* (as the NASB implies) but rather on what the idolater will fail to *receive* from God (mercy, steadfast love, grace). All of these translations contain theological truth, but which of them best expresses the intent of the author? The Hebrew word that is translated as *faithfulness, grace, mercy,* or *steadfast love* in our English translations is an important one: *hesed.* It is used at least 250 times in the Old Testament, and is most commonly translated as *lovingkindness.* Most often, the word is used to describe God's affections and actions toward humanity. In Psalm 144, David says That the Lord Himself *is* his *hesed.* It is God's *hesed,* His lovingkindness, that manifests itself to us as grace, mercy, faithfulness, and steadfast love. *Hesed* is what salvation from sin is all about. God rescues sinful human beings because He loves us, because He is rich in grace and mercy, and because He is faithful to His promises. So, while the NASB is theologically correct in saying that idolaters forsake their faithfulness to

God, the point here seems to rest on the forsaking of such a great salvation that comes from the Lord in His lovingkindness.

Verse 9 says, "Salvation is from the Lord!", but those who cling to idols forfeit that salvation which is so freely offered to them. They turn away from the Lord, who alone can save, to empty nothings which can never save. And this is the consequence of idolatry. Our idols may bring us a fleeting and temporary satisfaction in the thing we want, but that satisfaction is brief and hollow. Moreover, idols cannot deliver that which we most desperately *need*. Idols lie and tell us that life is all about our success, our beauty, our possessions, our intelligence, our coolness, our power. They tell us that if we will work harder, try harder, do better, then we will be okay. But God tells us a different story, a better story, a true story that we call the Gospel, the good news.

The Gospel tells us that our greatest need is not acceptance, beauty, power, or money. The Gospel tells us that our greatest need is God, and we are cut off from Him. We are not cut off because we are too ugly to be loved, too weak to be powerful, too poor to be rich, or too lame to be cool. The Gospel tells us that we are cut off because we are too sinful to be in God's presence. The solution is not to do more, to be better, or to try harder. The Gospel tells us that the solution is not something *we do* but something that *God has done* for us. In His lovingkindness, His grace and mercy, God has become one of us in the person of Jesus Christ. He has lived the righteous life that we cannot live, and in His death, He became a sacrificial substitute for us. Jesus has borne in His own body on the cross the wrath that the righteous justice of God requires, not for His own sins (for He had none) but for ours – for my sins and for yours. And He has conquered death through His resurrection, and ever lives to save those who turn from sin to trust in Him alone as Lord and Savior. The Gospel tells us that God cleanses us from our sins through the blood of Christ, and He covers us with the righteousness of Christ. He comes to dwell within us in the person of His Holy Spirit to empower us and to transform us. And He gives to us eternal life, not so we can attain heaven as the goal of all, but so that, in heaven, we come face-to-face with the one true God in whom all of our deepest longings are satisfied forever.

Salvation is from the Lord. And He offers it to all who will turn to Him and call upon Him. But many will choose to cling to their idols, and in so doing, they forfeit the steadfast and faithful love of God that alone can save us. Hebrews 2:3 warns us: "How will we escape if we neglect so great a salvation?" Jesus said, "What will it profit a man if he gains the whole world and forfeits his soul? Or what will a man give in exchange for his soul?" (Matt. 16:26). He said, "No one can serve two masters; for either he will hate the one and love the other, or he will be devoted to one and despise the other. You cannot serve God and wealth" (Matt. 6:24). The Apostle Paul said, "Do not be idolators," and "beloved, flee from idolatry" (1 Cor 10:7, 14). Otherwise, by clinging to your idols, you forsake the grace of God that can save you. Believers, do not think you are immune to idols. They woo you to turn away from the grace that is saving you. It was, after all, to us who believe upon Jesus that the Apostle John wrote, "Little children, guard yourselves from idols" (1 John 5:21).

XIII

Salvation is From the Lord
Jonah 2:9-10

"But I will sacrifice to You With the voice of thanksgiving.
That which I have vowed I will pay. Salvation is from the LORD."
Then the LORD commanded the fish,
and it vomited Jonah up onto the dry land.

Language can be a tricky thing. Words have shades of meaning, and sometimes we use words to express ourselves in ways that make perfect sense to ourselves but confuse our hearers, even when we speak the same language. One Sunday many years ago, a church member said to me, "After church, come to my house for dinner." I told her I would be there! Around 1:45 that afternoon, she called to ask why we weren't there. I didn't realize that when she said "dinner," she meant "lunch." I thought she meant "dinner," you know, like you eat at night. When she said, "after church," I assumed she meant the evening service. In my mind, there was no difference between dinner and supper—they both referred to the evening meal. I learned that day that dinner means supper, unless it's Sunday. On Sunday, dinner means lunch. Now I know, so if any of you want to invite me over for dinner, or supper, or lunch, I will be there and I won't be late!

Sometimes Christians can be guilty of using language that confuses our hearers. A few years ago, I asked a man if he had trusted Christ as His Savior, and he said, "That depends on the meaning of the word 'trust.'" I suddenly began to wonder if I had stumbled into a congressional hearing or something. Another case happened when I came to know Christ. I was asked by my pastor if I wanted to give my life to Jesus and to receive Him as my Lord and Savior. I accepted the offer with great joy! A few days later, someone said to me, "Hey, I heard you got saved!" I was taken aback. I had not heard that term used in connection with my experience with Jesus. So I said, "Saved? Saved from what?" But as it was explained to me, I was nodding my head in agreement and said, "Yes, that is exactly what happened to me! I got saved!"

When we talk about salvation, someone could get easily confused. They may think, "Saved from what?" In their minds, being saved is something that happens to people who are buried under the rubble of an earthquake, or who are drowning, or who are being chased by a swarm of killer bees or something like that. And even in so-called Christian circles, there is some confusion about what it means to be saved. There are some who believe and teach that Jesus saves us from all poverty or from all sickness. In their view, a poor or sickly person is someone who has not exercised the right amount or the right kind of saving faith in Jesus. But these kinds of things are not what the Gospel, the good news of Jesus Christ, promises us—at least not immediately in the here and now. The Gospel does assure us that a day is coming when we will be set free from sickness and poverty and the other hardships of life in this fallen world, but those matters are not primary in the Gospel; they are secondary at best. When the Gospel promises salvation to those who believe on Jesus, the primary idea is that we are saved from our sin and from the eternal consequences of sin.

The truth we find in Scripture is validated in our everyday experience: we are all sinners by nature and by choice. Romans 3:23 says that all have sinned and fallen short of the glory of God, and Romans 3:10 says that there is none righteous, not even one. This sin separates us from God, as stated in Isaiah 59:2, "Your iniquities have made a separation between you and your God, and your sins have hidden His face from you so that He does not hear." Since Romans 6:23 tells us that the wages of sin is death, the person who dies in his or her sin dies separated from God and will not enter His presence. Rather, that individual will suffer the torment of eternal separation from God in that horrible place the Bible calls hell. There His infinite justice will be experienced as His holy wrath is poured out against sin. It is described in Scripture as a lake of fire, spoken of in Revelation 20 and 21 as "the second death." Now, as uncomfortable as these facts are to reckon with, the fact is that this is what each of us deserve because of our sins. This is what it means to be lost.

This sounds like bad news, not good news. But the Gospel is good news. In fact, it is *very* good news. The Gospel is good news because it tells us that though we deserve this horrible penalty for our sins, God has made a way of escape, a way of salvation. In the person of Jesus Christ, God has come to dwell among us. Jesus lived the righteous and sinless life that God requires of us all, and in His death, He has become our substitute. He has borne our sins on the cross, and He has borne the wrath that our sins deserve. He has overcome sin and death through His resurrection from the dead, and He offers us forgiveness of our sins, the covering of His perfect righteousness, and eternal life in the presence of God if we will turn from sin and trust in Him. And this is what it means to be saved.

In these verses, Jonah says that salvation is *from the Lord*. Now, in Jonah's circumstance it is easy to see that the salvation of which he speaks includes a physical rescue from his certain death beneath the waves of the sea. God has miraculously saved him by sending the great fish to swallow and preserve him. But Jonah is not unaware of his need for a spiritual salvation as well. He has recognized that his rebellion from the Lord testifies strongly against his spiritual well-being. It is not that he has lost his salvation, for as we have examined several times in our study of Jonah, this is impossible. Rather, it is that Jonah's stubborn refusal to obey the Lord has suggested the possibility that he has never been spiritually saved at all. He has heard the call of the Lord to go to Nineveh, where the Lord desires to save a pagan people from their sins and the judgment they will face because of their sins. But Jonah was too hard-hearted to have compassion on these lost souls. He has encountered a group of idolatrous sailors who were eager to turn to the Lord for this salvation. And the experience of all of this has taught Jonah the important lesson that salvation is from the Lord. In his ordeal we see a wonderful picture of what it truly means to be saved.

I. Salvation originates with the Lord.

There is a song that we often sing that says, "I have decided to follow Jesus." I like that song, and you probably do too. But when I stop to think about the moment I believed upon Jesus, I do not recall there being any deliberation in my mind about whether or not I would choose to believe this. I woke up one morning and I didn't believe in Jesus. By 9:00 that night, I did. Was it because I decided to believe in Him? Or was it because I suddenly realized that I could not deny it any longer? C. S. Lewis writes of his own conversion in similar terms. The story goes that he and his brother set out for the zoo one morning. Lewis was riding in the sidecar of his brother's motorcycle. He recalls, "When we set out I did not believe that Jesus Christ is the Son of God, and we reached the zoo I did. Yet I had not exactly spent the journey in thought. Nor in great emotion. ... It was more like when a man, after long sleep, still lying motionless in bed, becomes aware that he is now awake."[190]

I have come to the conclusion that belief is rarely the result of a decision. I am convinced that belief is something that happens to you. On Tuesday afternoon, August 23, 2011, at ten minutes until 2:00, I was in my office and felt a rumbling that lasted for about fifteen seconds. My first thought was *not* that we had just experienced an earthquake. I thought there was some heavy machinery at work on the property beside of our church. I happened to be talking to my father on the phone at the time, and I said, "That's odd, the building is shaking!" My dad lives an hour away from me. He said, "That's funny, my house is shaking too." The plausibility of an earthquake was beginning to be more attractive at this point. I looked on Twitter and saw posts from friends all up and down the East Coast saying that they had felt a shaking as well. I quickly pulled up the website of the U.S. Geological Survey. There I saw the indicator that a 5.8 magnitude earthquake had struck in Virginia, and I could no longer deny that the shaking I had felt was indeed an earthquake. I didn't *decide* to believe it. Belief overcame me and I could no longer deny it.

This is what happens in salvation. The faith involved in salvation is not something that a person chooses to exercise. According to Scripture, human beings are incapable of exercising this faith on their own. Man is dead in trespasses and sin (Eph 2:1), and the faith that is exercised in God's saving work in Jesus is supplied to us as a gift of His grace at the moment in which God saves us (Eph 2:8-9). It is not the result of a

---

[190]C. S. Lewis, *Surprised by Joy.* In *The Inspirational Writings of C. S. Lewis* (New York: Inspirational Press, 1994), 130.

decision. It is something that happens in our soul as a result of God's sovereign work in salvation. This is what Jonah is talking about when he says, "Salvation is from the Lord." He is talking about the origin of salvation. It originates in the Lord who, in His sovereign power and grace, and for reasons of His own choosing, saves sinners who are unworthy of saving.

Jonah had seen the sailors. There was nothing in them that moved or prompted God to save them. He saved them because He chose to in His mercy and grace. And Jonah had experienced this for himself. He had done nothing to earn the favor of a divine rescue as he sank to a watery death. On the contrary, Jonah knew that what he had done was worthy of death. But salvation came in the form of a fish, appointed in the sovereign grace of God to rescue Jonah. Jonah did not decide to turn to God in faith to plead for salvation. He did not decide to climb into the fish's mouth. God had determined to save Jonah, and from the inside of the fish, Jonah could no longer deny that the Lord was a saving God who rescues sinners by His mercy. He could no longer refuse to go to Nineveh, for if God could save sailors who worshiped idols and prophets who ran away from their calling, He could save a pagan city as well.

Who are we to say who God can and cannot save? Our mission is not to decide this, but rather to proclaim to a lost world the glorious gospel of Jesus Christ, which the Apostle Paul says *is* the power of God unto salvation to those who believe (Romans 1:16). As we make this truth known, the Holy Spirit will work in His sovereign grace to draw some to believe in a way that they can neither deny nor resist.

Salvation originates in the Lord. For Jonah the vessel of salvation was a divinely appointed fish that rescued him from drowning and preserved his life. But God has not chosen to send a fish to save us. He has chosen to send His Son, the Lord Jesus. His very name, *Yeshua* in the Hebrew language, means "The Lord Saves." His Hebrew name is here in this very verse. Salvation is from the Lord. Yeshua is from the Lord, and He is salvation for those who believe on Him.

II. Salvation transforms those who are saved.

I love watching this television show called *Overhaulin'*. On this show, a crew of expert mechanics sets up a fake car theft. While the owner goes through the emotional ups and downs of dealing with a stolen car, the crew takes a week and transforms the car from whatever state they found it in to a completely overhauled masterpiece. It gets a new paint job, custom body modifications, and an all new interior. When they finally reveal the overhauled car to the owner (who still thinks their old clunker has been stolen), their reaction is predictable. Most of them find it hard to believe that it is the same car. It looks better than they ever imagined. But the real surprise comes when they open the hood and see a brand new, top of the line, high performance engine. The car has been radically transformed and will never again be like it once was. And the car owner has done nothing to bring this about. They never got their hands greasy, they didn't turn a wrench, and they didn't pay a dime. It is done as a completely free gift. All the owner has to do is get in the car at the end of the show and drive away in his or her overhauled car.

Today, all around you are people who have been spiritually overhauled because they have been saved by God's grace through faith in Jesus Christ. This is not just an external change, like a new paint job. There is a completely new power source at work in the person! The Holy Spirit has come into that person's life in a powerful way and He is transforming them. They haven't done anything to earn or deserve this. They didn't pay for it, and they didn't work for it. This new life has been given to them by God's grace in Christ. Cost nothing; required nothing; but a transformation has begun in them which will cause them to never be the same.

In the beginning of verse 9, Jonah says, "I will sacrifice to You with the voice of thanksgiving. That which I have vowed I will pay." He is committing himself to a life of worship and service to the Lord. Now, it is wrong to think that this commitment is the reason why the Lord has saved him. His salvation has occurred already, but he speaks of these works that he will do in the future tense. Salvation did not come by any works on Jonah's part, but solely by the grace of God. Jonah is keenly aware that "salvation is from the Lord." But though Jonah was not saved by his works, his salvation had an effect on him that produced a change of heart that led to a change of life. Because of the workings of salvation by grace in his life, Jonah has committed himself to worship and serve the living God.

Prior to the Protestant Reformation, many within the Church were confused about the relationship between works and salvation. As a young Catholic scholar, Martin Luther began to see a growing discrepancy between the teachings and practice of Roman Catholicism and the teachings of Scripture. One of his primary concerns, indeed the single most important factor that led him to post the 95 Theses, was the sale of indulgences. An Archbishop had circulated a letter to the churches that instructed the clergy to offer to the people an indulgence in exchange for a monetary contribution to the church for the construction of St. Peter's Basilica in Rome. The most prominent preacher of these ideas was Johan Tetzel, who proclaimed that "all who confess and in penance put alms into the coffer … will obtain complete remission of all their sins."[191] Luther was irate as he saw the impoverished people of Germany giving all they had to the church for this promise which had no basis whatsoever in God's Word. The people were being financially broken by the church, and no spiritual benefit was gained at all by them in exchange. So Luther set out to make clear, wherever he had influence, the truth of God concerning salvation by grace alone through faith alone, and the relationship between salvation and works. Luther was convinced of the truth of Scripture by passages like Ephesians 2:8-9, which says that it is "by grace that you have been saved through faith; and that not of yourselves, it is the gift of God; not as a result of works, so that no one may boast."

Luther rightly proclaimed that salvation comes by grace through faith, and that works have no part to play in making a person righteous. But Luther also knew that it was an error to say that one can be saved and have no works to validate his or her salvation. He said, "Works themselves do not justify him before God, but he does the works out of spontaneous love in

---

[191] Albert of Hohenzollern, Archbishop of Mainz, "Summary Instructions for Indulgence Preachers," and John Tetzel, "A Sermon," in Hans J. Hillerbrand, *The Protestant Reformation* (rev. ed., New York: Harper, 2009), 14-21.

obedience to God."[192] In other words, though we are not saved by our works, once we are saved, we work in the power of the Holy Spirit, so that it becomes evident to others and even to ourselves that we are saved. This is exactly what the Apostle Paul says in Ephesians 2:10, after declaring emphatically that we are saved by grace through faith and not by works, that "we are Christ's workmanship created in Christ Jesus to do good works."

So, salvation has this transforming effect upon the saved. It is not received by works but it produces works in us. Like Jonah, once we have been saved through faith in Christ, the worship and service of Christ become priorities for us, as the Holy Spirit within us prompts and empowers us. Praise and worship given to the God who is worthy is what Jonah's words about sacrifice and thanksgiving are all about. We do not bring to God an animal sacrifice as Jonah may have, for the blood of bulls and goats can add nothing to the shed blood of Jesus Christ, who is the ultimate and final sacrifice for sin. Those ancient sacrifices were given as an act of worship before a worthy God, and throughout each day you and I may make worshipful sacrifices to God with thanksgiving for His saving grace. As we cling to the sacrifice of Christ for our redemption, we make sacrifices of our own. Vocal sacrifices of praise; moral sacrifices of denying ourselves in moments of temptation; obedient sacrifices of proclaiming His truth in love to others; these and others are the sacrifices that we joyfully and thankfully render to the Lord. The fulfillment of vows speaks to our service to Him. Serving God in tangible ways that have no other aim but to bring Him glory and advance His Kingdom; serving God by serving our brothers and sisters in Christ and the least of humanity in ways that meet their needs; serving God in ways that no one else sees, and for no other reward than the applause of heaven; these are our vows of service to God. Because He has saved us with such a gracious salvation, we will pay these vows. This is how salvation transforms the saved.

---

[192] Martin Luther, "The Freedom of a Christian," in Hillerbrand, 47.

III. Salvation is leading us toward a triumphant end.

When I was translating the book of Jonah from Hebrew into English at Seminary, we were not allowed to use our English Bibles as helps. We simply had to translate word by word often without knowledge of what the verse was supposed to say. In a familiar story like Jonah, you kind of know what is coming, and when I got to verse 10 I remember thinking, "OK, this is where the fish spits Jonah out." So I was translating along, a word and a phrase at a time, "And he spoke ... the Lord spoke ... the Lord spoke to the fish ... the Lord spoke to the fish and it ... what? What did it do?" It was a word I had not encountered in my translations or vocabulary studies before: *vayaq*. So I began to scour the lexicons. I guess you expect to find something sophisticated in these dusty old volumes filled with brilliant wisdom. And there it was, the root *qyay*, meaning "to vomit." When you see that word "vomit" in your English Bible you might wonder, "What does that mean in Hebrew?" It means vomit.

What was the triumphant end of Jonah's experience of salvation? He became fish vomit. And that is glorious. You say, "It doesn't sound glorious." Oh but it is! You see, for Jonah to be vomited, he had to be swallowed up. And if he hadn't been swallowed up he would have died. And if he had died, he would have died in a state of spiritual rebellion and only God knows what his fate would have been. Might he have perished? We can but speculate. But God saved him by His wondrous grace. That fish that God had appointed swallowed Jonah, and Jonah was miraculously kept alive in the belly of that beast for three days, and then he was vomited out on dry land. That may sound inglorious to you, but to Jonah, I imagine nothing more glorious had ever happened before or ever would again. He had been transported from death to life, and he stood on the dry land as a saved man with a brand new opportunity to serve the living God. The worship and service he promised to God from inside the fish, he could now render because he had been vomited out on dry land by the great fish.

What does this have to do with you and me? Everything! When Jesus was asked for a sign to validate Himself and His claims, He pointed to the sign of Jonah, saying, "for just as Jonah was three days and three nights in the belly of the sea monster, so will the Son of Man be three days and three nights in the heart of the earth" (Matthew 12:40). On that third day, unable to hold Him any longer in its grasp, death *vomited* the Risen Lord Jesus. In resurrected glory, the Lord Jesus passed from death to life, victorious over sin and death forever. And Paul speaks of the promise of resurrection, saying that Christ has emerged as the "firstfruits," and "after that those who are Christ's" will rise at His coming (1 Corinthians 15:23). Because of the wondrous salvation that the Lord has bestowed on us freely by His grace in Christ, we have a triumphant end to anticipate. After death has swallowed us whole, we will be *vomited* upon the dry land of glory, sharing in the resurrection of Jesus, and passing from death to life eternal.

Look at that prophet standing on the dry land! Do you think for a moment that he is thinking, "Oh how undignified and inglorious! I have been vomited by this great fish!" No way! If we could hear Jonah in that moment, I imagine his cry may be, "Oh great mercy of God! I have been saved! I have passed from death to life. Praise His holy name!" And there, my friends, is our picture of the triumphant end of our salvation. When death has swallowed us, it will not be able to hold us, for we will be vomited forth from death in a glorious resurrection, following our Master in like manner. And we will stand face to face with Him in glory, and we will say there, "Oh how great is the mercy and grace of God which has saved me! I have passed from death to life eternal. Praise His holy name." And all eternity will lie before us, where face-to-face with Christ our Savior, we will worship and serve Him like never before. As Paul exclaims in worshipful wonder, "Death is swallowed up in victory. O death, where is your victory? O death where is your sting? The sting of death is sin, and the power of sin is the law; but thanks be to God, who gives us the victory through our Lord Jesus Christ. Therefore, my beloved brethren, be steadfast, immovable, always abounding in the work of the Lord, knowing that your toil is not in vain in the Lord" (1 Corinthians 15:54-58).

XIV

When the Word of the Lord Comes
Jonah 3:1-3a

Now the word of the LORD came to Jonah the second time,
saying, "Arise, go to Nineveh the great city
and proclaim to it the proclamation which I am going to tell you."
So Jonah arose and went to Nineveh according to the word of the LORD.

A few years ago I noticed an annoying habit that I had somehow developed. I walked past someone in the corridors of the hospital, and I said what I suppose I have said thousands of times: "How you doin'?" And I kept walking. Suddenly I was convicted by the Holy Spirit. Why would I ask that person how they are doing if I do not care enough to stop and listen for a response? I tried to justify it by telling myself, "Well, it's just something we do in small talk." But then I realized that there are plenty of other things I could say, like "Hello," or "Hi," or something like that without saying, "How you doin'?" when I have no intention of hanging around for an answer to that question. I haven't completely kicked the habit yet, but I am trying to make a conscious effort to not say, "How you doin'?" to anyone as I pass by them, and if I do say it, to stop and wait for a response.

I guess the reason we say things like this, or talk about the weather, or make any kind of small talk when we are around other people is that silence tends to be awkward. It makes us uncomfortable. That is why we surround ourselves with music, the noise of television, and conversation, even when it is meaningless. We generally just really don't like silence, but especially when someone else is around and not speaking. Small talk arises because we feel like if there are two or more of us in the same space, someone should be saying something.

Here stands Jonah, back on the shores from whence he set out in his rebellious attempt to escape the Lord and His calling earlier in the story. Here Jonah has been, shall we say, "deposited" onto dry land. He has prayed for deliverance and God has answered. He has prayed to rededicate himself to the Lord's service. And now he stands here on the beach. Will God speak? We do not know how much time passes between Jonah 2:10 and Jonah 3:1. It might have been minutes or seconds. But what if it wasn't? What if it was days or months? However long it was, in the moments, hours, or months that elapsed between 2:10 and 3:1, God's silence must have been terribly awkward for Jonah. He knew God was there. He had learned the hard way what he should have known from Psalm 139, that there is nowhere to flee from God's presence. But for whatever amount of time passed, he waited for God to speak. And now, as Chapter 3 begins, the Word of the Lord comes to Jonah. We aren't told how long he waited, and we aren't told how the Word came. Was it a vision? Was it an audible voice? Was it an impression on his soul? We don't know. But what we do know is sufficient for us. God has not revealed all that we may want to know, but He has revealed all that we need to know to know Him, to worship Him, and to serve Him. And as we look at the coming of the Word of the Lord to Jonah here in these verses, we understand something about how the Word of the Lord comes to us.

I. When the Word of the Lord comes, it comes in sovereign grace.

Have you ever applied for a job and waited to get called back or invited to come for an interview? It can get nerve-wracking while you wait day after day and you wonder if you are ever going to get that phone call. Somewhere along the way, you come to the realization that once the application is submitted, you are no longer in control. You can't make them call you, and you don't have any control over what they say to you if they do. The company is in control, and they operate on their own schedule, according to their own agenda and priorities.

That's not a great analogy to use when we are talking about the coming of the Word of the Lord. We never make the first move. God always moves first and we aren't "waiting" for Him to catch up with our ambitions. But there is one similarity with this analogy: we aren't in control of when or how God speaks, or what He says when He does. God doesn't take orders from anyone or bend His will to accommodate the will of others. And though Jonah may wonder what will come next, one lesson that he learns, and that we learn through his experience, is that *God speaks when He wants to*. Verse one opens by saying, "Now the word of the Lord came to Jonah." But we need to understand that the Word didn't have to come at all, it didn't have to come to Jonah, and it didn't have to come when it did.

The big picture of what we are talking about here concerns the doctrine of revelation (not the book of Revelation, but the doctrine of revelation). Revelation, the doctrine, concerns the act of God by which He makes Himself known to us. Here's a crash course in this important doctrine: the only way any of us can know anything about God at all is if He decides to make Himself known to us. So, God must sovereignly decide to graciously condescend to us to give us His truth, His word, His revelation about Himself. We can't make Him do that, and we can't specify when or how we want to receive that message. That is up to God. The fact is that because of our sinful nature, if God hadn't already begun to reveal Himself to us, we wouldn't even want Him to. As Paul says in Romans 3, no one is seeking after God. But in His sovereign grace, He determines to reveal Himself to us through His word in His own time and in His own way.

Just as we have no control over *when* or *how* God will reveal Himself, we also have no control over *what* God will reveal. What God revealed to Jonah was a gracious opportunity to be restored into the Lord's service. Notice that the text says in verse 1 that the Word of the Lord came to Jonah *the second time*. You understand that Jonah didn't deserve this, don't you? After rejecting the Word of the Lord the first time, there was no guarantee that he would ever have a second opportunity. As the writer of Hebrews says, borrowing from Psalm 95, "Today if you hear His voice, do not harden your hearts" (Hebrews 4:7). If you reject the Word of the Lord that comes, you have no guarantee that you will ever have another opportunity to hear and heed His word again. But God, in His grace, according to His sovereign purpose, does mercifully grant to some a second chance to hear and to heed. To others He grants a third, a fourth, a fifth, a fiftieth, a four-hundred-ninetieth chance even. As Frank Page has written, "Although God's word came to Jonah a second time, demonstrating his forbearance and mercy, examples in Scripture show that not everyone has a second chance to do what God has commanded. ... However, this text should bring thanksgiving to the heart of every believer who has been given another opportunity to do what God requires."[193]

When the Word of the Lord comes, it comes in sovereign grace. It does not come when and in what manner we choose, but in the time and manner that God determines. It doesn't always say what we want to hear; it says what He wants to say. But it is a gift of grace for Him to speak at all, and what He says to us is saturated in His revealing and restoring grace. You may wonder, "When will God speak to me?" He has spoken! He has spoken through the incarnate Word, the Lord Jesus, who is the Word made flesh, and He has spoken in His written Word, the Bible. We do not have to wonder and wait for new words to come. These words are what we have. And we have them because God has spoken in sovereign grace.

II. When the Word of the Lord comes, it comes unchanging and unfolding.

In September of 2011, Pat Robertson made the news AGAIN for saying something ridiculous. In his comments on the 700 Club, Robertson said that he thought it was permissible for a person to divorce a spouse suffering from Alzheimers.[194] Thankfully, the response of the evangelical community was loud and univocal in denouncing Robertson's statements. What he said flies in direct opposition to clear biblical teaching about marriage and divorce. In order to believe what Robertson said to be true, one would have to believe that the Word of God has either become irrelevant or else it has somehow changed in our day. Surely there are some out there who do believe these claims, and a number of them claim to be Christians and are in nearly every church in America. Unfortunately, no small number of them are pastors and other church leaders. And this has given rise over the years to a number of divergent groups of churches. Twentieth century liberalism believed to some degree that many portions of the Word of God had become irrelevant because of the passage of time and changes of culture. Cults such as Mormonism and Jehovah's

---

[193] Page, 255.

[194] He later, predictably, sought to withdraw his statement and distance himself from it.

Witnesses believe that God's Word has changed over time, and proclaim either that new revelation has been given to them, or that they alone possess the true original or authentic words of the Lord. So amid this chaotic spiritual climate, one might ask, "Has God's word changed?" Does the passage of time or the changing of circumstances change what the Lord says? And here in this passage of Jonah we see a microscopic illustration of two important concepts when it comes to hearing and heeding God's Word. His word is unchanging, and it is unfolding.

When we say that God's word is unchanging, we mean that God doesn't change His mind about what He has previously spoken. When Jude was writing to first century Christians, he says that he is writing to appeal to them to "contend earnestly for the faith which was *once for all* handed down to the saints" (Jude 1:3). The orthodox[195] Christian faith is built upon what God has revealed in His Word which has been handed down to us once and for all. In Jude's day there were many who were attempting to revise and supplement God's Word, and he was writing to admonish the church to stand against this. In Jesus' prayer in John 17:17, He asks the Father to sanctify His followers in "the truth," and then He says, "Thy word is truth." As a true Word, this word is not in danger of ever becoming untrue. It does not change.

We see this illustrated as the Word of the Lord comes to Jonah "the second time." When the Word of the Lord came the first time, in Jonah 1:2, God's command to Jonah was, "Arise, go to Nineveh the great city." Now, after all that Jonah has been through, the Word of the Lord comes to him again, and what does it say? It says exactly the same thing: "Arise, go to Nineveh the great city." It reads exactly the same in English because it reads exactly the same in Hebrew. God's message to Jonah has not changed because of the passage of time or the change of his circumstances. If you want to know what God's word to us today is, we have to go back and read what His word was to Abraham, and to Moses, David, Peter, Paul, John, and

---

[195] The word "orthodox" means essentially "right doctrine." There is a difference between an orthodox (lowercase "o") Christian and an Orthodox (capital "O") Christian. The former refers to those who hold to an essential, undeniable core of Christian doctrine, such as the Apostle's or Nicene Creeds. The latter is a distinct denomination that originated from the Great Schism in 1054 AD. Not all of the orthodox are Orthodox, and sadly many Orthodox are not orthodox.

others, for His word has not changed. Though twenty centuries have past since the last book of the Bible was written, and though the world has changed tremendously, God's word to humanity has not changed.

Now, some will undoubtedly say, "But God spoke different things to John than He did to Moses," or "He spoke different things to Paul than He did to Abraham." There is some truth to this, but the key factor for us to consider is that what came later in time did not invalidate what came before, but expanded and built upon it. This is what Jesus was talking about when He said in Matthew 5:17-19,

> *Do not think that I came to abolish the Law or the Prophets; I did not come to abolish but to fulfill. For truly I say to you, until heaven and earth pass away, not the smallest letter or stroke shall pass from the Law until all is accomplished. Whoever then annuls one of the least of these commandments, and teaches others to do the same, shall be called least in the kingdom of heaven; but whoever keeps and teaches them, he shall be called great in the kingdom of heaven.*

But does the New Testament not also say things like, "For the Law was given through Moses; grace and truth were realized through Jesus Christ" (John 1:17)? Indeed it does, but this does not mean that Jesus was invalidating what had been spoken by Moses. It means that He was giving fullness to the words that God revealed to and through Moses. This is what we mean when we say that God's word is *unfolding*. The theological term is "progressive revelation," meaning that in each era of revelation, God builds upon, without contradicting or invalidating, what has been revealed before.

Notice how the word of the Lord unfolds from Jonah 1 to Jonah 3, even in such a short span of time. In Jonah 1, the call of God is for Jonah to go to Nineveh and "cry against it." But in Jonah 3, the wording undergoes a slight change. Now the command is to go and "proclaim to it the proclamation which I am going to tell you." In the first case, the context seems to indicate that Jonah's message is to be one of condemnation. It is a confrontational announcement "against" the city of Nineveh because, the Lord says, "their wickedness has come up before Me" (1:2). But here the wording is different. As we will see in Jonah 3:4, it is still a message of warning about a judgment that is about to come to Nineveh because of their sins. In that sense the word has not changed. But it has unfolded. Now it is a proclamation *to* Nineveh rather than a cry *against*, as if God was calling out to Nineveh to repent of its sins so that the judgment would not come. Of course, if they refuse to repent, the judgment will still come. God's Word hasn't changed, but it has unfolded to include more information than was revealed before.

Now, someone may ask, "How then has God's Word progressed or unfolded in the 2,000 years since the New Testament writings were completed?" And the simple answer is that it hasn't. Revelation was unfolding and progressing throughout the centuries until it culminated fully and finally in Christ and His word that comes to us through His chosen apostles. The writer of Hebrews makes this clear in Hebrews 1:1-2 when he says, "God, after He spoke long ago to the fathers in the prophets in many portions and in many ways, in these last days has spoken to us in His Son." According to John 1, Jesus is the Word of God made flesh. And John's Gospel records two promises that Jesus gave to His apostles concerning the revelation that would come to and through them as they composed, under the inspiration of the Holy Spirit, the writings that would become the New Testament. In John 14:25, Jesus told them that the Spirit would teach them all things, and bring to their remembrance all that Jesus had said to them. And in John 16:13, Jesus promised the apostles that the Spirit would disclose to them what is to come. Now, many Christians have misapplied these promises to themselves. In fact, nearly every cult that has ever arisen has used these verses as foundations for their so-called new revelations. But the promises were given to those men whom God would use to complete the written revelation, the written Word concerning the living and incarnate Word, the Lord Jesus. So the process of unfolding is complete now. After the Lord Jesus and the completion of the New Testament writings, there is no "new" word from God. Now, we stand upon a faith that has been, as Jude said, "once for all handed down to the saints." It is unchanging, and it is no longer unfolding.

III. When the Word of the Lord comes, it comes bearing expectations on those who hear it.

In September of 2011, we invited Dr. Danny Akin to speak at our church. Following the service, Dr. Akin joined me and another pastor for lunch. Our lunch table conversation turned into a crash course in church history. Dr. Akin's doctoral dissertation was on Bernard of Clairvaux., whom Dr. Akin calls "An Evangelical of the 12th Century." One of the many brilliant things that Bernard said long ago is this: "Some seek knowledge for the sake of knowledge. That is curiosity. Some seek knowledge to be known by others. That is vanity. Some seek knowledge to serve. That is love."[196] When it comes to the knowledge of God's word, we have to realize that His word is not given to satisfy our curiosity or our quest for vanity. The purpose of revelation is not merely to convey information, it is to produce *transformation*! That transformation results in loving service to the Lord, to His people, and to the World. And that transformation occurs as we depend on the Word of God and obey it.

Notice in verse two that the Lord says, "proclaim to it the proclamation which I am going to tell you." Now, if Jonah is anything like me, he's probably thinking, "OK, and what is that?" But God doesn't specify here what that message is. In a sense, it isn't important for Jonah to know now. God will let him know when he needs to know. But what is important at this point is for Jonah to be committed to delivering the Word of the Lord "as-is." His calling is not to expand, elaborate, modify, or adjust the Word of the Lord. What God wants from Jonah at this point is a commitment to total dependence on the word when it comes. Jonah is not responsible for producing effects or results; he isn't called upon to be creative or to exercise artistic license. He is being commissioned to deliver the word precisely as it is given. He must be totally dependent on God's Word.

Over the years, I have had a lot of folks ask me why I preach through books of the Bible verse-by-verse rather than preaching on particular subjects or contemporary issues. The simple reason is that I have absolutely NOTHING important to say, but EVERYTHING God has said

---

[196] Timothy Paul Jones, *Christian History Made Easy* (Torrance, Cal.: Rose, 2009), 84.

is important. So, preaching is never about a pastor's opinion or his take on contemporary events. It is always about what God has spoken. When I answered God's call to preach, I made a declaration, not of *independence* but of *dependence*. I would depend on the Word of God, for there is nothing else in which I can safely place my confidence.

If you are a follower of Jesus, you are His spokesman. Acts 1:8 says that when the Holy Spirit comes upon you, which happened the moment you gave your life to Jesus, you become Christ's witness—His messengers who spread His good news to a lost world. We don't need sophisticated surveys and statistics to demonstrate that a vast majority of Christians are NOT doing this. We are far too often like Jonah after his first calling. We are running away from the people to whom God has called us to be witnesses. And why do we do this? One reason I have heard many Christians give over the years is that they just don't know what to say. I have some *really* good news for you! You never have to *come up with* the right words! What you have to do is to commit yourself to speaking God's words. Being Christ's witness means telling others what the Lord has spoken through His Word, particularly what He has spoken about Jesus Christ, including His life, death and resurrection and the promise of eternal life. So in calling you to be His witnesses, God is not calling you to be clever and eloquent orators. He is calling you, just like He called Jonah, to be totally dependent on His words. Proclaim to the lost world the proclamation that He has told us.

Not only does the word of the Lord come to us with the expectation of total dependence, it also comes with the expectation of total obedience. If all you had was these two and a half verses, what would you know about Jonah? You would know that he arose and went to Nineveh according to the word of the Lord. And that would be all you need to know about Jonah. In fact, sometimes I wish the story ended right here, with Jonah being totally obedient to the word of God. That would be a happier ending than the one we have.

We don't know how he got to Nineveh. Did he take a camel or a donkey or a 747? We don't know. Did it take hours, days, weeks, or months? We don't know; it doesn't really matter. What matters is what we do know.

Jonah did exactly what God told him to do. In Chapter 1, the Lord said to Jonah, "Arise, go to Nineveh." And we read there that Jonah "rose up" but it was "to flee to Tarshish from the presence of the Lord." He obeyed part of what God said: the "arise" part. I heard a preacher say many years ago that *partial obedience* is *total disobedience*. God hasn't called us to obey part of what He said. The calling is to total obedience.

The Lord Jesus said that total obedience is the evidence of our love for Him. He said "If you love Me, you will keep My commandments," and "If anyone loves Me, he will keep My word" (John 14:15, 23). Thankfully, we are not saved by our ability to totally obey, for if that were so then none of us could be saved. We are saved by grace through faith that we place in the Lord Jesus, and when He saves us He declares us to be righteous. But He also fills us with His Spirit who empowers us to live in righteousness. We have a power that is not our own to enable us to live in obedience to God's word. Though we will continually waver in our obedience, we are without excuse when we do. We have the Word, and we have the Spirit. In our love for the Lord Jesus, we submit to His authority and live in obedience to His word. Total obedience is God's expectation when His word comes.

If you've ever been lost while you were traveling, you know how helpless, confused and disoriented you feel. In those moments you would give anything for some kind of accurate road map or reliable set of directions. When we travel with our GPS nowadays, we often say, "Do you remember what it was like before we had this?" Have you ever considered what it would be like if God had not given us His word? We would be helpless, confused, disoriented, and ultimately lost forever. But thanks be to God, in His sovereign grace, He has revealed Himself. His word has come to us, like it did to Jonah, but even better. Second Peter 1:19 says that we have the "prophetic word made more sure," for it has come to us unchanging yet fully unfolded in the Lord Jesus and in the New Testament which testifies to Him. And the Word comes to us with the expectation that we will totally depend upon it and totally obey it.

XV

God's Gifts to Unbelieving People
Jonah 3:3-5

So Jonah arose and went to Nineveh according to the word of the Lord.
Now Nineveh was an exceedingly great city, a three days' walk.
Then Jonah began to go through the city one day's walk; and he cried out
and said, "Yet forty days and Nineveh will be overthrown."
Then the people of Nineveh believed in God; and they called a fast
and put on sackcloth from the greatest to the least of them.

Have you ever heard anyone say, "Don't look a gift horse in the mouth"? It has to do with being appreciative of what is given to you. Because a horse's age can be determined by its teeth, the idea is that if someone gives you a gift, you don't study it to see what the value of it is before you decide whether or not you want it. I didn't always understand this saying. I have never known much about horses. I rode a horse once. I repeat: *once.* Not long into my ride, the horse decided it was time to go back to the barn, and he seemed to be in a hurry to get there, and he didn't seem to care what my thoughts were on the matter. Thus, my equestrian career ended on the same day it began. Since I know more about history than I do about horses, I had always assumed that the saying about looking a gift horse in the mouth had to do with what may have been the most famous "gift horse" in history. Whether it is an event of history or mythology we may never fully know, but the legendary Trojan Wars were said to have come to an end when the Greeks surprised the people of Troy with a "gift horse," a massive statue of a horse as a supposed act of surrender. Had the people of Troy looked this "gift horse" in the mouth before bringing it into their city, they would have known that it was filled with soldiers who would emerge under the cover of darkness and sack the city. So, for years I misunderstood the saying, "Don't look a gift horse in the mouth," to mean something like, "If you look a gift horse in the mouth, you might get shot in the eye with an arrow."

Of course, the greatest giver of gifts the world has ever known is God. Like the Trojan Horse, His gifts are often unexpected and full of surprises. But unlike the Trojan Horse, His gifts are always good. As a perfect Father He gives good gifts to His children. One of my favorite promises to remember in prayer is what Jesus said in the Sermon on the Mount, that even earthly fathers do not give their children stones when they ask for bread or snakes when they ask for fish. Therefore, He said, " If you then, being evil, know how to give good gifts to your children, how much more will your Father who is in heaven give what is good to those who ask Him!" (Matthew 7:11). As God's children, we have great confidence that when we ask our Father for good gifts, He will grant us what we ask, or else what He grants will be even better than what we ask. His children are those who, according to John 1:12, have been adopted into His family through faith in Jesus Christ. But what about those who neither believe nor ask God for good gifts? Even for them, we have promises in God's word that assure us that God is a gracious giver of good gifts. As it is written in James 1:17, "Every good thing given and every perfect gift is from above, coming down from the Father of lights, with whom there is no variation or shifting shadow." The Lord Jesus also said, "He causes His sun to rise on the evil and the good, and sends rain on the righteous and the unrighteous" (Matt 5:45). Because grace is an element of God's unchanging nature, He is a giver. And we, as His people, should be most grateful of all that He gives abundantly and generously to the undeserving, for this is what we are. Therefore, we shouldn't be surprised at how He blesses and gives good gifts to those who do not know Him or believe in Him, for it is through these gifts that He is revealing Himself to them and drawing them to Himself.

That is what is going on here in this portion of Jonah. Nineveh is a major city in the Assyrian Empire. The Assyrians were known for their evil and wickedness. Using today's vocabulary, we might say that Assyria was a world leader in state-sponsored terrorism at that time in history. The people of Nineveh were pagan polytheists, worshiping a host of idols, entirely unconcerned for the one true God. But in spite of this, God was deeply concerned for Nineveh. In Jonah 3:3, we read in our English Bibles that Nineveh was "an exceedingly great city." But this is not how this sentence reads in the Hebrew Bible. Translators have made an interpretive decision to render the verse this way, and it has been preserved through several generations of English translation. Literally, the sentence would read this way: "Nineveh was a great city to God." We may want to ask, "Why would God be so concerned with such an evil and wicked people?" But then we must stop short and actually give thanks to God that He is concerned for evil and wicked people, for otherwise we would have no hope. God is concerned for the people of Nineveh because they are people. He created them. As human beings, they bear His divine image. As sinful human beings, they are perishing apart from the knowledge of God, and they face the certain future of being separated from Him for eternity. Because God is a giver of good gifts, He has determined to give good gifts to Nineveh, even though they are undeserving, in order to turn their hearts to Himself. In a similar way, God gave good gifts to us when we were separated from Him in sin and unbelief, and He continues to give good gifts to unbelieving people. And as we look at the gracious gifts of God to unbelieving Nineveh, we see how He is using His good gifts to draw unbelievers to Himself today.

I. God graciously gives unbelievers a messenger.

These days, with all of our technology, communication is easier than ever. In the same week that I first wrote these words you are now reading, I was able to communicate with a Marine in Afghanistan via Skype, with the president of a Bible College in Asia and a Christian book publisher in England via email, with a church planter in Arizona via mobile phone, with a fellow pastor in our city via text message, with a university president in Tennessee via Twitter, and with an old high school buddy on Facebook. I did all of that without leaving my desk. But there are times when those methods, for all of their convenience, are inappropriate. When I received the news that a member of our church died during the same week, I knew that a personal, face-to-face visit with the family was necessary.

Jonah lived just shy of 3,000 years ago. There was no Twitter or text messaging available in that day. But God, being God, could have communicated with Nineveh in any way He so desired. And the way He chose to do it was by sending a messenger, a living and breathing human being, to them.

The journey from Israel to Nineveh was not without its risks. Jonah would have to travel treacherous terrain and face untold dangers. Upon arriving in Nineveh, there was no guarantee that he would be received well. He may face injury or even death at the hands of the Ninevites, a reality that undoubtedly factored into his initial attempt to flee from the Lord's calling. Recently, I journeyed with several members of our church to Richmond to witness a missionary appointment service. We were celebrating with 144 new missionaries and their 50 children the opportunity on which they were preparing to embark to points all over the globe. The joyful and celebratory tone of our fellowship with these precious servants of the Lord was fully grounded in realism. The main speaker in the service spoke about the dangers of life on the field. Hanging in the very room where newly appointed missionaries, their parents, friends, and well-wishers celebrated, there was a plaque containing the name of every Southern Baptist missionary who has died on the mission field. Seeing that sobering reminder of the dangers of going into hostile territory as the Lord's messenger, one may be tempted to ask, "Is it worth it?" And if you ask any one of those 144 new missionaries, they will tell you, "Yes it is." God's love and compassionate concern for an unbelieving world are absolutely worth the risk of being His messenger amidst a people who do not know Him.

Jesus told a parable in Mark 12 of a landowner who leased his vineyard out to tenant farmers. They would work the land, and in return they would pay the landowner with a portion of their crops. When the landowner sent his servant to collect a portion of the produce, the workers beat the servant and sent him away empty-handed. He sent another servant, and he was beaten even worse. A third servant came, and he was killed. Finally, the landowner sent his son, thinking, "Surely they will respect my son." But when the son came, the workers beat and killed him as well. With this parable, Jesus was foreshadowing His own future. After God had sent one prophet after another as His messengers into the world, in the fullness of time He sent His own Son. He incarnated Himself as a man, the Lord Jesus, and came as the greatest messenger of all. And those to whom He came as a messenger put Him to death on a cross, the most heinous form of execution the world has ever known. But God considered the redemption of an unbelieving world worth the sacrifice, so He did not spare even His only Son. God so loved the world that He *gave* His only begotten Son.

God so loved Nineveh (that city filled with unbelievers) that He gave them His prophet Jonah as His messenger. God so loved this world, filled as it was with unbelievers, that He came to us in the person of the Lord Jesus, one greater than Jonah, as a messenger. And God so loves the unbelieving nations of the world today that He is still sending out our church members, our children, and our grandchildren to go be His messengers there. Do you have an unbelieving friend, neighbor, co-worker, or family member? Do you think God loves them? I tell you He does. He loves them so much that He is sending them a messenger – you are His messenger. Filled with His Spirit, you are His representative messenger to the unbelievers in your life, placed into their midst because of God's great loving concern for them.

II. God graciously gives unbelievers a message.

St. Francis of Assisi is one of those Christians from Church History that everyone has heard of, but most know very little about. If any average Christian can name one thing Francis ever said, most likely it is this famous quote: "Preach the Gospel at all times; when necessary, use words." Have you ever heard that? There are a couple of problems with that statement, not the least of which is that Francis never said it. No biography written within 200 years of his death ever attributes anything like this to Francis.[197] Moreover, the words hardly fit Francis' lifestyle. He was, after all, a *preacher* who was known for his preaching, sometimes preaching in up to five villages a day. But most problematic about the expression, notwithstanding its spurious origins, is that it really clouds the question of what it means to preach the Gospel. "When necessary, use words." That seems to imply that there are times when words are not necessary. Now, certainly we would want to affirm that words always need to be validated by action, but action without words is hardly sufficient to communicate the good news of Jesus to a lost world. Francis was not a messenger without a message. He lived what he preached, but be sure of

---

[197] Mark Galli, "*Speak* the Gospel." http://www.christianitytoday.com/ct/2009/mayweb-only/120-42.0.html. Accessed September 22, 2011.

this: he also preached what he lived! He was a messenger *because* he had a message. A messenger without a message is no messenger. He is just a guy standing around with a really confused look on his face wondering what he's supposed to be doing. Preaching the Gospel involves more than words, but certainly not less. Words are always necessary.

God loves unbelieving people so much that He sends them not only messengers; He sends them messages through His messengers. He sent Jonah to Nineveh, saying in verse 3, "proclaim ... the proclamation which I am going to tell you." So Jonah's instructions were to receive the word from God, and deliver it without modification to Nineveh. And in verse 4, he does. Now, Jonah's sermon was only eight words long. In Hebrew it is actually only five words long. Some of you may think you would like to have sermons every Sunday that short. But you might have second thoughts when you consider the content of his message. He said, "Yet forty days and Nineveh will be overthrown." This was not a message that sent everyone away a smile on their face. These were hard words of judgment, a real fire and brimstone kind of message. In fact, the first mention of "fire and brimstone" in the Bible comes from the judgment that came upon Sodom in Genesis 19, and three times in that passage, the words are very similar to those found here in Jonah 3:4. The Lord is threatening to "overthrow" Nineveh, just as He did Sodom.

This was a hard message to these unbelievers, but it was a true one. In forty days Nineveh would be destroyed. The reason was stated in 1:2, "their wickedness has come up before me." Messages like this will NOT grow your church or win you any popularity contests, even if they do get you to the cafeteria before the Methodists. But these messages have to be stated anyway. God loves the unbelievers of Nineveh too much to let this calamity come upon them without warning. So He sent them a message. This message is a good gift from a gracious God. Now, you say, "Well it doesn't seem like a good gift. This seems like very bad news." But here is the thing: it doesn't have to be bad news. You see, God loves unbelieving people so much that He has given us a message. He has told us in no uncertain terms that the wages of sin is death (Romans 6:23). And He has told us that it is appointed unto man once to die, and then the judgment (Hebrews 9:27). But He has also told us that He so loves the world that He has given His only begotten Son, so that whosoever believes in Him will not perish but have everlasting life (John 3:16). And that message makes it very clear that some (those who do not believe in the Lord Jesus) will indeed perish. But this message also tells us that those who believe will not perish, but will have everlasting life. This is not merely "not bad" news. It is good news. It is great and glorious news!

What if you knew that you would die in 40 days? Would you spend the rest of your days doing life as usual? Would you waste those days chasing vanity and frivolity? Or would the realization that six weeks from now you will stand before your Maker and Judge cause you to reconsider your ways? Would the knowledge of that serve as a warning to you? Now, you might say, "Well, that is a moot point, because none of us ever know for sure when we are going to die." That may be true, but all of us know *that* we are going to die. You may not know that you have 40 days. The truth is that you may have 40 years. Or, you may be like a church member I visited recently in the hospital; 40 hours later I met with his family to plan his funeral following his death. Or you may be like another church member I shook hands with after the service one Sunday. She said, "That was the best sermon you have ever preached." She stopped by her mother's house on her way home from church to tell her about the wonderful worship service she had been to that morning. Then, she went home, walked in her front door, and dropped dead, just 40 minutes after shaking my hand after the service. You may only have 40 seconds; you could be dead before you finish reading this page! You don't know *when* you will die, but you know *that* you will die. And you know that when you do, you will stand before your Creator and Judge to give an account. That ought to be a sobering realization for us. God has made this truth known to us; He has given us a message, like He did to Nineveh, to serve as a warning.

III. God graciously gives unbelievers an opportunity for redemption.

Skeptics and critics of the Bible have said that God lied to Nineveh. He told them they would be destroyed in 40 days, but they weren't. So they say that there is a problem with the Bible here. That would be true were it not for other clear passages of Scripture that explain the mind and ways of God to us. For instance, in Jeremiah 18:7-8, the Lord said, "I might speak concerning a nation or concerning a kingdom to uproot, to pull down, or to destroy it." That is exactly what God has done here through Jonah to the people of Nineveh. He has spoken concerning their destruction. But He goes on to say, "if that nation against which I have spoken turns from its evil, I will relent concerning the calamity I planned to bring on it." God has a condition underlying His proclamation. Sometimes it is clearly stated, and sometimes it is implicit. But always there is a gracious offer to repent of sin and to turn to the Lord in faith.

Now the reality of our human condition is that we are so radically corrupted by sin that we cannot and will not just decide to turn to the Lord in repentance and faith. Paul said in Ephesians 2 that we are dead in our trespasses and sins. Dead people don't make decisions or take actions on their own. But God, in His great love for unbelieving people, actually moves upon the hearts of those to whom He imparts life, and He enables them to repent and believe. That is why we read things like we do in Acts 5:31, where God is said to "grant repentance" to Israel which leads to forgiveness of sins. But this is not a promise for Israel alone, as we find in Acts 11:18 that God also *grants* to Gentiles "the repentance that leads to life." Similarly in 2 Timothy 2:25 we read that the servant of the Lord must gently correct those who are in error, "if perhaps God may *grant* them repentance leading to the knowledge of the truth."

Not only does God give us the ability to repent, He also gives us the ability to believe. In Ephesians 2, Paul writes that we are "saved by grace through faith," and he says there that even the faith by which we believe on the saving promises of God in the Lord Jesus Christ is "not of yourselves, it is the gift of God." In Philippians 1:29, Paul speaks of belief in Jesus as something that has been "granted to you." Everything we need in order to come to Jesus, namely repentance and faith, is given to us as a gracious gift from God.

One of the most common questions Christians have about the Old Testament is this: If repentance and belief in Jesus is required for salvation (and it most definitely is), then how were people saved in the Old Testament? And the answer is the same. But how could they believe in Jesus when He had not yet come? The answer to this is that they believed in God's promises to save, based on the revelation that they had at the time, all of which have been fully realized in the person of Jesus. So every saving promise of the Old Testament pointed people *forward* to the coming of Christ, to His life, death, and resurrection, just as every saving promise of the New Testament points us *back* to the coming of Christ and His life, death, and resurrection.

Notice what happened in our text when Jonah came in as God's messenger delivering God's message to Nineveh: "The people of Nineveh believed in God and they called a fast and put on sackcloth, from the greatest to the least of them" (verse 5). Sackcloth and fasting were acts of self-denial frequently associated with the repentance of sin. They were visible, outward demonstrations that reflected their conviction of sin and their desire to turn away from sin. But more than just a turning away from their wicked past, they were turning to something, or more accurately, to Someone. That Someone was the God who loved them and saved them from perishing. And this may well be the greatest miracle recorded in the book of Jonah, a far more astounding miracle than Jonah being swallowed by the fish.

God had given Nineveh a messenger. He gave them a message. He gave them an opportunity for redemption, and He granted to them, by His grace, a faith to believe in Him and a repentance that turned them from their wickedness. I would say that few, if any, prophets ever had this kind of response from their audience, even among the people of Israel! When the Ninevites heard the promise of God concerning their impending judgment, what they were hearing was the Gospel. It was incomplete and imperfect, having not been fully unfolded and fulfilled yet in the person of Jesus. But when they heard it, they believed it, and moreover they put their faith in God, and turned from their sins.

History shows us how the story evolved from that moment. The city of Nineveh and the Assyrian Empire was spared from judgment as they turned to God. Israel continued to follow after idols and resisted the calls of God's prophets and His offers of redemption. Eventually the Assyrian Empire became a tool that God would use to bring judgment upon Israel, as they conquered the Northern Kingdom in 722 BC. But Nineveh's season of revival was short lived. In time they would return to their wickedness and idolatry, and eventually they too would be judged and wiped out. But for at least one generation, the people of Nineveh became a testimony to the love and patience of God and to His gracious gifts that He lavishes upon unbelieving people to draw them to Himself. And of course, in time, God would send the ultimate Messenger, the Lord Jesus into the world. And He would proclaim the ultimate message, that He had come to save all who would turn from sin and trust in Him. But rather than believing in Him, the people of His day hated Him and eventually conspired to put Him to death on the cross. But before they did, Jesus denounced that unbelieving generation by way of a surprising contrast.

When the people pressed Jesus for a sign to prove that His mission and His message were genuinely of God, He said in Luke 11:29-32,

> *This generation is a wicked generation; it seeks for a sign, and yet no sign will be given to it but the sign of Jonah. For just as Jonah became a sign to the Ninevites, so will the Son of Man be to this generation. ... The men of Nineveh will stand up with this generation at the judgment and condemn it, because they repented at the preaching of Jonah; and behold, something greater than Jonah is here.*

Jesus was saying that there would be a multitude of saved souls from Nineveh standing present at the judgment bar of God whose testimony of repentance and faith in God would be an added condemnation to the unbelievers of Jesus' day. They had turned to the Lord in response to the preaching of Jonah, that flawed and stubborn prophet. But the people of Jesus' day had rejected God's message that came to them through an even greater Messenger. And Jesus would say the same thing to our present generation. The Messenger has come, and the message has been proclaimed. All of those who have turned from sin and believed on Him have been now commissioned as messengers themselves, pointing an unbelieving generation to Christ and His Gospel promise. If they reject the offer of redemption in Jesus, they will perish, and the redeemed people of Nineveh will testify against them and add to their condemnation when they stand before God to give account.

I pray that this will not be the case with any who are reading these words. You have heard the message. You know that God's ultimate Messenger, the Lord Jesus, lived a life fully pleasing unto God, and died in your place to bear your sins on the cross. You know that He has conquered sin and death by His resurrection. You know that turning to Him in repentance and faith is your only hope of redemption. If you never have before, I pray that even this very day, you would receive God's gracious Messenger and His glorious message, and His miraculous gifts of repentance and faith.

If you already have come to know Him and trust in Him, then you are a testimony to God and to His gracious gifts to unbelieving people. For such were you until God brought you to Himself and saved you. He has made you to be His messenger now, bearing His message of the greatest Messenger. God loves your unbelieving friend and family member, neighbor, coworker, and that stranger you pass by, and the one who lives in the farthest reaches of the globe. Because He loves them, He has given them wonderful gifts. He has given them a Messenger, the Lord Jesus. He has given them a message, the gospel. He has given them the opportunity to repent and believe and be saved. And you yourself are also God's gift to them as you bear witness for Jesus in their lives. Would you ask the Lord to lay on your heart someone with whom you can share this good news and these great gifts of God?

XVI

Leading with True Greatness
Jonah 3:6-9

When the word reached the king of Nineveh, he arose from
his throne, laid aside his robe from him, covered himself with sackcloth
and sat on the ashes. He issued a proclamation and it said,
"In Nineveh by the decree of the king and his nobles:
Do not let man, beast, herd, or flock taste a thing.
Do not let them eat or drink water.
But both man and beast must be covered with sackcloth;
and let men call on God earnestly that each may turn
from his wicked way and from the violence which is in his hands.
Who knows, God may turn and relent and withdraw
His burning anger so that we will not perish."

What makes a great leader? According to John Maxwell, a very popular Christian writer on the subject of leadership, "The true measure of leadership is influence—nothing more, nothing less."[198] If this is our guiding principle for understanding leadership, then any number of people in the world today and throughout history can be called great leaders. The person who sold you the car you drive had some influence over your decision. Is he or she a great leader? Probably not. Adolf Hitler influenced an entire nation to follow him in an epically horrific direction. Was he a great leader? I don't think anyone would want to express that. This brief measure of leadership does not, by itself, address essential qualities such as the moral character of the leader or the direction in which he or she seeks to influence others. If were to take a poll to determine who the truly great leaders of recent history have been, it would include people like Winston Churchill, Abraham Lincoln, and Martin Luther King, Jr. If we expand beyond recent history, we would find people like Julius Caesar, Queen

---

[198] John Maxwell, *The 21 Irrefutable Laws of Leadership* (Nashville: Nelson, 1998), 11.

Elizabeth, and in an altogether qualitatively different way, the Lord Jesus Christ. The great leaders of history are people who are known to us, not just because they influenced people, but because of the positive impact they made on the world or on their society. They influenced people for the better. Sometimes, the legacy of great leaders lives on for centuries. Perhaps more often, great leaders are forgotten rather quickly once their own generation exits the stage of history. A recent feature on Life Magazine's website chronicled 15 great leaders through history. Among them are some we have mentioned, including Martin Luther King and Winston Churchill. Others, such as Mohandas Gandhi, Nelson Mandela, and Golda Meir will long be remembered for their work on behalf of their fellow countrymen. But among this list of 15 great leaders are some surprises like Oprah Winfrey and Steve Jobs, the founder of Apple Computers.[199] None of us are omniscient, and none of us can accurately predict the future, but I would suspect that 100 years from now, several of these names would reappear on a list of 15 great leaders through history. But one has to wonder if Oprah Winfrey or Steve Jobs will be considered great leaders once the present generation of Americans has expired. Their influence in our day is significant, but they may be forgotten in the future while the legacies of these others will live on.

Through the pages of the Bible we encounter many great leaders. The greatest is Jesus, but also there is Moses, King David, Solomon, Queen Esther, and many others. Some are better known than others, and there are some whose names are completely lost to us. Such is the case with the Assyrian King in Nineveh of whom we read in this brief portion of Scripture. What is his name? We do not know. When and for how long did he reign? We do not know. Was he a great leader? How could we think he was great when we don't even know his name? The event that is recorded here is not even mentioned in the historical records of his own country. In spite of this, when we think of leadership as the ability to influence people to unite for the purpose of seeking a better future, we can conclude that Assyria never had a greater leader than this king. Forgotten by history though he may be, few leaders of fame and notoriety could be called

[199] "15 Great Leaders Through History." http://www.life.com/gallery/36522/image/53370403/15-great-leaders-through-history#index/0. Accessed October 24, 2011.

greater leaders than this anonymous king. As we examine this text, we will see what sets him apart as a great leader. From this, we will discover the keys to leading with true greatness for ourselves.

Now, you may say, "I am not a leader." Not everyone is, and that is okay. But many are leaders in some arenas of life whether they realize it or even desire to be. Some of you are leaders at your workplace. Some of you are leaders in your church or community. Others are leaders in your home. Among those who *are* leaders, or who *should be*, some have shrunk from the massive responsibility and others have pursued it wrongly. And for those who are not leaders by nature or calling, there is still a need to understand what it means to be a great leader so that you will know who to follow. This is important to you as you go into the voting booth, as you choose your friends and marriage partners, as you work in your career, as you involve yourself in community activities, and even as you seek to be responsible church members. We are not all leaders, but we are all followers. By understanding the keys to leading with greatness, we are prepared to follow well and, if and when the time comes, to lead well also. Our unnamed king in these verses shows us some keys to leading with true greatness.

I. Great leaders lead in submission to the Word of God.

I remember a day in my hermeneutics class when the professor walked in and found several of us passing our Bibles around to each other. We were feeling them and examining them, some were even smelling them. The professor asked what we were doing and we said, "We are comparing the different kinds of leather that our Bibles are bound in." He said, "Brothers, if it ain't in your shoe leather, it really doesn't matter what other kind of leather it's in." Of course, what he meant was that we can spend lots of money on expensive Bibles, but if we aren't personally applying the Word to our lives and living in obedience to it, then it is all for nothing. You can have a nice, beautiful Bible, you can even read and study it, commit it to memory, and teach and preach it to others. You can command others to put themselves under the authority of God's Word without being personally submitted to the Word. Great leaders, however, are those who are personally submitting themselves to the authority of the Word in their lives, and who are leading others to join them under the authority of the Word of God.

The prophet Jonah has been in Nineveh for a day or so preaching God's message to the people, saying "Yet forty days and Nineveh will be overthrown." Now, we do not know if he got a private audience with the king, or if this message came in some kind of report to the king from his counselors, but the king was made aware of what the prophet was saying. Notice how verse 6 says, "When the word reached the King of Nineveh…." The word "reached" here is a little weak, unless we mean "it reached out and smacked him." That might be a more literal rendering of the Hebrew term. One Hebrew dictionary lists the meanings of this term as, "to touch," explaining, "to make contact with a … part of the body, implying, in some contexts, damage to the object touched," or "to strike," as in, "to make violent impact on an object."[200] The idea is not just that the king got wind of the message. He was impacted and affected by it! It struck him! And the striking of the Word produced a radical change in this king. He began suddenly to lead his people to submit themselves to the same word of God that had impacted him.

The world has certain characteristics that they look for in leaders, and so does God. In Isaiah 66:2, the Lord says, "But to this one I will look, to him who is humble and contrite of spirit, and who trembles at My word." I would venture to say that in the history of the world, few leaders have ever trembled at the hearing of the word of God like this unnamed Ninevite king did. So, the question for us is, "What is our attitude when God's word reaches us?" If your response to His word is indifference or antagonism, then you may be able to influence people, but you will not lead with greatness because you will not lead them toward God's purposes. But if you are struck by the word, if it affects you and impacts you, leading you to tremble in submission to it, then you will lead with true greatness for you will lead others to join you under the authority of the Word.

---

[200] James Swanson, *Dictionary of Biblical Languages With Semantic Domains : Hebrew (Old Testament)*. Electronic ed. Oak Harbor: Logos Research Systems, Inc., 1997.

II. Great leaders lead in humility.

Humility is a quality that is hard to define but easy to recognize. We detect it when people have it. We detect it more easily when people don't. History has remembered General George S. Patton as a very arrogant and self-absorbed man. After all, he said himself, "All very successful commanders are prima donnas, and must be so treated."[201] But the men who served under Patton also saw in him another quality that they respected. He said, "Always do everything you expect of the men you command."[202] Patton understood the power of leading by example, and he never commanded his men to do something that he was unwilling to do himself. The king of Nineveh that we meet in this passage is another leader who seems more than willing to do everything that he asks of those he commands. He leads by example and nowhere more evident than in his humility.

When the king was struck by the word of the Lord, he did not respond like the Pharaoh of Egypt in the days of Moses, who retorted, "Who is the Lord that I should obey his voice?" (Exodus 5:2). Instead this king "arose from his throne" and "laid aside his robe from him." His extravagant throne and his lavish robe were visible symbols of his extensive authority. But when God spoke, this king realized that his authority was nothing in comparison to that of the God of the universe. Quickly he was humbled into the recognition that his throne, his robe, and all the other symbols of his power were meaningless. He had possessed the power to lay other world empires to waste, but now he has met up with a power that can lay his own empire to waste and extinguish his very life. He doesn't argue the point! Instead he humbles himself before the Lord, putting away all of the pretenses of his own self-importance. Instead of his royal robe, which set him apart from the people of his empire, he joins them in wearing sackcloth. He is not a man ruling over a troubled nation. He is a fellow-citizen of a troubled nation, at one with his people under the looming judgment of God. Rather than sitting on his cushioned throne in the seclusion of his royal palace, he sits now out in public view of society upon a heap of ashes. The ashes may symbolize that all of the king's empire and even his own life is at the

---

[201] George S. Patton, *War as I Knew It* (New York: Houghton Mifflin, 1947), 355.
[202] Porter B. Williamson, *Patton's Principles* (New York: Simon and Schuster, 1982), 14.

mercy of the God who can burn it all down, return it all to dust, and wash it away like a castle made from sand.

Leaders are often seen as those who exert their own greatness over others and who never expose the chinks in their own armor. But the truly great leader is one who is brought low in humility before God. A great leader, like this king, recognizes that our earthly empires that we are building are nothing before God, and nothing apart from Him. The great leader knows that his thrones and robes are not impressive to the Lord, and so he humbles himself and leads those who follow him to humble themselves as well.

Perhaps you've heard about the man who was awarded a medal for his humility? They had to take it away from him because he started wearing it. Like that man, some people have questioned the humility of the man that Numbers 12:3 says was more humble than any man on the earth: Moses. The problem that some seem to have with this statement is that Moses supposedly wrote these words about himself. Many scholars have said that Moses could not have been truly humble if he wrote this about himself. I believe that Moses could have said this about himself, and it could still be true. Moses knew something about himself that no one else knew. Moses had met face-to-face with God, and only Moses knew what that time in God's presence did in his heart and soul. I believe Moses could say that he was the most humble man in the world because Moses *had been humbled* more than anyone in the world in the presence of God. We might expect Moses to say, "I met with God, so I am better than everyone else." Instead Moses said, "I met with God, and as a result there is no one on earth who is more humble than I am." Like Moses, this king of Nineveh has been struck by God's word, and it has humbled him. So rather than whipping his people into an inflated estimation of themselves or their great leader, he leads them into humility knowing that none of us can boast of anything before the awesome power of God.

III. Great leaders lead in repentance.

There is a fascinating thing in the early chapters of the book of Isaiah involving the repetition of the word "woe." Between Isaiah 3 and Isaiah 5, seven times Isaiah pronounces a "woe" of judgment on all the wicked people around him. But in Isaiah 6 something happens. Isaiah has a vision of the Lord seated on His throne, and the angels around Him crying out, "Holy, Holy, Holy is the Lord of Hosts!" And the first thing Isaiah says when he sees this is *not*, "Yes, Lord you are holy! Now smite all these wicked sinners with your holy wrath!" Rather, Isaiah is immediately convicted of his own sin and he says, "Woe is me, for I am ruined! Because I am a man of unclean lips and I live among a people of unclean lips; for my eyes have seen the King, the Lord of hosts." A glimpse of the holiness of God did not make Isaiah more aware of the sinfulness of others. It made him aware of his own sinfulness, and only as he dealt with that was he able to be used by the Lord as a prophet to his nation.

When the word of the Lord struck this king of Nineveh, notice that he did not go out on his portico and shout down to his people, "Alright you heathens! You people better straighten up or else God's gonna get ya!" Instead, he put the sackcloth on himself and sat on the ashes in repentance over his own sins before calling on his people to join him in repentance. Only after dealing with his own sins before God does he call his noblemen together for the purpose of issuing a proclamation to the people. And when he does, he gets right to the heart of the matter. He announces a complete fast, saying, "Don't taste anything, no food or water at all, and don't even let your animals eat." Then he orders the people to put on sackcloth as a demonstration of their self-denial and the turning of their hearts in repentance. Every person is to wear the sackcloth and put it on their animals too!

There are lots of opinions on why they included the animals in these rituals, and ultimately we do not know why. We are told here *what* they did, not *why* they did it. It is possible that they were just doing the best they could do with very little knowledge of how to approach God, and they wanted to be as thorough as possible in their call to repentance. More important than what they wore, or what they didn't eat or drink, or how they treated their animals, the people of Nineveh are instructed by this king to call on God "earnestly" (literally, "with strength") and each one is to "turn from his wicked way and from the violence which is in his hands."

I would imagine that within your lifetime, you have probably heard some leader, either the president, or your boss, or your dad, or your pastor, say, "Look folks, times are hard, and so we better pray." But have you ever heard a leader say, "Folks, things look very bad. And I have personally repented of my sin, and I am calling on you to do the same!" This king is leading like few others ever have, leading his people in repentance of their wickedness before the Lord. And yet, this is perpetually our greatest need. We are sinners by nature and by choice, and that sin drives a wedge between us and God. If God were to give us what we deserve, we would perish eternally apart from Him in hell. But repentance is the means that God has granted to us that we may turn to Him in faith, renouncing our sins and asking Him for mercy instead of justice.

At the heart of the preaching of Jesus, John the Baptist, and all of the prophets and apostles is the call to repentance. To repent is to turn away from the wickedness of sin, and toward the holiness of God. J. I. Packer speaks of repentance as a change of mind issuing in a change of life.[203] True repentance has both inward and outward components. We see several of the outward components of repentance here in this passage: fasting, sackcloth, ashes. But don't you know that it is possible to perform all of the outward signs of repentance without any corresponding internal spiritual realities? One could fast, wear sackcloth, and sit in ashes thinking that these rituals alone will secure the favor of God; meanwhile they do nothing about their hard, cold, and unbelieving hearts. That is not true repentance. It is superstition and hollow religion that seeks to earn God's favor by the performance of works. As Calvin said, the outward signs, "when not genuine, do nothing else but provoke the wrath of God."[204] But true repentance is an internal condition that may or may not be accompanied by these specific outward demonstrations, but it will always have some outward demonstration. John the Baptist preached to the Pharisees and Sadducees that they should "bear fruit in keeping with repentance." In other words, if our repentance is genuine, it will be evident by the actions that our internal condition produces. The internal is the key.

---

[203] J. I. Packer, *A Passion for Faithfulness: Wisdom from the Book of Nehemiah* (Wheaton, Ill.: Crossway, 1995), 58.
[204] John Calvin, *Calvin's Bible Commentaries: Jonah, Micah, Nahum* (trans. John King; reprint, Forgotten Books, 2007), 78.

You can do the external without the internal, but if you have the internal the external will be present as well.

What are the internal conditions of repentance? First, repentance involves a mourning over one's sin. This is not the same as remorse. Remorse often has to do with grieving over being caught in one's sin or being sorry for the consequences of one's sin. True repentance grieves over the wickedness of one's sin (the *sinfulness* of sin) because of its offense against the holiness of God. We see this in the king's willingness to address the sins of Nineveh for what they are: "wickedness and violence." Second, true repentance involves a sincere turning away from sin. It was not enough for the king and the people to recognize that their deeds were wicked and violent, they must "turn from" them in a decisive act of putting their evil deeds away. Third, true repentance involves a turning to God in faith.

Repentance and faith are often treated as two different things, and there is a sense in which they are. But there is another sense in which they are inseparable. You cannot turn away from one thing without turning toward another. And if a person is not turning toward God in faith, then he or she is not truly turning away from sin in repentance. They are merely turning from one sin to another. So the king says that the people of Nineveh must "call on God earnestly."

True repentance is not something that we do once and are done with it forever. No, true repentance is a daily, even moment by moment, condition of the heart in which we despise the sin that is present within us, and in which we deeply desire to be free from that sin, willing to put it aside to never return to it, and in which we humbly seek the face of God and the grace that He supplies to forgive us and reconcile us to Himself. Great leaders do this, and they lead others to do so by their example.

IV. Great leaders lead in hope.

I love this king's honesty. He is the first to admit that he doesn't have all the information, but he hopes that he knows enough to rescue his people from doom. He knows that his sins and the sins of his people have landed them in deep weeds with the Lord, and He knows that they have a great need to turn to God for mercy. He says in verse 9, "Who knows? God may turn and relent and withdraw His burning anger so that we will not perish." Don't you just love his candor? "Who knows? God might just do this!" Whenever anyone in my family says, "Who knows?" about something, my four-year-old nephew usually responds by saying, "God knows!" That's pretty good theology for a four-year-old. In fact, that is good theology for anyone. Who knows? God knows! The king doesn't know what God will do, but he has one great and final hope that God will see that the repentance of Nineveh is genuine and that He might spare them from destruction. And he holds that hope out for his people to find shelter in it. All is not lost just yet! God has given us 40 days! Let us do what we know is right and turn to him in hope that we may be saved! That is a great leader.

Indeed, God does know, and the only way any of us can know what God knows is if God chooses to reveal it to us. And He has! Every promise that God ever made concerning His justice, His grace, and His mercy, has come to fruition in the person of Jesus Christ. Like a truly great leader, the Lord Jesus has come, in perfect obedience to the will and word of His Father. He has set aside His magnificent robe of glory and left His eternal throne in heaven to become one of us. He has taken our sins upon Himself and bore them to the cross where He died in our place. And because of what He has done in His life, death, and resurrection, we do not have to say, "Who knows? God might save us!" We have a more certain hope than this. We have the assurance of God's promise that, if we will turn from sin and commit ourselves by faith to Christ as our Lord and Savior, we will be saved. If, like this king of Nineveh, we will put aside all that we are tempted to boast in – our earthly thrones and robes, as it were – and recognize that our own greatness is but filthy rags, nothing more than a castle made of sand that can be swept away in a moment by the just judgment of God, and turn to Him in sorrowful repentance for our sins and in the great hope of His mercy and grace demonstrated in Jesus, we *will be* saved. Who knows? God knows! And because He has made this truth known to us, we know as well. Ours is not a hollow wish that God *might do* something to save us. Ours is the confident expectation that He *has done* something to save us, and that He *will* uphold His promise to save every sinner who turns to Jesus in repentance and faith.

By God's grace, He allows every person He saves to enjoy the glorious privilege of leading others into this hope as well. And in eternity, as we stand together with the redeemed of all the ages, we will come to know that the truly great leaders of history are those who have led others to know the hope of Jesus Christ. Their names may never be recorded in the history books of earth, but they will be recorded in the Lamb's Book of Life.[205] I wouldn't be surprised to find this king's name listed there, along with yours and mine if we are in Christ, and a whole host of Ninevites who found the saving mercy of the Lord through the influence of this anonymous Assyrian king.

Do you want to lead with true greatness? Then lead others under the word of God that has struck and transformed you. Lead others in humility and genuine repentance. But most of all, lead others into the hope of Jesus Christ. This is true greatness in leadership. And if you would follow a great leader, then you must look for these same attributes. You won't find them anywhere more perfectly exhibited than in the Lord Jesus Himself. Follow Him faithfully, and as you do, you will be able to see glimpses of these characteristics in other people that He will use to lead you in life. Follow those who lead you to follow Jesus more closely. And as you do that, you may be surprised to find that you are leading others to Him as well.

---

[205] See Revelation 20:12-15; Philippians 4:3; et al.

XVII

God in the Hands of an Angry Sinner
Jonah 3:10-4:4

When God saw their deeds, that they turned from their wicked way,
then God relented concerning the calamity which He had declared
He would bring upon them. And He did not do it.
But it greatly displeased Jonah and he became angry.
He prayed to the LORD and said,
"Please LORD, was not this what I said
while I was still in my own country?
Therefore in order to forestall this I fled to Tarshish,
for I knew that You are a gracious and compassionate God,
slow to anger and abundant in lovingkindness,
and one who relents concerning calamity.
Therefore now, O LORD, please take my life from me,
for death is better to me than life."
The LORD said, "Do you have good reason to be angry?"

On the door of my office, I have a little picture of Jonathan Edwards surrounded by the words, "Jonathan Edwards is my homeboy." Edwards is called by some the greatest American theologian and philosopher who ever lived; by some, the last of the great line of Puritans; and by others, the most excellent and prolific writer and preacher of American history. He is perhaps most well-known for a sermon he preached in 1741 called "Sinners in the Hands of an Angry God." Edwards has been criticized by some who have probably never read this sermon, simply because of its provocative title, but the content of this sermon is thoroughly biblical and brilliant. If you have never read this sermon, I'd encourage you to do so and also to read some of his other excellent sermons to get a better understanding of this giant of a man.

In a way, the title "Sinners in the Hands of an Angry God" could have been a fitting title to Jonah's brief sermon that he delivered to the people of Nineveh in Jonah 3:4 – "Yet forty days and Nineveh will be overthrown." Like Edwards' sermon centuries later, those hard words that Jonah preached were used by the Spirit of God to spark genuine repentance, conversion, and revival among those who heard it. Few prophets in the history of Israel, and few preachers since, have ever experienced the kind of response that Jonah experienced in the preaching of this message. Here in Jonah 3:10, we learn that God saw their deeds, demonstrating that their repentance was sincere and genuine, and in His sovereign grace He saved them from the destruction which He had warned was coming. Rather than rejoicing over the success of the mission and the power of God and His Word, Jonah was "greatly displeased" and "angry." The Hebrew of Jonah 4:1 indicates that Jonah considered God's dealings with Nineveh to be "evil," "troubling," or "disastrous." It would be just as accurate to render verse 1 this way: "But Jonah considered this to be a terribly evil thing, and he burned with anger."

The significance of this is hard to overstate. Jonah was angry. That's not the problem; anger is not always a sin. But Jonah is angry at God because of what He has done. Jonah has placed himself in the judgment seat over God, charging the God of the universe with committing a terrible evil in saving the Ninevites from their destruction. If Jonah's sermon could be called "Sinners in the Hands of an Angry God," then Jonah's present condition of heart and state of mind could be just as well called, "God in the Hands of an Angry Sinner." And if we were truly honest with ourselves, we would admit that there have been times when we have felt the same way. Haven't all of us have had times when we were angry with God, and in which we were tempted to cast judgment on God as being unfair, unkind, or, as Jonah accused, even evil? On our best days, that kind of thing would strike us as absurd. How can we, depraved and sinful people, sinners by nature and by choice, place ourselves in judgment over the holy and righteous God of the universe who is perfect in justice, perfect in love, and perfect in grace and mercy? It is ridiculous, isn't it? But when His providence becomes uncomfortable for us to bear and His will is somewhat contrary to our own, things start to get turned upside down. I suppose that when I am angry with God that my reasons are not so different than Jonah's, nor are yours. As we look at Jonah's prayer we see some of the reasons for his anger at God and this shines a light on us in those moments when we are angry with God.

I. We get angry with God when we misunderstand His ways.

It is an effect of being made in God's image that we are all born with a sense of right and wrong, of good and bad. We may not all agree on all of the particulars of what is good and what is bad, but we are all aware that such categories exist, and we grow into an understanding that they are categories that were established by God. From this, we develop a sort of expectation that God will bless good people with good things and bring bad things upon bad people. Here is where something else is at work in our minds. Not only are we influenced from birth by the lingering presence of His divine image, but we are also affected by sin. Because we were born with a fallen, sinful condition, our thoughts about God and fairness, right and wrong, good and bad, are corrupted. Often we are just wrong about these things. If life consisted only of people getting what they deserved, then we would all be in bad shape. None of us *really* want what we deserve from God.

Part of our problem comes from a false idea in our heads about what it means to be a good or bad person. We make those kinds of judgments about others by comparing them to ourselves. We think people who do things like we do are probably good people, and people who do other things are probably bad people. Even if we do understand that we are all sinners, we think that there are your garden variety sinners (like me and you), and then there are SINNERS (like Hitler and, well, no one really wants to lump anyone else into a category with Hitler). But God never intended for us to measure people's goodness or badness by comparing ourselves with each other. The true evaluation of our condition comes when we compare ourselves with God. And we can do that most vividly by comparing ourselves to Jesus Christ, who is God in the flesh. And when we consider ourselves in comparison to Him, we realize that we are ALL bad; we are all VERY bad. The human race is not like a Western movie where the good guys wear white hats and the bad guys wear black hats. If life were like a Western movie, then we would all be wearing black hats, and Jesus would be the only one with the white hat.

I like to illustrate it like this: if we were to go down to a track and field venue and compete with one another in the long jump, undoubtedly many of you could jump farther than I could. But let's suppose that we were standing on the edge of the Grand Canyon and we were forced to try to jump across from the South Rim to the North Rim. In that scenario, it really wouldn't matter that you could out-jump me by six feet. We would all fall flat to the bottom of the Canyon (actually, we wouldn't even make it all the way to the bottom). Similarly, there are some people out there who I may think are "better than me" or "worse than me" in some ways. But when all of humanity lines up in comparison to the holiness of God, the shades of goodness and badness that distinguish us from each other become miniscule. All of us fall so far short of His glory that it really doesn't matter how much better or worse we are than each other. This is Paul's point in Romans 3 when he says, "There is none righteous, not even one," and "all have sinned and fall short of the glory of God."

Now, it wasn't that Jonah thought that he was good and the Ninevites were bad. Jonah knew that he was a sinner. He made that clear in his prayer of repentance in Chapter 2. And it wasn't that Jonah thought that God couldn't forgive sinners. He had experienced the saving mercy of God in Chapter 2, and had seen God do it for Israel throughout his prophetic ministry. But in Jonah's mind, there were *sinners* (like himself and the rest of his countrymen in Israel), and then there were *SINNERS* (like Nineveh). And because the people of Nineveh were so much more evil in his mind than himself or the people of Israel, he misunderstood the ways of God toward Nineveh. What angered Jonah was what he considered to be an evil thing that God had done in *not* bringing judgment upon Nineveh. But what Jonah misunderstood was that it is the way of God to forgive sin when there is confession, repentance, and a turning to Him in faith, regardless of how bad the sin is, and regardless of the ethnicity or nationality of the sinner.

It did not anger Jonah when God saved him from his sin. It did not anger Jonah when God blessed Israel, even though they seemed unrepentant of their sin. But it angered Jonah when God saved Nineveh. This was scandalous! Indeed, when God saves sinners and treats the guilty as if they are not, it is scandalous. How could God operate this way? Every case like this in the Old Testament serves as a pointer, directing our focus to the cross of Jesus Christ. There, the ways of God that the world considers scandalous are demonstrated vividly. In the person of Christ, Paul says in Romans 3:26, God is *just* and the *justifier*. He is just in that He punishes sin with the full measure of judgment that it deserves. The brutality of Christ's death is a visible image of the grotesqueness of our sin and the penalty that it warrants in the righteous justice of God. But because Christ endured this on our behalf as our substitute, God is also the justifier of the sinner who turns to Him in repentance and faith. He declares the guilty to be not guilty, the sinner to be righteous. God's ways are to punish sin and to bless the righteous. And in the cross of Jesus, He does both, and the benefits of His saving work in Jesus are made available to all humanity – even to those, like the Ninevites, who lived centuries prior to the cross, and to us, who live centuries after it. That is why we call this the Gospel, a word that means "Good News!" It is the best news we could ever hear. It is too bad that we so often misunderstand it.

Have you ever been angry at God when you saw or experienced something bad happening to yourself or someone else you think is a good person? Have you ever been angry at God when you saw something good happen to someone you think is bad or undeserving? Have you ever been mad at God because something in life seemed unfair? If so, then you have misunderstood the ways of God. It should not anger us that God forgives sin, even in the worst of sinners. This is the glory of the believer, for it assures us that we ourselves are never beyond hope! When we protest like Jonah that someone didn't get what they deserve, we prove that we have misunderstood the ways of God. And we must beware of that lest it reveal a hardness of heart which indicates that we ourselves have not partaken of the saving mercy of God. If we've truly experienced the saving ways of God, then we should rejoice when others experience it as well!

II. We get angry with God when we misunderstand His nature.

These two thoughts are related because God's ways (the things He does) are an expression of His nature (who He is). God acts in justice and in mercy because He is righteous and He is merciful. When we speak of God's nature, we are talking about His attributes. In my library, I have a book by Stephen Charnock, a seventeenth-century Puritan, entitled *Discourses Upon the Existence and Attributes of God.* Altogether, it weighs in at a hefty 1,200 pages or so. Reading that book will certainly explain a lot about God's attributes, but thankfully it is not necessary for us to read a volume like that to understand God's nature. All that we *need* to know about His nature is revealed to us in Scripture. In some passages we see a glimpse of one attribute or another, and as we weave them together systematically, we come to understand more about who He is. But then there are passages like Exodus 34:6-7 in which God reveals immediately a thorough description of Himself. There He describes Himself as, "The LORD, the LORD God, compassionate and gracious, slow to anger, and abounding in lovingkindness and truth; who keeps lovingkindness for thousands, who forgives iniquity, transgression and sin; yet He will by no means leave the guilty unpunished, visiting the iniquity of fathers on the children and on the grandchildren to the third and fourth generations." This passage was committed to memory by the faithful people of God as a means of learning God's nature. Jonah knew it well, for he recites the better part of it here in verse 2. When God revealed Himself in these words to Moses, Exodus 34:8 says that Moses "made haste to bow low toward the earth and worship." That is what a right understanding of God's nature should lead us to do—worship! But Jonah is not drawn to worship by this understanding of God's nature. Instead, he is drawn into anger over it.

Now, it is important to recognize here that Jonah does not have a defective theology. He says, "I knew that you are a gracious and compassionate God, slow to anger and abundant in lovingkindness, and one who relents concerning calamity." These things are true of God, and Jonah *knew* it! The problem was not in Jonah's head; the problem was in his heart. And now, finally, we are told the reason why he fled from the Lord. Chapter one presents Jonah's attempt to run away as a matter of fact with no explanation. At times during our study of Jonah, we have speculated about some of the factors that might have influenced that decision: he might have feared how he would be treated in Nineveh; he might have had a bitter prejudice against the Ninevites. Certainly these reasons are partly true. But now the whole truth is told. Jonah admits that his orthodox theology – his knowledge of who God is – is what drove him to disobedience. His running didn't have anything to do with what he feared among the people of Nineveh; it had everything to do with what he knew about God!

He tries to pull the "I told you so" bit on God. "Was not this what I said while I as still in my own country?" And here is where we see his error. He knew these things to be true about God, but he earnestly expected, or at least hoped, that by running away from the Lord, he could cause God to act in a way that is contrary to His nature. But that is something that God cannot and will not do. Jonah acts as if he knew more about the situation than God did, thus misunderstanding God's omniscience. He acts as if he knows better what should be done with Nineveh than God does, thus misunderstanding God's sovereignty. Jonah's complaint amounts to something like this: "Oh God, You blew it! Oh God, You should have listened to me! If You would just let me run the universe for a day or two, I could really show You how it is done!" Isn't that a ridiculous thing to think? Well, if so, then why do we think that way so often?

Often when we become angry with God, it is because we misunderstand His nature. We think God would have done something different if He knew what we knew. We think He chose something second-best or worse, and that we could have handled the situation better than He did. We think the task was too big for Him to handle. We think that when He poured out His grace, He hit the wrong target, or that when He allowed the bitter consequences of sin and this fallen world to land on someone that He had a bad aim. Our complaint is something akin to what Jonah is saying: "God, You should have listened to me! You should have sought my advice about how to handle this situation! You should have just let me do it my way!" These don't sound like the words or thoughts of someone who truly knows God's nature. Now matter how sound our theology is, when anger against God arises, there is surely some misunderstanding of His nature at work.

There is a great hymn that doesn't get sung much anymore, written in 1889 by Thomas Benson Pollock called, "We Have Not Known Thee As We Ought." The first line says, "We have not known Thee as we ought, or learned Thy wisdom, grace, and power. The things of earth have filled our thought, and trifles of the passing hour. Lord, give us light Thy truth to see, and make us wise in knowing Thee." Whenever we are angry with God, these are words we should sing.

III. We get angry with God when we misunderstand His will.

Have you ever seen a child hold his breath in defiance of his parents? Whenever I see a kid do that, I think, "What good is that going to do?" But to a child, it makes sense, right? "If you don't let me have my way, then I am just going to stand here and die." Doesn't that sound like what Jonah is saying in verse 3? "God since You think Your way is better than my way, You might as well just strike me dead." It's a wonder the book doesn't end right there. It is truly amazing that it doesn't say, "'Lord, please take my life from me.' *Poof. The End.*" It is an evidence of God's nature and His ways that He continues to lean toward Jonah in grace. But Jonah is not so much different that you and me. When he gets angry with God because God didn't do what Jonah wanted, he begins to pray with death wishes. If God is truly this kind of God, who truly does things this way, then we can sometimes think, like Jonah did, that "death is better than life".

Ultimately, all of our anger, frustration, and disappointment comes down to a clash of competing wills. God's will is one thing, and ours is something different. There are sometimes lengthy seasons in life when it seems that our will is sovereign. We want something, we get it. We want to do something, we do it. But then we come running full speed into the immovable object of God's ultimately sovereign will. Suddenly we realize that we are not the ones who are in charge, and we don't like it. Here we have a choice. We can recognize that God's will is bigger and better than ours, and we can bend our will into submission to His, praying as Jesus taught us to, "Thy will be done on earth as it is in heaven" (Matthew 6:10). Or we can stiffen our necks and harden our hearts and insist on having our way. Jonah is doing that here, holding himself out like a hostage: "Okay God, listen here: one false move and the prophet here is gonna get it!" That doesn't threaten God at all, because God is ultimately in control even of Jonah's life and death, and he can no more choose when his life is going to end than he chose when it would begin. You may say, "That's not true. I know a guy who chose to take his own life, so he chose when he would die." Well, have you ever known anyone who tried to take their own life and it didn't work? I have. And they live on, in whatever state they survive, as a reminder to everyone that ultimately we do not choose when or how we leave this world.

Our notion of unlimited free will is a myth. The reality is that God's will is what prevails. It doesn't often look like we want it to look. It doesn't often happen in the timeframe we think it should. It is often punctuated with more mercy or less judgment than we think it should have. It is sometimes seasoned with more unpleasantness than we think we deserve. And we get angry – angry enough to die. But if we truly knew the Lord, we would be thankful that His will prevails over ours. What a dreadful thing it would be for the Lord to say to us, "Okay then, thy will, and not Mine, be done." That would be a catastrophic nightmare and would certainly lead us down the broad path of destruction.

Jonah burned with anger against the Lord. Some of us know how that feels, and it is a miserable state to be in. In fact, I wouldn't be surprised if someone reading these words feels that way right now. Maybe God hasn't done what you think He should in your life or the life of a loved one. Maybe there is someone out there that God hasn't dealt with as harshly as you'd like for Him to. Maybe you think you could have handled this circumstance better than He did, or you are frustrated that He just doesn't seem to see things your way. What is it? Was it that death that happened? Or the one that didn't happen? Was it what the doctor told you? Was it how your boss treated you, or what your spouse did, or what your children said? Was it the way your friend treated you, or the way your enemy seems to go from blessing to blessing, while you suffer in misery and agony? You may be like Jonah, burning in anger toward God over this thing in your life. What would God say about that? I imagine He might say to you what He said to Jonah. Jonah had his reasons for being mad at God, but God says in verse 4, "Do you have *good* reason to be angry?" And ultimately, our reasons for being mad at God are never good ones.

Jonah did a lot that was wrong, but I want to point out two things Jonah did that were right. First, he wasn't just complaining *about* God, he was complaining *to* God. He prayed to the Lord in his anger. It's hard to pray when you are angry, especially when you are angry at God, but never do we need to pray more than we do in these moments. If we can't say anything else good about the Jonah we see here in these verses, we can say this: his anger drove him to God and not away from Him. You may not be comfortable admitting your anger toward God in prayer, but here's a secret: He already knows about it, so you might as well talk to Him about it. Often, when I am angry at God (and yes, that happens to me more often than I wish it did) I don't want to pray because I know that as I do, I will begin to see how foolish I am acting. But when I pray anyway, God begins to remind me of who He is and how He acts, and that His will is far superior to mine. This realization breaks down my anger and brings me to confession, and repentance, and worship. Sometimes those end up being the most precious times ever spent in prayer.

Secondly, there is something else I think Jonah got right. He recognized that he couldn't go on living like this. He wanted to die rather than to go on living like this. That's bad, isn't it? Maybe it is, but I try to look at it like this: Jonah knew he couldn't go on like this, but he didn't have to go on like this. Do you remember when Elijah got depressed and wanted to die (1 Kings 19:4)? Have you ever felt like that? I tell you I have. I remember one afternoon some years ago when I was feeling down and discouraged, and ultimately angry at God. I walked out of my office and went down into the sanctuary of the church I was serving at that time, and I began to saturate the altar with tears and pound my fists into the carpet. I remember saying, "God, I just want to die!" And two verses of Scripture came into my mind in that moment. One was the words of Jesus: "If anyone wishes to come after Me, he must deny himself, take up his cross, and follow Me." Taking up the cross means dying. My calling was to die to myself! And that led me to another passage—Paul's words in Galatians 2:20: "I have been crucified with Christ; and it is no longer I who live, but Christ lives in me; and the life which I now live in the flesh, I live by faith in the Son of God who loved me and gave Himself up for me." I realized in that moment that Jesus wanted what I wanted. I didn't want to live anymore, and He didn't want me to. That was my problem all along. He wanted me to die to myself and to let Him live through me. As best as I could, that very moment, I did just that. And it was like a weight was lifted off my shoulders and instantly my perspective was changed.

I don't know where you are in your journey with the Lord right now. Maybe you haven't even begun. Maybe you are still trying to think your way to God with thoughts that seem right to you, but which are corrupted and twisted by your sin nature. You think that you are a good person and that God will therefore bless you. That is not what God says about you. God says that you are a sinner and that you are spiritually dead, and that you are separated from Him. But He also says He loves you, and He wants to save you. So, in the person of Jesus, God has dealt with your sins fully and finally, and He offers to forgive you and declare you righteous in His sight if you will turn from sin and trust in Christ to save you.

You might be angry with God. Is He not letting you have your way? Is He not handling things the way you think He should? Is there something about Him that you think is flawed, imperfect, or, as Jonah thought, even evil? Why don't you do what Jonah did – talk to Him about those things. He already knows so you might as well. And as you do, allow His Word to shape your understanding about who He truly is and how He works in justice and grace, and how His will is ultimately far better than yours. And as you consider that, just give yourself up to Him – die to yourself and allow His life to live through you. And as you do that, your perspective will be transformed, the fire of anger will die out, and you will be brought to repentance, confession, worship, and ultimately into the abundant life that comes through the taking up of your cross and following Jesus.

XVIII

A Sheltered Life
Jonah 4:5-6

Then Jonah went out from the city and sat east of it.
There he made a shelter for himself and sat under it
in the shade until he could see what would happen in the city.
So the LORD God appointed a plant and it grew up over Jonah
to be a shade over his head to deliver him from his discomfort.
And Jonah was extremely happy about the plant.

Whenever my family heads out to the local shopping center, we drive past a large synagogue in our city. Recently, as we drove by, we saw a little hut that had been erected in the front lawn of the synagogue. It happened to be the time of the Feast of Tabernacles on the Jewish Calendar, sometimes referred to as *Sukkot,* the Feast of Booths, or the Feast of Ingathering.[206] During this weeklong observance, some Jewish families will construct a simple little booth called a *sukkah* in their yards, and others will make use of "communal" booths erected at their synagogues. Some will "camp out" under the shelter, while others just use it for family meals. This is one of the most popular and joyous festivals for Jewish people. It was commanded in Leviticus 23 for the people of Israel to dwell in booths for seven days as a two-fold memorial. First, it celebrates the end of the harvest in an act of worship and thanksgiving to the Lord who has provided. It is kind of like a Jewish Thanksgiving. Some have said that the early Puritan settlers in America, who were familiar with the Old Testament Law, patterned American Thanksgiving after Sukkot. Secondly, it remembers the time of the Exodus, when the people lived in tents and booths during their sojourn through the wilderness, and when the Lord Himself dwelt among the people in the Tabernacle. On the first and last day of the feast, the Israelites were commanded to cease from their

---

[206] This sermon was originally preached during the week of the Feast of Tabernacles, 2011.

ordinary work, and on each day there were to be sacrifices and meals shared together in joyful celebration of the dwelling of God among men and the faithful provision of the Lord for the people's needs.

Because Israel was called to be a light to the nations, there was even a sense in which the Feast of Tabernacles celebrated God's desire for all nations to know and worship Him. Numbers 29 prescribed a total of 70 bulls to be sacrificed during the week of the feast, interpreted by some rabbis to represent the 70 nations of the world that were enumerated in Genesis 10. It is commonly believed that the dedication of Solomon's Temple in Jerusalem took place during the season of Sukkot. One cannot read Solomon's prayer of dedication in 1 Kings without seeing the repeated emphasis on the Gentile nations coming to worship the God of Israel at this temple. In Zechariah 14:16-17, the Lord spoke of a coming day when all the nations who had warred against Israel would come together in Jerusalem to celebrate the Feast of Tabernacles. But as we know from reading our Bibles, Israel had neglected their responsibility to be a light to the nations. They became calloused and unconcerned about the nations, content to believe that God was concerned only for Israel.

Now what does any of this have to do with Jonah? Well, actually it has quite a lot to do with him, particularly in this little portion of Chapter 4. As I was translating the Hebrew text of Jonah 4, I came across this little word in verse 5: *sukkah*. "Jonah went out from the city and he sat to the east of the city and he made for himself there a *sukkah*." Now, we don't know anything about Jonah outside of what we are told about him here and in a brief mention in 2 Kings 14. Was he a carpenter or a mason by trade? We don't know. But as a faithful Jew, he knew what a *sukkah* was and how to go about building one. Even though the festival had been abandoned by and large in Israel since the days of Joshua when they first occupied the land of promise (Nehemiah 8:17), as a prophet Jonah would have known what the feast of tabernacles was all about. And though there are plenty of Hebrew words that could have been used to describe what Jonah built for himself there, I believe there is some significance in the fact that the word *sukkah* is used.

Traditions have arisen beyond what the Bible specifies that say that a *sukkah* is to be a three walled booth with one side open. The roof has to be made from material that grows from the ground: wood, branches, leaves, etc., all delicately placed, not fastened, overhead. The roof should provide more shade than sunshine, still allowing for a little rain to pass through and for the family to see the stars through the roof at night. Looking up at the stars would surely remind a Jewish person of the promise of God to Abraham that his descendants would be as numerous as the stars in the heavens (Genesis 15:5), indicating a fulfillment of the covenant promise in Genesis 12:3 that through Abraham all the families of the earth would be blessed.

So here sits Jonah in his *sukkah,* translated here as "shelter." And there in his shelter, Jonah continued his little pity party as he looked down upon the city where he had just preached. It is quite ironic. He is sitting inside of a structure that was intended to be a place of joy, but Jonah is not very joyous. The *sukkah* was to be a place where God was worshiped and thanked for His goodness, but there is no worship or thanksgiving going on in Jonah's *sukkah*. In fact, Jonah is not concentrating at all on the goodness of God. In verse 1, the Hebrew language indicates that he has accused God of committing an evil deed. He is angry at God, and he has gone into his shelter to pout about it. In some ways, Jonah's time in that shelter is reflective of his entire outlook on life, and that of the better part of his nation. It might be appropriate to refer to Jonah – and to Israel, who had cut themselves off from the nations to whom God had called them to bear witness – as a *sheltered* people. Rather than infecting the godless nations around them with the good news of the one true God, they had insulated themselves from them. As we see the prophet sitting there pouting in his little shelter, we should ask ourselves whether or not we have become sheltered in the same way. Jonah forces us to raise some questions about our sheltered lives.

I. Is there room for anyone else inside of your shelter?

Jonah may have feared at one time that the people of Nineveh would not receive him well. What he experienced there had to come as a surprise to him. He was not only received well, but the short sermon he had preached in Nineveh had sparked a genuine turning to God among the people in the city. One can imagine that he might have been considered a hero in the city. He might have been welcome to spend the rest of his life there, but he didn't. Instead, he chose to leave by himself. He didn't even bother to go back through the city to leave on the same side he came in on. He made no attempt even to head back home to Israel. He left out the east side and went up on a high spot where he could overlook the city of Nineveh, and he built this little sukkah *for himself* and sat under it in the shade.

The unusual thing about this is that a true *sukkah* is not built for one. The idea is to gather under the sukkah with your loved ones and to share meals together. One interesting feature of the typical sukkah is a plaque called an *ushpizin* that bears a prayer of welcome for holy guests. This tradition points back to Genesis 18 when Abraham welcomed three visitors who had come with a message from God about the birth of his son Isaac. This episode likely underlies the statement in Hebrews 13:2, "Do not neglect to show hospitality to strangers, for by this some have entertained angels without knowing it." So the *ushpizin* says essentially that anyone who should happen to come by is welcome to join us in the *sukkah*. That would include the poor, the hungry, the unbelieving, and the Gentiles, on the chance that God could be bringing those visitors in for a holy purpose.

But Jonah's *sukkah* had room for only one. If he had any family or true friends, they were a long distance away, but Jonah did not even make room for strangers in his *sukkah*. His little *sukkah* was built for one, and this is an illustration of the condition of his sheltered life. In his view of the world, there was no room in the shelter of the Lord for anyone other than himself and his own people. He had done what God told him to do, but he had not enlarged his heart and mind, or even his *sukkah*, to make room for the people of Nineveh. Just as the Feast of Tabernacles commemorates the conclusion of the harvest, so God had brought about a great harvest of souls in Nineveh, but Jonah had made no room in his storehouses for the harvest. He was content to let it rot in the fields.

This forces the question on our hearts: is there room for anyone else in our shelter? Have you understood that God did not create your life to be lived in isolation but in community? Is there room in the shelter you have made in your life for your spiritual family, your brothers and sisters in Christ? Is there room in your shelter for you to show hospitality to strangers? Is there room in your shelter for people whose skin is a different color or whose native language is different from yours? Have you come to the understanding that God's purposes are greater than just your individual life, your immediate family, your nation of origin, and your ethno-linguistic people? Perhaps God is challenging you to enlarge your tent and make room for others in your life. In so doing, you may find that God is bringing holy visitors into your life to bless you and to bless them through you.

Jonah has either not understood or not adjusted his life to this reality, and so here he sits in a booth made for one. He is depressed. In my career as a pastor I have learned a lot about depression. It is not because I have read a lot of books about it or counseled a lot of people about it, though I have done my share of both. It is rather because, as a pastor, I have experienced depression personally in ways that I never imagined I would. And one of the things I have learned about it is that depression makes me feel like I want to withdraw myself from others. I want to just pull away from everyone and build a little shelter for myself and have a pity party inside of it. But I have also learned that doing this never helps my depression get better. I only get worse in that little shelter. It is only by enlarging my shelter to welcome others into it that the darkness begins to lift.

George MacDonald once gave this counsel about the darkness of depression: "Fold the arms of your faith and wait quietly for light to arise in your darkness. Fold the arms of your faith, but not of your action: think of something that you ought to do, and go do it, even if it is merely sweeping the room or preparing a meal, or visiting a friend. Don't heed your feelings: do your work!"[207] Long before MacDonald, the Puritan Richard Baxter said similarly, "Be sure that you live not idly.... Idleness is but the devil's home for temptation, and for unprofitable, distracting musings. Labor profits others and ourselves; both soul and body need it. ... *I have known grievous, despairing melancholy cured and turned into a life*

---

[207] Cited in its original vernacular in John Piper, *When I Don't Desire God* (Wheaton, Ill.: Crossway, 2004), 219. I have updated the antiquated wording for ease of understanding.

of godly cheerfulness, principally by setting upon constancy and diligence in the business of families and callings."[208]

I have come to wonder if one cause of so much depression today is that we have allowed ourselves to become too disconnected from the lives of others. God did not create you for this. He created you for interaction with others. And He has called you, in Christ, to invest your life into the lives of others, even and perhaps particularly to those who are different from yourself. So, is there room in your shelter for others? Is there room in your shelter for strangers? Is there room in your shelter for those whom God would have you reach for His glory? Is there room for those who are different? If not, if your shelter is built just for one, then God would have you expand it, and welcome others into your sheltered life. Thus far, it seems that Jonah has been unwilling to do this. What about you?

II. Is there any joy in your shelter?

Jewish people refer to Sukkot, or the Feast of Tabernacles, as "the time of our rejoicing." Of all the festivals of the Hebrew calendar, this one is the only one in Scripture where rejoicing is actually *commanded*. Leviticus 23:40 says "you shall rejoice before the LORD your God for seven days." It was once said that "the person who had not been to Jerusalem during the Feast of Tabernacles just didn't know what rejoicing really meant."[209] That seems to be a stark contrast with the attitude of Jonah here in his *sukkah*. There is no joy in his shelter: only the miserable outlook of a sour disposition waiting hopefully for disaster to strike. Like a Fourth of July spectator, Jonah has built his little booth in a place where he can see the fireworks of destruction from a safe distance.

Of course he is hoping in vain. God has already declared that the disaster will not happen. Nineveh has avoided judgment by turning to God in repentance and faith. But Jonah is so calloused in his heart that he has not received God's word, and he hopes the disaster will strike anyway. How strange! Instead of coddling his hard heart, he could be rejoicing in what God has done! Instead of sitting alone and miserable in the desert, he could

---

[208] Ibid. I have made slight modification to antiquated wording.
[209] Richard Booker, *Jesus in the Feasts of Israel* (Shippensburg, Pa.: Destiny Image, 1987), 103.

be either enjoying the blessings of God in Nineveh, or else going back to Israel to share the report of what God has done. But there is no joy in Jonah's shelter because there is no room for the joy of the Lord in his heart.

I have spotted some times in my life when I am kind of like Jonah in this regard, and perhaps you have too. In the midst of God doing some great things, I choose to focus instead on what He doesn't appear to be doing, or on how He isn't doing what I think He should, or that He isn't doing it the way I think He should. This misdirected focus causes me to miss out on the joy of what the Lord *is* doing! This can happen to all of us from time to time, but there are some who seem to have this negative outlook on everything perpetually. Like Jonah, they sit back at a safe distance hoping to see a disaster happen.

We used to live near the birthplace of Robert Fulton in southern Lancaster County, Pennsylvania. There were lots of things named after him around the area, so we thought we'd better learn something about the hometown hero. One of the most interesting anecdotes I discovered about Fulton concerned the skeptical critics who came out to see the launch of the first steamboat. I have not been able to find out if the story is true or not, but it is amusing. According to the legendary tale, while Fulton was trying to start the engine, the critics shouted "You'll never get it started!" But, once the engine began to rumble and the boat began to move, the critics began to shout, "You'll never get it stopped!" Are you like that? Do you always find something to complain about and find fault with? If so, you probably don't recognize it, so you will have to ask your friends to tell you (if you have any left). And if you are that kind of person, you have no idea of the joy that you are missing out on! Your inability to find joy will soon enough create a situation where there is no one left in your shelter but fellow grumblers and complainers, and that is a sad place to be.

So what is the mood there in the shelter of your life? Is there any joy? If not, you may well be missing out on something that God is doing that deserves celebration. You may be hopelessly hoping for something to happen that God has declared will not, or vice versa. Your bitterness is not going to change Him, but it may harm you and isolate you more and more.

Better for you to accept His word and His will, and allow Him to transform your perspective accordingly so there is room for joy in your shelter.

III. Have you found the shelter of the Lord God?

I love being *at* the beach. I do not particularly care for being *on* the beach, especially when it is extremely hot. Something about the recipe of sweat, sand, saltwater, and sunscreen just kind of bothers me. My wife and kids, on the other hand, love it! The hotter the better! They love to bury each other in the sand, and they are proud to come in after a long day glowing red with sunburn. So, I try to be a supportive husband and father and join them out there on the beach, even though I don't really care for it. A few years ago my wife had a brilliant idea: take an umbrella to the beach, then I can sit in the shade and read a book in a comfy chair while they enjoy the beach. That sounded good to me. "So, how did you like the beach then?" you may ask. Well, the wind on the beach blows about 300 miles per hour, so I spent the better part of the afternoon chasing after the umbrella and trying to keep it from collapsing or folding up inside-out. In spite of all my efforts to provide a shady resting place for myself, I was not able to enjoy it any more than I had without the umbrella.

There sits Jonah, not on the beach but in the desert, in a *sukkah* built for one. He's got a nice canopy over himself. He's built the walls; he's covered the roof to provide himself some shade from the desert sun. Forgetting for a moment his mental and emotional state, which is obviously miserable, what kind of physical state is he in? Is he comfortable there resting in the shade he has built? No! Verse 6 describes him as being in "discomfort." That is a pretty weak rendering of the Hebrew word. In fact, the Hebrew word is one that has been used repeatedly throughout Jonah, probably with intentionality in order to capture the reader's attention. It is used, for instance, to describe the "wickedness" of Nineveh in 1:2 and 3:8, the "calamity" that has come upon the ship in 1:7-8, the "calamity" that God declared He would bring upon Nineveh in 3:10, the "displeasure" of Jonah in 4:1, and now the "discomfort" of Jonah here in 4:6. It is not a pleasant word. We might be right to call it *misery*.

In spite of all of his handiwork to construct a shady shelter for himself, he is not comfortable and at ease. He is miserable. And you and I look at that and say, "Serves him right! He deserves to be miserable. In fact, he deserves to be dead!" There might have been times people said that about us. Aren't you glad that God doesn't treat us like we deserve? He is always leaning in toward us in grace and mercy because He loves us. And that is what He does for Jonah here.

Seeing the prophet in his physical discomfort under his hand-made shelter, "the Lord God[210] appointed a plant to grow up over Jonah to be a shade over his head." He didn't have to do this, but He did it in His sovereign grace. And why? We will see in the verses that follow that God was also going to use this plant to teach Jonah an important lesson, but first things first. The Bible tells us that God caused this plant to grow up over him to "deliver him from his discomfort." Jonah had done all he could do in his own effort to provide himself relief from his misery, but it was not enough. In God's saving grace, He provided for Jonah the shelter that Jonah could make for himself. And finally, perhaps for the first time in Jonah's pitiful story, he is happy. Literally, the Hebrew says, "He rejoiced over the plant with a great joy." Joy was nowhere to be found in the *sukkah* that he had built for himself, but here in the shelter of the Lord, Jonah found the comfort and joy that had eluded him for so long.

There is a lesson here for us and for the whole world. Try as we may to make ourselves comfortable, secure, and happy in this world, we can never seem to attain it. There is something we are seeking that is always just beyond our grasp. The work of our hands can never reach it. Even in the joyous Feast of Tabernacles, the most joyous event on the Hebrew Calendar, there is still a sense of dissatisfaction and longing for something more. The roof of the *sukkah* is constructed so that the heat of the sun still comes in, and the rain still falls through. It is not until we come under the true shelter of the Lord God that we find what it is that we have been missing. Where is this shelter, this tabernacle of the Lord, found? The answer to that is found in the New Testament, in John 1:14. There we find that God "became flesh and dwelt among us." Literally in the Greek

---

[210] This is the only time in Jonah that the compound name "Lord God" appears.

language, He *"tabernacled* among us." Just as in the ancient days, when the Shekinah Glory of God rested upon the Tabernacle of Israel in the wilderness, John says that the Word became flesh and tabernacled among us, and "we beheld His glory."

In Jesus Christ, all that the Feast of Tabernacles represents finds its fulfillment. In Him, we rest from all of our labors and rejoice in the salvation that He has provided for us from our sins through His life, His death, and His resurrection. In Him there is the joy of knowing that God dwells among His people once again. And in Him the way into God's presence for all nations has been opened and the harvest of those from every tribe and tongue and nation is completed. In Him we can rejoice with exceedingly great joy! He is our shelter, our Tabernacle, our deliverance and salvation. And in Him we look forward to a day when Revelation 21:3-4 promises, "Behold, the *tabernacle* of God is among men, and He will dwell among them, and they shall be His people, and God Himself will be among them, and He will wipe away every tear from their eyes; and there will no longer be any death; there will no longer be any mourning, or crying, or pain." There will be no more of any of life's misery there because there will be no sin there. It was dealt with fully and finally in the cross of Jesus, where He took the penalty of all human sin upon Himself. And just as He has removed the penalty of sin from those who believe in Him, so shall we be removed from the presence of sin forever in the glory of His eternal tabernacle where we will live in His presence forevermore.

The Feast of Tabernacles, like each of the seven biblical festivals of Israel, points to Jesus Christ, in whom all of them find their fulfillment. And though Jonah didn't understand it, another of Israel's prophets did. The prophet Ezekiel was given a vision of a day far off in Israel's future, one that is still future today. And in Ezekiel 45, he envisions a day in which Israel will not celebrate seven festivals as they did in the Old Testament, or nine as they do today, but only two. Those two will be the Feast of Tabernacles, which is fulfilled in the coming of Christ as the Messiah, and the Passover, which is fulfilled in the Cross where Christ died for our sins. Is it coincidence that these two feasts correspond with our celebrations of

Christmas and Easter?[211] These two events are our continual reminders that Christ has become our shelter and our salvation, and in Him we rest and we rejoice. And we beckon every nation, including the nation of Israel, to come into His shelter and enjoy His salvation.

Have you entered into the shelter of the Lord Jesus Christ? Or are you still trying to construct a shelter in life with your own hands? It will never do! Come to Him and call upon Him and be saved! And if you have, is there joy in your shelter? If not, then you are not experiencing the joy of the salvation of the Lord! Fix your thoughts on what God has done for you in Christ, and what He is doing in you, through you, and around you in Christ, and find joy! Is there room for anyone else in your shelter? If not, then enlarge your shelter, and bid others to come in and find the rest and the joy of the Lord Jesus!

---

[211] Though the date of the Feast of Tabernacles is actually in the Fall and Christmas is December 25, the theological correspondence is that to which I am referring. Most scholars are agreed that, whenever Jesus' actual birth date was, it was certainly not December 25. Good arguments have been made to place the date of His birth in the Fall, and it is no stretch to conclude further that it may have occurred during or around the time of the Feast of Tabernacles.

XIX

A Lesson in Right Affections
Jonah 4:6-11

So the LORD God appointed a plant and it grew up over Jonah to be a shade over his head to deliver him from his discomfort. And Jonah was extremely happy about the plant. But God appointed a worm when dawn came the next day and it attacked the plant and it withered. When the sun came up God appointed a scorching east wind, and the sun beat down on Jonah's head so that he became faint and begged with all his soul to die, saying, "Death is better to me than life."

Then God said to Jonah, "Do you have good reason to be angry about the plant?" And he said, "I have good reason to be angry, even to death." Then the LORD said, "You had compassion on the plant for which you did not work and which you did not cause to grow, which came up overnight and perished overnight. Should I not have compassion on Nineveh, the great city in which there are more than 120,000 persons who do not know the difference between their right and left hand, as well as many animals?"

A portion of this final passage in Jonah was at the center of an infamous fight between two remarkable Christian leaders in the late 300s and early 400s. During that time period, the two most well known Christians were Augustine and Jerome. Both left indelible marks on the church that are still evident today. In 390, Jerome began to translate the Old Testament into Latin directly from Hebrew. Prior to that time, the Latin Old Testament had been based on a Greek text, the Septuagint. Augustine feared that Jerome's version would create confusion and controversy because the wording of some familiar texts would undoubtedly be changed. When Jerome's version began to grow in popularity and common usage, a twelve year war of letter writing took place between the Jerome and Augustine over the issue. At the heart of the debate for some period of that time was the identification of the plant found in Jonah 4:6. The Latin Bibles which were based on the Greek Septuagint had identified the plant as a gourd. When Jerome translated it from Hebrew, he used a word that means "ivy."

In a letter to Jerome in 403, Augustine tells that a certain pastor had begun to use Jerome's version, and in the course of expounding the book of Jonah, he came upon this word, which in Augustine's words, had "a very different rendering from that which had been of old familiar to the senses and memory of all the worshippers." Augustine relates, "Thereupon arose such a tumult in the congregation, ... correcting what had been read, and denouncing the translation as false," that this pastor, "was compelled to correct [Jerome's] version in that passage as if it had been falsely translated." Had he not done this, Augustine assured Jerome that the pastor would have been terminated from his position.[212]

In John Calvin's reflections on this embarrassing episode in church history, he states that Jerome had been slandered and accused of sacrilege over the translation of this plant.[213] It is interesting that today most Bible commentators are content to say that we do not know, nor does it matter, what species of plant this was. Calvin says concerning the entire affair: "Those men were certainly thoughtless and foolish who were so offended for a matter so trifling."[214] So much emotionally fueled rhetoric, and for what? A plant!

That is not only the point of the debate concerning the translation of the word referring to the plant; it is also the point that God sought to teach Jonah by way of the plant. He might well be saying to the prodigal prophet, "Jonah, you are certainly thoughtless and foolish to be so offended for a matter so trifling." Like those who would argue vehemently about the identification of the plant centuries later, Jonah had some raw emotions on display concerning the plant. Through the entire ordeal, God was seeking to teach Jonah a lesson in right affections. Jonah is a man who is driven by his emotions, from the beginning of this book until its end. But thus far, his affections and emotions have not corresponded to those of the Lord. What brings joy to the Lord brings anger to the prophet. God desires to transform Jonah. He doesn't just want Jonah to *do* the right things; He wants him to

---

[212] "Correspondence of Augustine and Jerome concerning the Latin Translation of the Bible." http://www.bible-researcher.com/vulgate2.html. Accessed October 20, 2011.
[213] Calvin, *Commentaries,* 104.
[214] Ibid., 103-104.

have the right heart—to love the things that God loves and to share in the compassion of the Lord.

Like Jonah, we also need to have our affections shaped by the Lord. We need to learn to be angry at what angers Him and to rejoice over what brings Him joy. So, if Jonah's experience with the plant and the lesson God sought to teach him there can inform us, we may avoid having to learn the lesson through more direct and personal ways. It would be better for us to learn the lesson in right affections through his ordeal than through our own!

I. We must beware of misguided affections.

Emotions are part of what makes us human. We all have them and we cannot escape them. They are the gifts of God, and they can serve as important messengers for us. Emotions are powerful motivators in our lives. They lead us to do certain things and to think certain ways. But our emotions are corrupted by our sinful nature, therefore they cannot always be trusted. Just because something *feels* right to us, that doesn't mean we should do it. Just because something prompts anger within us, for example, this does not mean that our anger is the right response to the situation.

Back in June of 2003, we went to Phoenix for the Southern Baptist Convention. I had reserved a rental car on the internet, and I went to the agency's counter to pick it up only to have the agent tell me that they didn't have any more cars. Now, I thought this was a joke. I had seen this bit before on Seinfeld, so I played along. I explained to the agent the meaning of the words "reservation," and "confirmation," but I was assured that there was nothing they could do for me. I could feel the anger rising up within me. I did what many other Christians would do in that situation: I took a deep breath, looked around to make sure there were no other preachers I knew nearby, and then I absolutely uncorked it on the agent! After a few moments of my unbridled fury, I noticed someone trying to get my attention. I looked slightly to the right, only about five feet away, and there was an agent from another company pointing to the sign on his counter that said, "We have cars available." I did one of those hard swallows, the kind you do when you are trying to get all of your pride down in one gulp, and I walked over to that counter where I very politely asked if I could rent one of their fine vehicles.

Later on that night, I became so convicted that I cared more about a stupid car than I did about the soul of that rental agent. No need to wonder what she thinks of Christians and Baptist preachers after her run-in with me! Instead of unleashing my anger on her, I could have helped her through what was obviously a very difficult shift by telling her the good news of Jesus Christ! But my emotions were misguided. Do you want to hear more stories like that? I have a whole bunch of them I could tell! See, I have been learning the hard way for many years that my emotions are not to be trusted, and when I forget that, I begin to be led astray by them.

That is the lesson that God is trying to teach Jonah here in this passage. He teaches him this lesson by three divinely appointed instruments. He "appoints" a plant, then a worm, then a scorching east wind. All of them do exactly what God appointed them to do, just as the "appointed" fish did previously. In fact, in this entire book, only Jonah refuses to do that for which God has appointed him.

The first thing the Lord appoints here in the text is a plant. What kind of plant was it? *What do you want to do, start another war in the church?* It doesn't matter what kind of plant it was! One commentator has said that it was a castor-oil plant, and that is what Jonah needed: a good dose of castor oil![215] Like the fish that swallowed Jonah, it is futile for us to debate the identity of the plant. This is not a lesson in botany! The point is that God appointed the plant, and it grew up miraculously ("overnight", verse 10) and provided shade for Jonah. You can buy this product called "Miracle-Gro," but it doesn't work like this. This is real *miraculous growth*. The shelter he had attempted to construct for himself was insufficient to provide him comfort. In the loving providence of God, He graciously provided Jonah with a better shelter "to deliver him from his discomfort." And this delighted Jonah. For the first time in the whole book, Jonah is a happy man!

---

[215] Ferguson, 81.

Now, here comes the hard question: Was Jonah happy in God, or was he happy in God's gifts? The average person will say, "What does it matter? If he was happy, that is all that matters!" No, that is not all that matters. To be happy in God's gifts without being happy in God is idolatry. It is an inversion of true Christianity which focuses on seeking the blessings of God rather than seeking God Himself. This is why God's people have engaged in fasting throughout the centuries. In fasting, we give up the gifts of God in order to attune our affections toward the Giver; to seek the glory of God's face rather than the gifts of God's hands.

So, which was it for Jonah? Was he happy in God or was he happy in God's gifts? There's really only one way to find out – *take the gift away*. After Jonah had enjoyed a full day of joy in the shade of the miracle-grow plant, God took it away. He appointed a worm, and before the sun came up the next day, the worm "attacked" the plant and it died. How does this expose whether Jonah's joy is in God or in His gifts? If his joy is in the Lord, then he will say what Job said. He knew what Job said; he had that book of the Bible during his lifetime. Job said, when all that was precious to him in this world had been taken away from him, "The LORD gave and the LORD has taken away. Blessed be the name of the LORD" (Job 1:21). Jonah didn't say this. He didn't say anything, at least not yet.

The next thing that happened was that the Lord appointed a "scorching east wind" to blow. In addition to the blast of the wind, the heat of the sun began to beat down on Jonah's head. The Hebrew word is the same for what the sun did to Jonah's head as for what the worm did to the plant. The sun *attacked* his head. So intense was the burning heat of the sun and the hot blast of the wind that Jonah became faint and delirious. Some have speculated that the wind appointed by the Lord may be the same kind of wind that blows in the Middle East still today which is known as a *scirocco*. Stuart writes that the *scirocco* wind blows with "constant hot air so full of positive ions that it affects the levels of serotonin and other brain neurotransmitters, causing exhaustion, depression, feelings of unreality, and, occasionally, bizarre behavior." In some Islamic countries, he notes, "the punishment for a crime committed while the *scirocco* is blowing may be reduced at judicial discretion, so strongly does the prolonged hot wind affect thinking and actions."[216] This may be why Jonah begins to beg with all his soul to die, saying, "Death is better to me than life." He might have literally been "crazy from the heat."

What is it with this prophet and his recurrent death wish? He became suicidal on the ship when he asked the sailors to throw him overboard. When Nineveh was spared from destruction, again he asked for death in 4:3. And now that God has taken away his little plant and let him feel the heat of the desert with full intensity, again he pleads for death. This brother has got some issues! Remember that he didn't even have to be out in the desert in the first place! He could have stayed in Nineveh and enjoyed a hero's treatment. He could have labored there, training the people in the ways of God. He could have gone home to Israel and reported the amazing work of God to his countrymen. But he chose to pout in the desert, and now he is mad because God is making him feel the heat. Have you ever done that? Have you ever wandered out into the deserts of life on your own volition, and then cursed God because it was hot?

As in the previous cases, it is a demonstration of grace that God doesn't grant his death wish! Rather than just zapping the prophet, God asks him with tenderness, "Do you have good reason to be angry about the plant?" And Jonah responds, "I have good reason to be angry, even to death." In other words, "Yes, I am angry enough to die! I will die for my right to be angry about this!"

Now the scab has been ripped off so we can see the cankerous sore on Jonah's soul. He has misguided affections. He has found delight in the gifts of God without delighting in the person of God. He has rejoiced over a plant – a plant! – that he did not plant, did not tend, and did not cause to grow. He thinks he has every right to be terminally angry about this plant, but obviously he does not. Through this object lesson, God has shown Jonah that he is just an angry little man. He started out being angry at God because he didn't get his way, and now he is angry about plants and worms.

---

[216] Stuart, 505-506.

Misguided affections lead us astray like this. We begin to think they are trustworthy guides, and we allow them to direct our thoughts and actions. How many of us have ever been mad at one thing, which we may have had the right to be angry about, only to find that we are then getting mad about everything? James Boice describes the process:

> First we are angry with God. Next we express our anger at circumstances, then minor circumstances. Finally, our shoelace breaks one morning, and we find ourselves swearing. God was showing this to Jonah, saying, in effect, 'Look where your anger has taken you, Jonah. Is this right? Is this the way you want to live? Do you want to spend the rest of your life swearing at petty annoyances?[217]

This is not the way Jonah wants to live. In fact, it seems that this is the way he wants to die. He seems more willing to die like this than to change his heart and live a different way. What about us? Do we want to live this way, being led up and down a tumultuous rollercoaster by our unbridled emotions? Rejoicing one moment because we have received something good, only to wallow in misery the next because it has broken, or been lost, or been taken away? If our joy were in the Lord rather than in the gifts He gives, there would be more constancy in our affections for He is unchanging. If we are in right relationship with Him and He is the object and source of our joy, then we get off the rollercoaster of emotional ups and downs and we begin to find joy in the ordinary things of life here on the flat ground. I don't know, maybe you like living on the rollercoaster? I doubt it, but you may say that you do anyway. And given the chance to get off the rollercoaster of misguided affections, will you accept it, or will you insist on staying on through the rest of your life and even unto death?

There is a lesson here in Jonah's predicament concerning misguided affections. We can learn it from his experience, or we can learn it from our own. But be sure, God will have us learn it in life or in death. He desires to move our affections away from the things of this world and place them where they belong – in the only place they can be satisfied – in Him. When

---

[217] Boice, 309.

that happens, we can say when our loved one dies, "My joy is in Christ." When the doctor says we have cancer, we can say, "My joy is in Christ." When the house burns down, we can say, "My joy is in Christ." When the cellphone dies, or the car crashes, or the stockmarket plummets, "My joy is in Christ, and He is enough!" And once He becomes the object of our delight and joy, our misguided affections begin to be transformed to reflect His affections.

II. We need transformed affections that reflect the heart of God

Rumors concerning the death of Muammar Gadaffi began to circulate early on the morning of October 20, 2011, and by midday it was confirmed. One comment on Twitter summed up the emotions of many people around the world. It said, "Hell has been busy this year." Now, before you say "Amen" to that, let me remind you that hell is busy every day. And the big question we need to ask is not "How does this make us feel?" The big question is "How does this make God feel?" The death of a ruthless tyrant is good for the world and good for the people who have suffered under his violent and oppressive regime. Therefore, the end of his reign is the cause for some measure of rejoicing. But if our rejoicing is not tempered with another reality, then we have not understood the affections of the God who said, "As I live! ... I take no pleasure in the death of the wicked, but rather that the wicked turn from his way and live" (Ezekiel 33:11). If our affections are undergoing transformation to reflect His, then there is a gravity in our emotions – a joy for the opportunity of the people to live in a freer society and for the world to be a safer place, mixed with the real horror that another lost soul has joined the population of hell for eternity. You may say, "Well, he got what he deserved!" But, please remember, you also deserve it, as do I. If you think that you are not as great a sinner as Gadaffi or any other ruthless tyrant in the world, then you have not grasped the sinfulness of all of our sin and how it is viewed in the affections of a just and holy God.

Let me throw out another case study. Most of us remember Jeffrey Dahmer, the serial killer whose grisly and perverted crimes tallied seventeen murders from the late seventies to early nineties. To read of the things that this man did to his victims is gut-wrenching. At some point during his imprisonment, Dahmer testified that he had become a born-again Christian. The pastor who baptized him in the prison has stated repeatedly that he is sure that Dahmer's conversion was sincere and genuine. If that is true, then when Jeffrey Dahmer was brutally beaten to death by a fellow inmate, he went to heaven. How does that make you feel? How do you feel when you think that Dahmer might be in heaven, but your neighbor who is a nice and friendly unbeliever will go to hell? Are you more outraged that Dahmer could be saved, or more sorrowful that your neighbor has not been saved?

We've migrated into the crevasse of weighty issues here. This is visceral stuff, but these kinds of questions are exactly the kinds of questions that God was asking Jonah to teach him about right affections. He asks, "Jonah, do you have a good reason (or a *right*) to be angry about the plant?" God caused the plant to grow with no help or permission from Jonah. God didn't need Jonah's permission to take it away. He gave, and He took away. Was Jonah able to bless His name? No, he was wrongfully angry.

Jonah's emotions are the same concerning the plant as they are concerning Nineveh. He was terminally angry about the repentance and salvation of Nineveh as well. God had already asked him in verse 4, "Do you have good reason to be angry" about what took place in Nineveh? Jonah didn't answer that time. But the answer he gave concerning the plant exposes the fact that Jonah felt like he did have a right to be angry about Nineveh. In fact, Jonah's tirade against God and his silence in the face of God's questions indicate that Jonah felt that God had *no right* to spare Nineveh. Now God has Jonah in the place where He wants him to teach him a lesson about right affections.

"Should I not have compassion on Nineveh?" Unlike Jonah's cherished plant, God had a good reason and a right to have compassion on Nineveh. He "planted" this seed. This city was filled with human beings whom God had created, and as such they bore His divine image. They were the objects of His love – the love of a Creator for His creation. Should God delight in their destruction, or does He have the right to spare them if He chooses?

If Jonah is unwilling to acknowledge God's right to have mercy on the adult population of Nineveh, many of whom (but certainly not all) have been guilty of heinous crimes against humanity, would he object to God sparing Nineveh's children? These may be the ones God is referring to when He speaks of more than 120,000 who cannot tell the difference between their right and left hand. If He wipes out the whole city, it will include these children who have committed no crimes against Jonah or Israel. Should God have mercy on them? Many commentators believe that this statement does not refer exclusively to the children of Nineveh, but to the entire population of the city. Not knowing their right from their left might speak of their moral and spiritual ignorance. Nineveh has been wicked because they didn't know any better. If that is so, should God not have mercy on them now that they have repented of their sin and turned to the Lord begging for mercy? And what of the animals? What have the cattle or flocks of Nineveh ever done to Jonah? If fire and brimstone should fall on Nineveh, they will be destroyed as well. Does God not have the right to spare Nineveh, if for no other reason than to spare these animals? Does God, or does He not, have permission to have mercy on whom He will have mercy and to show compassion to whom He shows compassion (Romans 9:15; Exodus 33:19)? Does God need Jonah's, or anyone else's, permission to save the lost wherever they may be found?

"Should I not have compassion on Nineveh?" the Lord asks. And then the story ends. Jonah gives no answer. If he wrote the book, or provided information to another writer (and one or the other of these options must be the case given the "eyewitness" details in the story), then we know that he didn't die there. He lived long enough to record the ordeal or provide the information to one who did, but we do not know how he answered the Lord, or if he ever did at all. Did he learn this lesson of right affections? I guess we will find out when we get to heaven.

There is a sense in which we really don't need to know how Jonah answered. We don't have to give account for him, but we do have to give account for ourselves. So, what is more important for us is whether or not we have learned this lesson. What is our response? Does God have the right to save whosoever He desires to save, wherever and whoever they are? Does God need your permission or mine to do what He desires to do?

Does He have the right to give and to take away, and shall His name be blessed when He does? If our affections are misguided, we will be angry at the Lord about things that should cause us to rejoice. We will be happy with His gifts when we receive them, but envious and angry when others receive them. But if our affections are being shaped to reflect the affections of the Lord, we will be angered by what angers Him, and we will rejoice over what brings Him joy. If there is more rejoicing in heaven over one sinner who repents than over ninety-nine righteous persons who need no repentance (Luke 15:7), then is that reflected in our affections? If so, it will be manifest in how we conduct ourselves in this world. We will be zealous proclaimers of the Good News of Jesus, and we will be glad when even the worst of sinners finds the saving mercy of God. We will be burdened when anyone departs this life without the hope of heaven that is found in Jesus. It will trouble us deeply that a significant percentage of the world's population has no access to the message of Jesus! And we will acknowledge that God is God, and God is good, and it will be our delight to join Him in His mission to spread His fame to the ends of the earth!

Jonah was not the first to wrestle with the question. And he won't be the last. Someone here today may be wrestling with it even now. Thomas Carlisle's poem "You Jonah" concludes with these words:

And Jonah stalked
to his shaded seat
and waited for God
to come around
to his way of thinking.
And God is still waiting for a host of Jonahs
in their comfortable houses
to come around
to His way of loving.[218]

He is waiting patiently for you. He longs to transform your affections so that they will reflect His. If you are struggling with the same burden that

[218] Quoted in John Piper, *Let the Nations Be Glad!* (Second Edition; Grand Rapids: Baker, 2003), 175.

Jonah was, call out to the Lord and offer Him all of your misguided affections that He might transform you for His glory.

But maybe you are struggling with the burden of Nineveh instead. Convicted of your sin, turned off by a host of hypocritical Jonahs you have known in life, you wonder if there may be any hope. The Gospel tells us that there is hope, and it is only found in Jesus. He is the One who is greater than Jonah (Matthew 12:41). He has taken your sin upon Himself and carried it to the cross where He received your penalty in Himself and He has conquered sin and death through His resurrection. He is alive today and will save you if you turn to Him. He is a God of mercy, and He will show it to whomever He chooses. He has announced that He will show His saving mercy to all who come to Him through repentance and faith in Jesus.

XX

How Great Is Our God?
The Abiding Message of Jonah
Jonah 1:1-3, 4:11

The word of the LORD came to Jonah the son of Amittai saying,
"Arise, go to Nineveh the great city and cry against it,
for their wickedness has come up before Me."
But Jonah rose up to flee to Tarshish from the presence of the LORD.
So he went down to Joppa, found a ship which was going to Tarshish,
paid the fare and went down into it to go with them to Tarshish
from the presence of the LORD.

...

"Should I not have compassion on Nineveh, the great city
in which there are more than 120,000 persons who do not know
the difference between their right and left hand, as well as many animals?"

When our congregation began to study this little book of Jonah together, few probably imagined that it would require six months and twenty sermons to do so. Yet, after all that, it is likely that we have not even scratched the surface of the timeless truths contained in Jonah. As we bring our study of Jonah to a close, we are looking at the big picture. We've looked at the individual trees, but now we want to look at the forest as a whole. Jonah is one of the smallest books of the Bible, at just four chapters and 48 verses, yet as we have seen, it makes a large impact on those who read, study, and apply it to their lives. As I have poured countless hours of study into this book, I have found it to be comforting, challenging, and convicting. Others shared similar sentiments with me throughout our study of it.

What do we take away from it after this lengthy study? I hope that you never look at this book again as being the story of a man and a whale. As we have seen, it's a fish, not a whale, and it only shows up in 3 of the 48 verses of the book (for the statisticians among us, that is 6.25% of the book). The great fish is a remarkable miracle, but it is no greater miracle than the storm, the plant, the worm, or the wind that God appointed to serve His purposes in this book. In fact, when we look at the book as a whole, we would have to say that God's communication with Jonah (the revelation of Himself through His word), and His grace toward Jonah and toward Nineveh are far greater miracles than any of those spectacular phenomena. G. Campbell Morgan said that, when it comes to studying Jonah, "some people are so busy with a tape measure trying to find the dimensions of a whale's belly that they never see God at all."[219] This is a terrible shame! More than a book about a fish or a book about a prophet, the book of Jonah is a book about God.

In spite of the relative simplicity of the story of Jonah, there is a brilliance at work in the telling of it that is sometimes lost on us English readers. One of the tools that the author uses is the repetition of certain important Hebrew words. We have mentioned how he repeats a word that means "down" to describe Jonah's progress as he rebels from God's calling. We have also mentioned the repetition of a Hebrew word that is translated as "evil," "calamity," "distress," among other English words, to indicate the trouble that comes upon Jonah and upon Nineveh. Another frequently occurring word in Jonah is a Hebrew word that we would translate as "great." It occurs 14 times in these 48 verses to describe the city of Nineveh (1:2; 3:2-3; 4:11), the wind and the storm on the sea (1:4, 12), the fear of the sailors (1:10, 16), the fish (1:17), the leaders of Nineveh (3:5, 7), and the emotions of Jonah (4:1, 6). But this word is never used to describe the greatest element of the story.

Greater than all of these is the greatness of God. God is the main character, the primary actor, and the hero of the story. All of the other components of the story (the ship, the sea, the storm, the fish, the plant, the worm, the wind, the city, and even the prophet) are what Morgan calls *incidental things* rather than *essential matters* in the book. He says, "These things are

---

[219] G. Campbell Morgan, *The Unfolding Message of the Bible* (Westwood, NJ: Revell, 1961), 188.

incidental because they were the instruments in the hand of the master Workman."[220] It seems to me that the single-most important abiding lesson of the book of Jonah concerns this master Workman. Like that favorite old hymn of many (which is not nearly as old as we imagine), the book of Jonah proclaims "How Great Thou Art!" Like the popular contemporary worship song, it asks and answers the question, "How Great is Our God?" And it provides for us four specific responses to that question.

I. God's love is greater than our circles of concern.

When I was a student at Fruitland Baptist Bible Institute, chapel services were a highlight of each day. There is nothing like singing the great hymns of the faith in a room filled with men who sing with passion and enthusiasm and hearing the faithful exposition of God's Word from some of the best preachers in America. During chapel services, from time to time, one of the faculty members would announce current opportunities for ministry that students may be interested in. I recall one day in chapel when Dr. Thad Dowdle, our hermeneutics professor and Academic Dean, announced that the Badlands Baptist Association in South Dakota was seeking pastors for several churches in the area. I remember thinking, "Who in the world would want to move to Badlands, South Dakota?" I can remember praying several times in those early years of ministry preparation, "Lord, send me anywhere to serve You. Anywhere, that is, except Badlands, South Dakota! Please don't send me there." I am sure it is a lovely place for someone to go serve the Lord—someone, but not me!

A short time later, Dr. John Bisagno came to preach in a worship service at my home church, Calvary Baptist Church of Winston-Salem, North Carolina, and he challenged us to consider serving the Lord wherever He called us to go. I remember praying in that service, "Lord, You name it! I will go anywhere, anytime, just let me serve You! And if possible, can I request that it not be in Badlands, South Dakota?" The next Sunday, I walked into church and was greeted by Ed Evans, a dear friend and brother in the Lord, whom I had known for most of my life. Ed said, "Russ, I have

---

[220] Morgan, *A Bible Survey: Genesis-Revelation* (Chattanooga, TN: AMG Publishers, 1993), 299. This book was originally published as *The Messages of the Books of the Bible*.

had to back out of a mission trip to Kenya, and I want you to go in my place. In fact, I have already paid for it in full. I want you to go." I said, "Well, Ed, thank you very much, but I don't really think I can go to Africa. Maybe you can find someone else." As I walked away from Ed, the Lord reminded me of my prayer that I would go anywhere, anytime. The Holy Spirit convicted me, as if to say, "Russ, you say you will go anywhere, anytime, but you won't go to Badlands and you won't go to Africa, so where will you go?" That afternoon, I called Ed back and told him I would go to Kenya, and that experience changed my life. Because of the lessons God taught me through that experience of following His calling anywhere, anytime, I subsequently served as a pastor in the small town of Conowingo, Maryland, and have since traveled to Eastern Europe, West Africa, and South Asia for short term volunteer missions projects. In fact, when the opportunity arose to serve the Lord near my hometown, it took much prayer and providence to convince me that the Lord was in that move. I had learned the lesson so thoroughly that I just assumed that the Lord would always lead me away from my comfort zone to serve Him.

From time to time, I counsel with young people who desire to serve the Lord in some way. Many of them say to me, "You know, I am willing to serve the Lord in any way, as long as it is here in North Carolina, or here in the South somewhere." And in those moments I have the opportunity to share my testimony of how God stretched me beyond my comfort zone and I challenge them to remove all geographic boundaries from their consideration of His calling.

In a similar way, whenever we share an opportunity to serve the Lord in international missions, there is always someone who will say, "Why should I go to Africa or to South Asia when there are so many lost people here at home?" My response to that is usually, "Well, what are you doing now, here at home, to reach the lost?" Surprisingly, very few of those individuals are actually doing *anything* to reach the lost at home. It seems, not that they want to stay home and serve the Lord, but rather that they really don't want to serve the Lord at all. For many of us, the lessons of the book of Jonah are greatly needed! And one of those lessons is that God's love is greater than our circles of concern.

To Jonah's credit, we can say that he was not in objection to serving the Lord at all. In 2 Kings 14:25, we read of how this prophet was already engaged in ministry in Israel. But when the call came for him to leave his home country and go outside of his own comfort zone to Nineveh, he ran away. Morgan isolates this as the primary abiding lesson of the book of Jonah. He says that in writing this book, "Jonah intended to teach his people the lesson of the inclusiveness of the Divine government, and thus to rebuke the exclusiveness of their attitude toward surrounding peoples."[221] He says, "The book is supremely the one of missionary teaching in the Old Testament," revealing "the attitudes and activities of God toward the nations, and toward His own for the sake of the nations."[222]

From the very beginning of their existence as a people, it was the commission of God for Israel that they should be a light to the nations. In God's call to Abram in Genesis 12, He announced that all the families of the earth would be blessed through him. The purpose of God's choosing Israel as His own people was never that Israel alone would be only people of God in the world. Throughout the Old Testament we find reminders that God intended to use them to draw the other nations into the knowledge and worship of the Lord. They were to be God's missionary people. But time and time again, Israel retreated into a "holy huddle" of exclusivism in which they sought to keep God to themselves. No individual in the Bible exemplifies this attitude more than the prophet Jonah. He refused to follow God's calling to Nineveh, and he became angry when God performed His saving work among them. All that Jonah experienced throughout these four chapters took place to teach him, to teach all Israel, and to teach us today, that God's love is greater than our circles of concern: it extends to all nations.

In the New Testament, the final command of Jesus to the church before His ascension was to be His witnesses in the whole world. Matthew records the Great Commission this way: "Go therefore and make disciples of all the nations, baptizing them in the name of the Father and the Son and the Holy Spirit, teaching them to observe all that I commanded you" (Matthew

---

[221] Morgan, *The Analyzed Bible* (Grand Rapids: Baker, 1964), 301.
[222] Morgan, *Bible Survey,* 299-300.

28:19-20). Luke records that Jesus instructed His followers to proclaim His death and resurrection and repentance for the forgiveness of sins in His name "to all the nations" (Luke 24:46-47). In Acts 1:8, we find these words of Jesus: "You will receive power when the Holy Spirit has come upon you; and you shall be My witnesses both in Jerusalem, and in all Judea and Samaria, and even to the remotest part of the earth."

Yet, the early followers of Jesus still struggled to comprehend the universal scope of God's love. We could point to the Apostle Peter as an example of this. In Acts 10, Peter was praying on the roof of the home of Simon the Tanner, unaware that a group of Gentiles was coming to meet with him in order to learn about Jesus. In order to prepare Peter for this meeting, God gave Peter a vision of a sheet being lowered from heaven, and spread upon it were all kinds of four-footed animals, crawling creatures, and birds. The word came to Peter saying, "Get up, Peter, kill and eat!" But Peter, being a good Jewish man, protested, saying, "By no means, Lord." By the way, that is always a bad thing to say. If He is truly Lord over us, then our response to His commands must never be, "By no means!" But Peter had a reason in his heart for rejecting this command. He said, "I have never eaten anything unholy and unclean." But the Lord said, "What God has cleansed, no longer consider unholy." This happened again and again, three times. And while Peter was considering what the Lord was trying to teach him through this vision, these Gentiles came in asking for Peter. Peter began to realize that the point of the vision was to teach him that there was a prejudice in his heart that would prevent him from fulfilling God's mission to reach Gentiles as long as he continued to think that God was only concerned for Jewish people.

Do you remember what Peter's full name was? In Matthew 16:17, Jesus calls him "Simon Barjona," meaning, "Simon son of Jonah." Now, we do not need to imagine that Peter was actually a descendant of the prophet Jonah. Jesus was speaking of Peter's earthly father, who happened to also be named Jonah. But in this episode in Acts 10, Peter shows us that the apple has not fallen far from the tree of the prophet who shared the same name as his father. In spite of the Lord's repeated commission to take the Gospel to all nations, Peter was still reluctant to embrace the Gentiles. And where did this episode take place? It took place in Joppa (Acts 10:5), the same place where Jonah boarded the ship to flee from God's calling. The Lord was teaching Peter, who had Jonah's name, who was staying in Jonah's town, and who seems to have had Jonah's heart, that His love is greater than our circles of concern.

Are we also sons of Jonah dwelling in our own town of Joppa? As we look at the world today, we find two alarming realities. First, we find the church in America, infected with carnality, consumerism, and competitiveness, building for ourselves larger and more comfortable buildings and spending more and more resources on ourselves than we have in the last 300 years or more. Compare that with the other startling reality: of 11,545 specific people groups in the world today, 6,672 of them are less than 2% Christian, and 3,575 of those are virtually isolated from any gospel witness![223] It would seem that we have, by and large, not learned the lesson of Jonah. It seems that, like Jonah, we have been content to stay in the confines of our comfort zones, content that we have the gospel, that we have the church, and that we have our basic needs met, while much of the world does not. If we would learn the abiding message of the book of Jonah, we would see that we serve a great God, and His love is greater than our circles of concern. His love extends to all nations, exemplified in His repeated call to Jonah to go there and preach His word, and in His saving work on their behalf when they turned to Him in repentance and faith. There are entire nations out there who may quickly turn to the Lord in repentance and faith, if only someone would come and share the good news of Jesus with them. So what are we waiting for? Why are we running from our calling to take the good news to the nations like Jonah did? Morgan supposes that our reasons are not all that much different from Jonah's. He says that we have halted "because we hate Nineveh. The Church does not want to see the world saved, does not want to see the heathen nations brought to Christ." Looking closer to home, Morgan said to his London congregation, "Why does the Church not reach the outcast people in London and save them? Because the Church does not like the outcast people, does not want them saved."[224]

---

[223] This information was current according to the Southern Baptist International Mission Board, November 16, 2011.
[224] Morgan, *Bible Survey,* 305.

The answer does not seem to be found in forcing ourselves to love the lost more than we do. I am not sure that is possible. But the answer may well be found in more love for Christ, for His love for the lost is unsurpassable. If we would love Him more, then His love for the lost, wherever they are found, may flow through us more freely! Through the book of Jonah, the Lord may be saying to us, "Arise, and go into all the nations, beyond your comfort zone, and tell them the good news about Me. Tell them of My glorious greatness and the great love I have for all people and every nation."

II. God's power is greater than our circumstances.

Throughout the Bible there are frequent reminders that God is able "to do exceeding abundantly above all that we ask or think" (Ephesians 3:20, KJV). As the prophet Jeremiah exclaimed, "Ah Lord God! Behold, You have made the heavens and the earth by Your great power and by Your outstretched arm! Nothing is too difficult for You" (Jeremiah 32:17). We find this point illustrated and reinforced throughout the book of Jonah. Nothing is too difficult for "the Lord God of heaven who made the sea and the dry land" (Jonah 1:9). We see this in Jonah by the power of God to "appoint" whatever is necessary to accomplish His purposes. The word "appoint" occurs four times, and twice more the idea of the Lord's sovereign appointment of agents to do His bidding is found, teaching us that His power is greater than our circumstances.

The first "appointment" that we find in the text is that of the prophet. The Word of the Lord comes to Jonah in the book's opening verses, calling him to go to Nineveh to proclaim God's message. Nineveh's circumstances were troubling, to say the least. In fact, there is some debate among scholars concerning the right way to translate Jonah 1:2, because the word rendered "wickedness" there can also refer to "trouble," even as it does elsewhere in Jonah. So here is the question: Was God sending Jonah to Nineveh because of their wickedness or because of the trouble that Nineveh was in danger of facing because of their wickedness? The most satisfactory answer may be that there is a double-entendre here. God is sending His prophet to them to announce that a destruction is coming because of their sin. Within that warning is an inherent condition that they may yet be saved if they repent and turn to the Lord in faith. Their circumstances were troubling, but not beyond the power of God who, in His sovereignty, could appoint a prophet to deliver His message to them.

Of course, we know that Jonah refused to go initially. He went to Joppa and boarded a ship bound for Tarshish. And on the ship, Jonah fell into a deep sleep hoping that he had escaped the Lord and His calling for good. But God's power is greater than our circumstances! He "hurled a great wind on the sea" which produced "a great storm" that threatened to destroy the ship, the sailors, and the prophet. As the captain urged him to wake up and pray, Jonah began to face the firing squad of interrogation from the sailors. As he answered their questions, he testified to his faith in the Lord, and as a result the sailors went from fearing the storm to fearing the Lord. So, though in Jonah's present circumstances he was running from God's call to reach Gentiles with His message, in God's power, He used a storm to awaken Jonah to reach Gentiles anyway! The sailors, freshly converted to faith in the one true God, threw Jonah overboard at his own request, and the sea became perfectly calm for them. God's power was greater than all of their circumstances.

In Chapter 2, Jonah reflects on how it felt for him to sink beneath the waves, certain that he was going to die and become entombed on the floor of the Mediterranean Sea. But the power of God was greater than Jonah's circumstances. He sovereignly appointed a great fish to swallow Jonah, and within the belly of that fish, Jonah was saved and preserved alive for three days and three nights. The fish carried him back to shore where he was once again presented with an opportunity to obey God's calling.

In Chapter 4, we find Jonah, after his mission trip to Nineveh, sitting out in the desert. Physically, he is in discomfort. Emotionally, he is angry. Spiritually, he is still hard-hearted toward the purposes of God. Those are not good circumstances to be in, but the power of God is greater than his circumstances. To save him from his discomfort, the Lord appointed a plant to grow up over him to provide him shade from the sun. But in order to deal with Jonah's emotional and spiritual circumstances, the Lord also appointed a worm to destroy the plant, and a scorching east wind to bring Jonah to the end of himself.

All of this speaks to us today because we are so prone to focus on the unpleasantness of our own circumstances rather than on the all-surpassing greatness of God's power. You recall how Paul prayed three times for the Lord to remove his thorn in the flesh (2 Corinthians 12:7-9). The answer he received from the Lord was, "My grace is sufficient for you, for power is perfected in your weakness." God's power was greater than Paul's circumstances, as it was in Jonah's situation and ours. Do you feel like you are drowning in your present circumstances? You must not forget that God's power is great enough to send His divinely appointed fish to swallow you. Do you feel like you are sweltering in the heat of your season in the desert of life? Remember that God is able, in His great power, to appoint a plant to grow up over you to give you shade and shelter. Do your present circumstances reveal a heart of disobedience or indifference to the Lord? Well, He can also do something about that! He can send storms your way to turn you back to Him. He can send His divinely appointed worms and winds to bring you to the end of yourself and turn your heart back to Himself! What we see in the book of Jonah is that God is powerful and sovereign over all creation – over people, over plants, over animals, and over the weather! He can make all of these things to be His servants for His purposes. And so Jonah teaches us this abiding lesson: that God's power is greater than our circumstances.

III. God's grace is greater than our sin.

Julia Harriette Johnston was the daughter of a Presbyterian pastor. She served as the director of Sunday School in her father's church in Peoria, Illinois for 40 years, and as President of the Presbyterian Missionary Society for 20 years. During her career of faithful service to the Lord, she wrote over 500 hymns.[225] The one that is most well known today is called "Grace Greater than Our Sin." Throughout the hymn, she speaks of the misery of sin. In the second stanza, she writes, "Sin and despair, like the sea waves cold, threaten the soul with infinite loss". In the third stanza she says, "Dark is the stain that we cannot hide. What can avail to wash it away?" But the song lifts our gaze beyond the cold waves and dark stains

---

[225] "Julia Harriette Johnston." http://www.cyberhymnal.org/bio/j/o/h/johnston_jh.htm. Accessed October 27, 2011.

of sin. Throughout we are pointed higher to the "marvelous grace of our loving Lord, grace that exceeds our sin and our guilt." And in the refrain, we sing repeatedly, "Grace, grace! God's grace! Grace that will pardon and cleanse within! Grace, grace! God's grace! Grace that is greater than all our sin!" Though it was written nearly three millennia after Jonah's experience, this song could be the soundtrack of Jonah's life and of Nineveh's experience.

We find God's grace displayed toward Jonah the prophet. In his stubborn rebellion, he flees from the Lord and is eventually thrown into the ocean to drown. Sin and despair, like the sea waves cold, threaten Jonah's soul with infinite loss. But God's grace is greater than Jonah's sin. We must understand that God is just; He is holy and righteous. As a just Judge, He has the full right and ability to administer perfect justice. He can see to it that everyone gets exactly what they deserve. And in His justice, He could let Jonah sink to the ocean floor, and die a miserable death by drowning. If Jonah dies in Chapter 1 or 2, we would have to say, "He got what he deserved. God is just." But although God is *completely* just, He is not *only* just. He is *perfectly* just, but justice is not the sum of His perfections! The Lord is also abundantly gracious! And in His great grace, He saves Jonah from drowning, and brings him back to shore by means of the appointed fish. If this were all that God did, it would be exceedingly gracious. But, as they say on the television infomercials, "But, wait! There's more!" In 3:1, we read, "Now the word of the Lord came to Jonah *the second time*." He is the God of second chances, and in His grace He gives Jonah a second chance. We might point to the end of Chapter 4, where we find God patiently working with Jonah and leading him toward an understanding of compassion, and say that God is giving Jonah even a *third* chance! Did he deserve any of this? No, if Jonah were to get what he deserved, if he were to get *justice* from God, then he would have died long before we reach the end of the book. But instead of justice, Jonah received grace! He received a grace from God that was greater than his sin.

Nineveh, the great city of the Assyrian Empire, could also say that they had experienced the marvelous grace of our loving Lord. Dark was their stain, and it could not be hidden. In 1:2, the Lord said, "their wickedness has come up before Me." He knew of their evil deeds. We recounted some of them in our study of the book, how they ruthlessly and viciously tortured and pillaged the inhabitants of other lands. These were deeds that their own historians recorded in an almost boastful way. Who knows what other evil they had committed? Surely God knew of all their wickedness. It had arisen before Him; He was aware and took notice of it. And He promised to also take action on it. His message to Nineveh through Jonah was one of justice: "Yet forty days and Nineveh will be overthrown!" But this message moved the people of Nineveh to repentance. They acknowledged the wickedness of their ways, and turned from the violence which was in their hands (3:8). God "relented concerning the calamity which He had declared He would bring upon them. And He did not do it" (3:10). Nineveh found the grace of God which was greater than their sins!

As you and I read this book, we may be like the king of Nineveh, who was "struck" (as the Hebrew literally reads in 3:6) by the word of the Lord, as we see our own sins. We may wonder like he did, saying, "Who knows? God may turn and relent and withdraw His burning anger so that we will not perish" (3:9). We may be like Jonah, who said, "While I was fainting away, I remembered the Lord, and my prayer came to You in Your holy temple" (2:7). And if we are struck in this way concerning our sin, and we turn to the Lord in repentance and faith, we will find that His grace is greater than our sins. We will find that He is a God of second and third chances. And this is so, not because of what we do about our own sins, but because of what God has done about our sins. Jonah recognizes that "Salvation is from the Lord" (2:9), and it is the Lord who has dealt with our sin fully and finally in the person of Jesus Christ. God's great grace does not merely overlook our sin; it faces our sin, and fights it, and destroys it in the death and resurrection of Jesus. So, Jonah and Nineveh are saved by a great grace of God that was yet to be revealed in its fullness. You and I can see that grace demonstrated vividly, perfectly, and fully in the substitutionary sacrifice of Jesus for our sins. The great hymn says this as well, pointing us in every stanza to Jesus. This great grace was "yonder on Calvary's mount outpoured, there where the blood of the Lamb was spilled." Grace points us "to the refuge, the mighty cross." "Look!" the hymn-writer says, "there is flowing a crimson tide!" And in that crimson tide of Christ's blood we are washed, cleansed of sin and forgiven. We see God's great grace portrayed in the story of Jonah. Yet, it is in the cross, and only in the cross, that we see the grace of God that is greater than our sin most clearly and most vividly!

IV. God's Son is greater than Jonah.

Recently, the noted atheist Richard Dawkins launched yet another attack on religion in general and Christianity in particular when he said, "Somebody as intelligent as Jesus would have been an atheist if he had known what we know today."[226] When I read that statement aloud in my home, my ten-year-old son said, "There is so much wrong with that statement, it's hard to know where to begin!" Indeed, my son is exactly right! It is hard to know where to begin a response to that statement! Obviously, one starting point for a response that comes to mind immediately is that Jesus knew that there was a God because Jesus *is* that very God! And He knew that about Himself! But the thing that really gets me is that Dawkins thinks he has access to more information than Jesus – that he is smarter than Jesus! What an arrogant and audacious claim! Yet Dawkins is not the first to claim that he knows more than Jesus, and he undoubtedly won't be the last.

When it comes to the book of Jonah, there have been many scholars who have claimed to know more than Jesus. Of course, most of them don't say it this way, but perhaps they have not considered the full ramifications of their theories. When critical scholars say that there is no historical truth to the story of Jonah (suggesting that it is merely a parable, an allegory, or midrash), they seem unaware or unconcerned that Jesus spoke of the story of Jonah as if it was a historical fact.[227] So, do they know more than Jesus knew? Can we just say for the record that *no one* knows more than Jesus knows! And we should be careful when anyone claims that they do!

Jesus said to the people of His own day, "The men of Nineveh will stand up with this generation at the judgment, and will condemn it because they

---

[226] Billy Hallowell, "Richard Dawkins: 'Jesus Would Have Been An Atheist if He Had Known What We Know Today.'" http://www.theblaze.com/stories/richard-dawkins-jesus-would-have-been-an-atheist-if-he-had-known-what-we-know-today/. Accessed October 27, 2011.

[227] For more on this discussion, I would commend the background study at the beginning of this volume.

repented at the preaching of Jonah; and behold, *something greater than Jonah* is here" (Matthew 12:41; Luke 11:32). He refers to Jonah and the people of Nineveh as real, historical figures, and He speaks of Nineveh's repentance and of the preaching of Jonah as real, historical events. But more importantly, He says that the people of Nineveh will testify against the people of Jesus' generation because, although they repented at the preaching of this severely flawed prophet, the people of Jesus' generation had not repented even though one *greater than Jonah* was among them.

This leads us to ask the question: *How is Jesus greater than Jonah?* As we compare the lives and ministries of Jesus and Jonah, we see at least four specific ways in which Jesus is greater than Jonah. First, we see this in *Christ obeying His calling.* When the call came for Jonah to go, the prophet's response was a resounding, "No!" Aren't you glad that the Lord Jesus didn't say "No!" to the call of His Father to redeem a lost and dying world? The mystery of the Trinity is thick here, and we may wander into dangerous speculations trying to imagine how that conversation between Father and Son took place. But we are helped in our attempt to imagine it by a statement in Hebrews 10:5-7. The writer of Hebrews takes up the language of Psalm 40:6-8 and invites us to imagine a conversation that may have taken place on Christmas Eve in heaven[228]:

> *When He* [Jesus] *comes into the world, He says, "Sacrifice and offering You have not desired, but a body You have prepared for Me; In whole burnt offerings and sacrifices for sin you have taken no pleasure. Then I said, 'Behold, I have come (in the scroll of the book it is written of me) to do Your will, O God.*

Paul explains it this way in Philippians 2:6-8:

> *Although He* [Jesus] *existed in the form of God, did not regard equality with God a thing to be grasped, but emptied Himself, taking the form of a bond-servant, and being made in the likeness*

---

[228] Harold John Ockenga preached a sermon on this text entitled "The Night Before Christmas." That sermon can be found in *Great Sermons on the Birth, Death, and Resurrection of Christ*, ed. Wilbur M. Smith (One-Volume Edition; Grand Rapids: Baker, 1996), 1:221ff.

of men. Being found in appearance as a man, He humbled Himself by becoming obedient to the point of death, even death on a cross.

Jesus is greater, because when He was called by His Father to come into the world for our salvation, He did not say "No!" Unlike Jonah, He obeyed His calling.

Jesus is greater than Jonah, and we see this secondly in *Christ calming the storm*. As we read the account of Jonah asleep the boat while the storm rages upon the sea, we are reminded of another storm on another sea. In Mark 4 we read about the Lord Jesus and His disciples encountering a great storm on the Sea of Galilee. Like Jonah's storm, this one was characterized by a "fierce gale of wind" and terrible waves (Jonah 1:4; Mark 4:37). Like Jonah's ship, which was "about to break up" (Jonah 1:4), Jesus' boat was filling up with water (Mark 4:37). Like Jonah (Jonah 1:5), Jesus was asleep in the stern of the boat (Mark 4:38), undisturbed by the raging storm. Jonah's traveling companions woke the sleeping prophet and compelled him to pray, saying, "Get up, call on your God. Perhaps your God will be concerned about us so that we will not perish" (Jonah 1:6). Jesus' companions similarly woke Him up saying, "Teacher, do You not care that we are perishing?" (Mark 4:38). But here is where the similarities end in these two accounts.

Unlike Jonah, who could only suggest that the sailors throw him overboard that the sea may become calm for them, the Lord Jesus "got up and rebuked the wind and said to the sea, 'Hush, be still'" (Mark 4:39). Immediately, "the wind died down and it became perfectly calm." And unlike Jonah's situation, in which the sailors began to fear and worship the prophet's God (Jonah 1:16), Jesus' companions began to fear and worship *Him as God*, saying, "Who then is this, that even the wind and the sea obey Him?" (Mark 4:41). While Jonah was on the receiving end of God's power, Jesus *possessed* the power to command the wind and seas to obey Him. He shows His disciples that He greater than Jonah. He is the One who has sovereign control over the forces of nature and who has the ability to appoint those forces to do His bidding.

We see thirdly that Jesus is greater than Jonah as we see *Christ conquering the grave*. When Jesus was asked by the scribes and Pharisees to produce a sign that would convince them that His claims about His divine nature and His mission of redemption were true, Jesus said, "no sign will be given to it but the sign of Jonah the prophet; for just as Jonah was three days and three nights in the belly of the sea monster, so will the Son of Man be three days and three nights in the heart of the earth" (Matthew 12:39-40; cf. 16:4; Luke 11:29-30). Of course, by this, Jesus was referring to His death and burial, in which He would be three days in the tomb.

But the glory of Jonah's experience in the belly of the fish was not that it swallowed him, and not that he was preserved alive within it for three days. For Jonah, the glory of that ordeal was that, at the command of the Lord, "the fish vomited Jonah up on the dry land" (Jonah 2:10). And Jesus is greater than Jonah. He was swallowed by death. His body was prepared and wrapped for burial and He was sealed in the tomb by a massive gravestone. But on that third day, just as Jonah was vomited by the fish, so the Lord Jesus was vomited from death, alive in resurrected glory. Repeatedly, Jesus told His disciples that He would suffer and die, and that He would rise on the third day (Matthew 16:21; 17:23; 20:19; Luke 9:22; 18:33; et al.). Those statements would be utterly ridiculous, unless He could actually do it. And His resurrection from the dead is the sign that validates His claims that He was the divine Son of God who had come to save humanity from sin.

Fourth, we find Jesus to be greater than Jonah as we see *Christ proclaiming salvation*. Not only was He greater than Jonah in His nature and His mission, His message was greater than Jonah's. Jonah came into Nineveh preaching a very short sermon: "Yet forty days, and Nineveh will be overthrown" (3:4). His message was one of judgment and condemnation. But, "God did not send His Son into the world to judge the world, but that the world might be saved through Him" (John 3:17). Jesus came preaching good news, the Gospel (Matthew 4:23; 9:35; Mark 1:14-15; Luke 4:18; 20:1). His message was better than Jonah's, for Jonah's message was one of condemnation, offering salvation only by way of an implicit and unstated condition. Jesus' message of salvation was explicit, clearly stated, and offered freely as an alternative to the condemnation that our sins deserve. The promise of Jesus was that "whosoever believes in Him shall not perish, but have eternal life" (John 3:16). And while He made no bones about the fact that those who do not believe will be condemned (John 3:16-18), He made it clear that He had come on a mission of redemption to reconcile men to God (Mark 10:45; Luke 19:10).

In Jonah 2:9, the prophet exclaims, "Salvation is from the Lord!" In the Hebrew text, that word *salvation* is rooted in the Hebrew word *yeshua*. This is same word from which we get the very name of Jesus. And when His birth was announced to Joseph, the angel said, "you shall call His name Jesus, for He will save His people from their sins" (Matthew 1:21). Jesus did not merely come proclaiming salvation. He came *to be* salvation from the Lord. In His death, burial and resurrection, He accomplished that salvation for those who believe upon Him. Salvation was His name, His message, and His mission, and in that, we see that Jesus is greater than Jonah.

And so as we close the book on Jonah, it seems that all we have encountered here in these pages is pointing our eyes upward so that we can gaze upon the greatness of our God. His love is greater than our circles of concern. His power is greater than our circumstances. His grace is greater than our sin. His Son, the Lord Jesus Christ, is greater than Jonah. So, if this is the abiding message of the book of Jonah, how do we know that we have learned the lesson?

1. If we have comprehended the greatness of God's love, we will enlarge our circles of concern to encompass every nation and all peoples. We will be compelled by love for the Lord to be involved in His task of proclaiming salvation to the ends of the earth.

2. If we have comprehended the greatness of God's power, we will understand that our circumstances are never beyond His ability to intervene by any means necessary to accomplish His will. We will rest in the assurance that all creation can be summoned in an instant to do His bidding. If we are walking in faithfulness with the Lord, this will be a great and precious comfort for us. But if we are in rebellion like Jonah was, this

truth should cause us to tremble and repent before the Lord, knowing that we will never escape Him or His purposes for us.

3. If we have comprehended the greatness of God's grace, we will be quick to turn from our sins and quick to forgive others of theirs. We will not envision ourselves as better than others or more deserving of God's favor, but will understand that none of us are righteous; none of us deserve the blessings of the Lord. Because we have received God's grace which is greater than our sins, we will readily give that grace away to others when they sin against us as well.

4. Finally, if we have comprehended the greatness of God's Son, the Lord Jesus, we will turn to Him in repentance and faith, calling upon Him to save us from our sins according to His promise and His atoning work. And once we have called upon Him as our Lord and Savior, we will seek to share the good news of this great salvation and point others to Jesus.

When we have seen beyond the fish, beyond the storm, beyond the plant, the worm, the wind, and even beyond Jonah and Nineveh, we will see the greatness of God through the pages of this book and we will exclaim with joyful adoration:

O Lord, my God, when I, in awesome wonder, consider all the worlds
Thy hands have made; I see the stars, I hear the rolling thunder,
Thy power throughout the universe displayed.

And when I think that God, His Son not sparing, sent Him to die,
I scarce can take it in: that on the cross, my burdens gladly bearing,
He bled and died to take away my sin.

Then sings my soul, my Savior, God, to Thee: How great Thou art!
How great Thou art! Then sings my soul, my Savior, God, to Thee:
How great Thou art! How great Thou art!

ABOUT THE AUTHOR

Russ Reaves has served as Pastor of Immanuel Baptist Church in Greensboro, North Carolina since September, 2005. He and his wife Donia have two children. Russ earned the Master of Divinity degree with a dual concentration in Christian Apologetics and Biblical Languages from Southeastern Baptist Theological Seminary. In addition, he also has studied at Lancaster Bible College and Graduate School, Fruitland Baptist Bible Institute, and the University of North Carolina at Charlotte. Prior to serving at Immanuel, Russ was the Pastor of Hillcrest Baptist Church in Kernersville, North Carolina and Conowingo Baptist Church of Conowingo, Maryland.

Follow @russreaves on Twitter and find his sermon podcast on iTunes by searching for Russ Reaves or Immanuel Greensboro.

Russ Reaves
Immanuel Baptist Church
2432 High Point Rd.
Greensboro, NC 27403
www.ibcgso.org

15577220R00146

Made in the USA
Charleston, SC
10 November 2012